Penguin Education

Society Against Crime

Society Against Crime

Penal Practise in Modern Britain

Edited by Howard Jones

Penguin Books

Penguin Books Ltd, Harmondsworth, Middlesex, England
Penguin Books, 625 Madison Avenue, New York, New York 10022, U.S.A.
Penguin Books Australia Ltd, Ringwood, Victoria, Australia
Penguin Books Canada Ltd, 2801 John Street, Markham, Ontario, Canada L3R 1B4
Penguin Books (N.Z.) Ltd, 182–190 Wairau Road, Auckland 10, New Zealand

First published 1981

Made and printed in Great Britain by
Richard Clay (The Chaucer Press) Ltd, Bungay, Suffolk
Set in Monophoto Times

Contents

Introduction: Setting the Scene

Howard Jones

Until the late sixties we knew where we were in penal thinking. People were either 'reformers' or 'traditionalists'. The former were humanistic, believing in a kinder, more rehabilitative penal system. The latter tended to believe more in deterrence and in making, in the words of Gilbert and Sullivan, 'the punishment fit the crime'. Of course, the borderline was blurred in places: the traditionalists were not always uncompassionate and the reformers would often express concern about punishments which they considered too severe in relation to the crime, e.g. long prison sentences needed for a training programme. The polarization of views was nevertheless very real and very clear.

Since then, new fashions have come to the fore in criminology. This has happened many times before and has often had its effect on penal methods. One could point to the growth of first psychiatric and then sociological ideas about the causes of crime and the impact these had upon the methods of correction adopted in prisons, probation, etc. No earlier vogue, however, affected basic thinking about the aims of punishment as much as has the growth of deviance theory during the seventies. While previous changes were confined to the advocates of rehabilitation and were concerned with improving methods of correction, the deviance theorists have straddled the time-honoured divide and, in particular, questioned whether the correctionalists were really the humanists they were thought to be.

This is not the place to offer a detailed account of deviance theory (Rubington and Weinberg, 1973). Such an account would have not only to include some assessment of the important new perspectives it has provided for penal thinking but also to describe the various competing and often conflicting themes within it, as well as its incompleteness. Though thus incomplete, it makes absolutist claims, but this, sadly, is to place it well within the criminological tradition. Most earlier developments have also claimed to usher in a new era, in which all existing theory and practice would be supplanted. In this case, however, the claim has begun to be accepted by both academics and practitioners within the penal field and may end by producing a transformation in penal practice such as we have not seen since the beginning of the century.

This revolution in thinking, as it affects ways of dealing with offenders, centres on two main ideas:

(1) That the machinery of law enforcement paradoxically increases the likelihood of further crime by offenders who are subject to it. This is because of the twin processes of stigmatization ('labelling'), and the more intensive interaction with other deviants, which trial and sentence are said to bring with them.

(2) That correctional methods in particular are ineffective, unjust and illiberal.

The claim for rehabilitative effectiveness (it is said), though unfounded, is used as a justification for intrusions upon personal privacy and for sentences which are more onerous than would be justified by the crime, as when, for example, a long period of training is said to be necessary for effective rehabilitation. The correctional approach, it is argued, is also 'deterministic', seeing behaviour as in the last resort determined by upbringing and social circumstances rather than by the free choice of self-determining individuals. So crime, for the correctionalists, is evidence of faulty development – a kind of personal or social sickness, requiring 'treatment' in exactly the same way as physical illness. That a person might *choose* to be a criminal is overlooked, which not only leads to a degraded model of man but also, by placing the emphasis on manipulative resocialization, glosses over the important question of whether we have any right to change people's values in this way.

That the penal system harms and corrupts the offenders with which it deals is not a new idea. The stigma of a sentence or even a court appearance and the contamination resulting from, say, a prison sentence have long been recognized. What was new was the discovery that penal experience may help to create in the offender a 'deviant identity' and thus produce in him a more established predisposition to criminality. Given this discovery, it was necessary to take the damaging effects of the penal system much more seriously. Some writers argued against criminal sanctions being imposed on drug addicts and other 'criminals without victims', on the grounds that otherwise non-criminals were criminalized. Proposals were made for the removal from legal punishment of other offences too. This would have carried much further earlier trends in Britain to 'decriminalize' acts such as homosexuality, abortion, suicide and the delinquent behaviour of young children.

Scope for decriminalization exists in relation to offences connected with drugs and drunkenness and sexual deviation; for failure to make payments (such as fines and maintenance allowances), legal attachment of wages could be extended. In spite of the rejection of rehabilitation by the deviance theorists, an even more fruitful area could be that in which an offence is better dealt with as a welfare matter than as a criminal infraction. We already do this in attempting to divert delinquent children from the courts into the social services departments of local authorities, but many other types of offence, especially those committed within the family and the trivial offences committed by inadequate offenders, would seem equally suitable for handling in this way. Diversion has seemed to have some attraction for deviance theorists, who have not always appeared to grasp the nettle of what you divert offenders *to*, if it is not to some kind of rehabilitative service.

It is in connection with their hostility to correction, however, that deviance theorists have blurred the borderline between the reformers and the traditionalists. The only equitable and liberal way to deal with offenders who are to be sentenced, they say, is as responsible individuals, who should receive punishment in accordance with the seriousness of the offence they have committed. The validity of this view is examined in Chapter 1 of this book, and it must be made clear that it does not exclude mitigation of punishment where this is justified, nor the 'treatment' of those who are clearly sick or disturbed. But, even with these concessions, this version of what is sometimes called the 'criminal justice model' is not greatly different from the position taken by all except the most punitive among the traditionalists. Many who take this view see themselves as 'radicals', but, if so, it is the radicalism of people like Thomas Szasz, whom Pearson (1975) described as 'radical conservatives'. For they have returned to the eighteenth century, to the classical model of man as an autonomous rational and responsible being, in spite of a hundred years of psychology and sociology which has taught us that this is true to only a limited extent. This must not, however, be seen as an argument between free will and determinism. The truth may lie on either side, but in the present state of our knowledge we do not need to search for it. Sufficient to recognize that if the free will of the criminal exists, it is neverthe less constrained by a variety of powerful crimogenic factors.

To move thus back from a position of limited but growing knowledge about responsibility to a more romantic and uncomplicated view must be seen as conservative. So must a philosophy which abandons the aim of helping criminals to conform and substitutes an appropriate meed of punishment. And the 'justice model', by asserting that there is a level of punishment which a crime 'deserves', implies a moral obligation to conform to the law which sits uneasily with the suggestion cited earlier that correction is open to criticism on the grounds of cultural imperialism. If society is culturally pluralistic (which, to do them justice, some deviance theorists like Matza (1964) deny) the law will reflect the ideas of dominant social groups. To impose a moral obligation on deviants to accept the law then becomes truly conservative in the political sense of operating to the advantage of the social elite. Because of the way in which deviance theorists see the early manifestations of deviance as being 'amplified' by social reactions to it, such as those of law enforcement, they are sometimes called 'social reaction' theorists. Some may feel this description to be also true in another, more familiar sense of the words 'social reaction'.

Various positions on these issues are taken up by different contributors to this book, all connected in one way or another with the Department of Social Administration, University College, Cardiff. It is obviously important that such a debate should take place. Monolithic fashions in criminology have too long received an unchallenged run, delaying the time when the contribution they have to make can be assessed and assimilated into the mainstream of our understanding of both crime and the penal system. It is to be hoped that readers will thus understand why they have been confronted in this book with conflicting basic conceptions of the nature and aims of a penal system. Apart from such philosophical differences, there will also obviously be others arising from the different professional backgrounds of the various authors. While most of them are academic teachers, one of social work and two of criminology, they also include a prison governor and a judge. It is thus possible for the observant reader to compare the views of prison and the courts held by those who work in them with the views of informed and concerned outsiders. Miss Elliott is in a rather special position here as she was once an approved school (community home) headmistress but has for some years been an academic with a special, but now outsider's interest in the field. This interplay of views will not give readers a clear lead on what they ought to believe, but we hope that it will make them aware of what the argument is all about, so that they make up their own minds on where the truth is most likely to be found.

Chapter 1 discusses the kinds of penal objectives – retribution, deterrence, incapacitation, correction – which have been proposed. Why courts (or the public) choose one or the other in a particular case often depends as much on emotional as rational considerations. A criminal whose circumstances arouse feelings of pity or whose bearing impresses the court favourably is more likely to receive a sentence with a correctional aim. A man who has committed a horrifying crime or shows defiance and independence may well find himself subjected to the full rigours of the tariff for his crime or even to a more severe, exemplary sentence. The judge may say that the latter is 'to deter others', but it is often not difficult to see in it also a reflection of his reaction to the nature of the crime itself or to the behaviour of the man in the dock.

Moral indignation is not out of place in a criminal court, but the rational element in sentencing needs to be strengthened; this chapter tries to tease out the strengths and weaknesses of the various sentencing aims. Needless to say, none is a panacea.

This subject is developed in Judge Stockdale's study of the courts as sentencers. While still at the bar, he was a keen and highly respected student of penological matters and wrote widely about them. He eschews further discussion of the aims of sentencing but instead sets himself the task of considering whether sentencing really should be the responsibility of courts of law. This eventually brings up many of the criticisms which have been levelled at the courts over the years. Being judge in your own case may not seem likely to produce an unbiased result, but on the way to his verdict of 'not guilty' Judge Stockdale gives us an admirable demonstration of the judicial mind setting out to ensure that both sides are given an airing.

With the recent decline in interest in correction, there has been a parallel decline in interest in non-judicial sentencing bodies, of which the California Youth Authority is probably the prototype. It looks as though we may be in for an era of strict legality in sentencing, with the 'justice model' in the ascendant. It is not so clear that this will be in the best interest of either society or the criminal himself.

Two chapters are devoted specifically to juvenile delinquency, written, as we have seen, from a knowledge of what it is like both to be directly involved in the correction of juvenile offenders and to stand a little apart and perhaps gain a more detached view. The juvenile courts and the modifications introduced by the Children and Young Persons Act 1969 are discussed first; Miss Elliott here explores the possible conflict between correction and traditional conceptions of justice. In the end she seems to want to compromise between the two, being perhaps more optimistic than the present writer about the extent to which oil and water can be successfully mixed. But she also makes it clear that there are many other, more immediate problems to be solved in our juvenile justice system and particularly emphasizes the lack of adequate resources for correctional work. Perhaps we ought to clear these up before we bite on the very controversial bullet of principle.

Chapter 3 reviews a wide range of provisions for delinquent children, extending from full-time residential correction in community homes and the short-term custody and rigour of detention centres, through the aptly named but still rather vaguely defined 'intermediate treatment', to correction within the community and even 'non-intervention'. Some attention is also paid to borstals for older teenagers. These developed as more constructive off-shoots of the adult custodial system and bring us straight up to the gates of the prison.

This is where the thread of argument is taken up by Mr McCarthy, one-time Governor of Cardiff Prison and now Governor of Wormwood Scrubs. One could not have a more authoritative guide to the way in which prisons are organized or how they work in reality – which is different in many ways from how they appear to work to the outsider. The effect of both inmate and staff anxieties upon their method of working, resulting in the emergence of 'wanting a quiet life' as the overall aim upon which all can agree, shows what powerful social and psychological forces have to be countered if prisons are to gain a positive correctional purpose. It has long been the present writer's view that smaller prisons would resolve many problems (Jones, 1959). Security and the control of inmates would be easier, the corrupting inmate culture would be weakened and real relationships between staff and prisoners would replace their present impersonal and mutually uncomprehending mode of interaction. Nor need it be any more expensive than the present prison system with its enormous capital costs and the large staffs required to keep those great fortresses ticking over. They were designed for containment, not correction; when we begin to design different and smaller prisons, it will be the first sign that the philosophy is also changing at last.

Mr Willis approaches prisons from the perspective of the academic researcher and rather more pessimistically than Mr McCarthy – which is itself a remarkable reversal of what used to be the case. It used to be staff in daily contact with the criminal population of the prisons who were inclined to become cynical about the possibility of correction and the criminologists who would press for the introduction into prison programmes of measures with a correctional end in view. This shift in relative positions may conceivably betoken the advent of a new generation of prison administrators more interested in correction, but it is more likely to be a reflection of the extent to which the criminologists have been won over to a position of at least neutrality and often outright hostility towards the correctional approach.

There is particular scepticism about the possibility of undertaking correction in prisons, with their tendency to institutionalize and criminalize. Many feel that the only solution is 'decarceration', keeping offenders out of prison whenever possible. They agree with Professor Sir Rupert Cross (1971) that having correctional aspirations for prisons is not only futile but positively harmful, in that it encourages imprisonment for offenders who can only be damaged by it. Cross suggests that we should concentrate instead on reforming prison so that they do less harm. Mr Willis, in Chapter 6, devotes much attention to this aspect, but it is difficult to see how abuses can be removed except by encouraging more positive trends, which might be very properly described as 'correctional'. No one has seriously suggested that prisons should eventually be dispensed with, and so long as we retain them, we must give up no line of attack which might enable us to put pressure on them for reform.

Probation, as the main non-custodial penal service, ought in theory to be a beneficiary from 'decarceration'. In practice, the use made of probation appears to be declining, mainly because of the popularity of other forms of disposition within the community, notably community service orders, which are examined in a later chapter. But probation faces a crisis on another front, which may not be without its impact on declining numbers. This is the by now familiar retreat from correction. Probation owes its existence to the correctional aim, and any widespread abandonment of this must threaten its survival. Attempts have been made (though not very convincing ones) to provide an alternative, 'policing' role for it (Bottoms and McWilliams, 1979).

Chapter 7, in recognizing the existence of these problems, asks what form the probation service ought to take if it is to revive – or, incidentally, if it is going to be able to provide the convincing alternative to prison that is necessary for 'decarceration' to take off.

The argument advanced is that probation is operating on an individual model of crime causation long after we have come to understand that crime is a social product. So, instead of seeking to change the offender's attitudes without much regard to his social background, we have to embark on a process of socializing him more effectively within his community. The probation officer's special casework skills will not cease to be relevant but will be applied within a broad social context in which ordinary citizens, as volunteers, may have a more important part to play. If probation can thus be criticized for focusing too much on the individual offender, this is even more true of prisons and other forms of custody. They separate him physically from his background, and such rehabilitation as they do attempt takes place within the enclosed and artificial society of the penal institution.

So there is a strong case for increasing the battery of non-custodial measures available to the courts; in Chapter 8, Mr Willis presents a critical survey of those we have at present. They include fines, which have the advantage of convenience in administration, but many disadvantages, not least of which is injustice between rich and poor. More recent arrivals on the scene are suspended sentences, community service orders and day training centres. Mr Willis also describes specialized day centres for habitual alcohol offenders. There seems scope for many other imaginative innovations along these lines, but the author of this chapter is not sanguine about the future for them and even questions whether there is any real prospect of 'decarceration' taking place on a substantial scale.

What then is the future of correction? If Chapter 1 (and this Introduction) are written by a supporter of the correctional approach, it seems right and proper in this controversial field that the last word should be entrusted to a writer with more reservations about it. He sees three trends beginning to take shape. Minor offenders are likely to receive non-custodial sentences or to be kept out of court entirely (i.e. in effect, 'decriminalized') by the use of cautions. On the other hand, Mr Willis's crystal ball shows an increase in the use of custody for major criminals, with longer sentences and the development of special kinds of regime for these prisoners. Rightly, he views this prospect with alarm. But the most disturbing of his predictions concerns the group in the middle, who represent the largest number but, because they are not sufficiently dangerous or dramatic to stir the public pulse, will receive little or no attention from our penal planners. In trouble for the most part because of their social inadequacy, he expects they will continue to receive sentences of imprisonment in largely unreformed regimes, which can only cause their social skills to deteriorate still further.

A grim prospect for them. But also a grim prospect for us all. For it is we who have to pay the heavy cost of their imprisonment and, when they are at length discharged, suffer the loss and inconvenience caused by their continued criminality. When the case for rational penal measures seems so clear, it is astonishing that people are so loath to accept it. We may have to face the fact that we maintain our penal system not so much as a means for the punishment and reduction of crime as to satisfy the widespread need for an emotional outlet. Amid all the stresses of everyday life, what a relief to have scapegoats on whom our feelings of anger and frustration can be legitimately vented!

If this is the case, real penal reform is going to be slow in coming. Certainly, in spite of superficial improvements, our prisons have not changed in essence in a century and a half. There are many things wrong with our society besides crime. Perhaps, if we broaden our reformist vision and work for the kind of society in which people can be happy and contented without the need for scapegoats, a more humane and effective penal system and lower crime rates will also be achievable. That may seem a somewhat unimportant by-product, but that is not how either the future victims of the penal system or the future victims of crime can be expected to feel about it.

References

Bottoms, A. E., and McWilliams, W., 1979: A Non-Treatment Paradigm for Probation Practice, *British Journal of Social Work*, vol. 9, no. 2, pp.159f.

Cross, Sir Rupert, 1971: *Punishment, Prison and the Public*, Stevens

Jones, Howard, 1959: *Prison Reform Now*, Fabian Society

Pearson, Geoffrey, 1975: *The Deviant Imagination*, Macmillan

Matza, David, 1964: *Delinquency and Drift*, John Wiley

Rubington, E., and Weinberg, M. S., (eds.) 1973: *Deviance, the Interactionist Perspective*, Macmillan

1. Punishment or Correction?

Howard Jones

Why do we have a penal system? What purpose does it serve for us? And what purpose ought it to serve? We do not lack answers to these questions. The problem is that we have too many, all of them plausible – and many of them contradictory. It becomes vitally necessary to tease them apart and examine their validity, in order that we may set ourselves clear and unambiguous penal aims – or, failing that, at least be aware when our motives are mixed and therefore self-defeating.

Penal policy is, of course, partly the creation of government, who must provide legislation and the facilities required. Nevertheless, these remain merely opportunities unless the courts choose to take advantage of them. Mandatory sentences, laid down by statute, are few, leaving the real decisions about penal policy to be made by judges and magistrates through the sentences which they enforce in particular cases before them. It is judicial sentencing practice, for example, which accounts for the fact that Britain sentences more people to prison than any country in Europe except West Germany.

The prison population is increased by the very long terms of imprisonment imposed – terms increasing in length all the time. Thus, between 1966 and 1975, the average length of prison sentence in England and Wales increased by over 50 per cent (Home Office, 1977, pp.158–9).

All of these factors set limits to the development and use of non-custodial measures (such as probation, community service, etc.) and by increasing congestion in the prisons severely restrict the options available to prison administrators in developing their regimes. Even where, as in the case of parole, the broad intention of the law is quite explicit, it is sometimes argued that the courts are frustrating that intention by imposing longer sentences, in order to ensure that even if prisoners are paroled they will spend at least a minimum period of time in confinement.

The sentencing philosophy of the judiciary is therefore crucial for any understanding of the aims of penal policy. Three motives loom largest in their thinking: retribution, the protection of the public and deterrence. Of these, by far the most influential is *retribution.*

It is this to which we refer when we talk about justice or fairness in sentencing. It received classical expression in the words of Lord Justice Fry, who wrote at the turn of the century: 'the object of punishment is to adjust the suffering to the sin' (Kenny, 1902, p. 32). A plausible case for the adoption of this 'justice model' of sentencing has been presented by the American Friends Service Committee (1971).

Leaving aside the theological implications of the word 'sin', the basic idea is that the criminal, in breaking the law, has committed a moral offence, thus disturbing the balance of justice. That balance can only be restored if he is punished and thus made to suffer in comparison with those who have not committed crimes. Although the main thrust of retribution is negative, i.e. concerned with punishing the guilty rather than rewarding the virtuous, it can sometimes operate in such a way as to temper the severity of punishment. If, in order to deter people from crime, a punishment is proposed which is severer than would be justified by the crime itself, then just retribution would argue for more lenient treatment. As we shall see, the longer sentences said to be required for the successful development of a training or rehabilitation programme are sometimes assailed on these grounds.

This idea of fairness is not confined to the criminal justice system. It permeates much of our moral thinking and transactions with one another. For example, it is a guiding principle in the training of our children – thus, incidentally, becoming firmly embedded in *their* moral consciousness too. It was probably more viable as a justification for the punishment of crime when there was greater moral consensus in society than there is at present. Certainly, many people would now feel under no sense of obligation to agree with particular laws. And the broader obligation to obey laws even if you disagree with them, because law is recognized as the main safeguard of the stability of society, has little conviction for those who either disagree with the kind of society within which they live or have a powerfully held belief that a particular law is so wrong that it has to be resisted. The older generation would point to Nazi Germany as a society which could not give moral legitimacy to its laws, and to Nazi ordinances about racial purity and the persecution of the Jews as particular laws which ought to be disobeyed. Socialists in the capitalist West or dissidents in Soviet Russia would have similar doubts. Homosexuals, women's rights campaigners, racial minorities and the property-less poor would be among those who could challenge the moral claim made upon them by parts of the legal code of even a liberal democracy like Britain.

It may be that we have to abandon the idea of consensus in society and recognize that the state is an expression of the will of those with power. The law will then reflect the interests of the powerful, even though it will be given a moral coloration. The task of the agencies of education (the family and the schools) and of re-education (social work, psychiatry, rehabilitative services, etc.) then becomes that of inculcating these moral principles in the population at large, and that of the more coercive organs of persuasion (in which the penal system figures prominently) of enforcing conformity with prescribed behaviour. The concept of justice, i.e. of retribution, would then be seen to be an attempt to provide a moral rationalization for the self-interested exercise of power through the state.

The Marxists have propounded this point of view the most vigorously, through their ideas about 'false consciousness' (Aron, 1968, pp.172ff.; Cohen, 1968, pp.80–81) and about the role of the state (Lenin, 1941), but it is not necessary to go so far in order to agree with G. B. Vold (1958, pp.208–9) that

> the whole political process of law-making, law-breaking, and law enforcement becomes a direct reflection of deep-seated and fundamental conflict between interest groups and their more general struggles for the control of the police power of the state. Those who produce legislative majorities win

control over the police power and dominate the policies that decide who is likely to be involved in violation of the law.

There is no suggestion that there are no areas of agreement between the warring interests in modern society. There would probably be much agreement about such general objectives as the protection of life, limb and property, the alleviation of suffering and advancement of welfare, and the preservation of liberty. It is when these vague concepts are given a more definite form and, in particular, when the means for attaining them are under discussion that the argument really starts. Does liberty include the right to take drugs or sell sexually explicit magazines? Does the protection of life and limb require laws against abortion, suicide or euthanasia? Could the advancement of welfare or the relief of suffering sometimes destroy personal incentives and thus be economically disadvantageous? On all these issues, and many more, there are divergent points of view.

To base retributive punishment on a shared sense of moral obligation is therefore probably unjustifiable. In so far as it has been generally accepted on such a basis, it is probably proof only of the success of the policy of cultural imperialism practised by the ruling groups in the society, buttressed, probably, by a fear among the powerless of a breakdown in even that framework of order under which they currently groan. Better the devil you know . . . especially when your interests so often cut across rather than coincide with those of other dissentient groups, so that no clear alternative consensus presents itself to you. If such a coincidence did exist, it would support the Marxist position which claims that the structure of society divides us neatly into two homogeneous groups and which portrays the struggle as one between the status quo and an identifiable alternative prescription. But such a simple dichotomy does not seem to fit the facts of a highly differentiated modern society like ours. The classical statement here is that of Max Weber (Gerth and Mills, 1961, pp.180ff.).

Even if the consensus view of society were more tenable, it probably would not save retribution from ethical criticism. Reference has been made above to the balance of justice – a metaphor often reified as a pair of scales, like those held aloft by the figure of

Justice on the dome of the Central Criminal Court at the Old Bailey in London. Into one pan of these scales goes the seriousness of the offence, the degree of 'sin', as Fry called it, and into the other, the punishment, the degree of 'suffering'. Only if these two quantities are equal – so that the scales are balanced – is justice being done. In theory, it is clear enough, in practice, it is more complicated.

Consider first the seriousness of the offence. How is this to be assessed? Is it measured, for example, by the consequences of the act? This often seems to enter into the calculations of judges: a great train robbery rates for a more severe punishment than petty thieving. It seems easy enough to justify the view that the greater the damage a criminal does to society, the greater his culpability. Yet we are talking about culpability and whether an offence has more or less serious consequences may often be a result of factors outside the offender's control and for which he can in no way be blamed.

Consider the case of the dangerous driver who happens to kill somebody. Because of a particular combination of circumstances the charge against him ceases to be one of dangerous driving and becomes the much more serious charge of manslaughter. There is, of course, no gainsaying the serious outcome of his behaviour, but was he more to blame than if he had travelled along that road a few minutes earlier or a few minutes later and had thus not encountered the man he killed? The classical legal test is, of course, a requirement of *mens rea*, the guilty mind, but this attempts the impossible, the reading of minds, and only too often, therefore, the courts have to assume that the offender intended the consequence of his action when it is clear that this is no more than a fiction to make law itself workable.

The difficulty of assessing culpability has been generally increased by the findings from criminological research. It is now well established that the prospect of being convicted of an offence is affected by a number of factors external to the individual and which he can in no way influence. One of these is sex: men are about six times as likely to be convicted as women. One must not leap to the facile conclusion that this is because women are better-behaved than men. No man who is married or who has sisters would accept this. Nor would any woman when referring to other women! It is probably largely a result of the still limited social opportunities available to women, including opportunities for crime, and this is something which arises out of forces within society itself. There is certainly nothing which the prospective male offender can do to reduce the risk of criminality to which he is exposed on this account.

Similarly with regard to the greater criminality recorded against young people. The following table (Home Office, 1978) sets out the statistics for England and Wales, but those for other countries tell the same story:

Table 1

Numbers of people found guilty of or cautioned for indictable offences 1973–7 per 100,000 of population.

	Age-groups				
	10–13	14–16	17–20	Over 20	All ages
Male	3,568	7,734	6,382	1,072	2,030
Female	894	1,457	838	242	388

The 14–16 age group has a much higher crime rate than others, and over 20, rates fall steeply.

Because sex and age are biological distinctions, the individual's helplessness in face of them is obvious enough, but there are social distinctions, equally significant for the incidence of crime, which he also has to accept as 'given'. One investigation after another has shown the much higher rates of crime among those who live in certain lower working-class areas than in other localities of the same cities. Yet people do not choose the class and neighbourhood in which they are brought up. It is open to argument whether the higher crime rates of these groups are due to discrimination against them by the law-enforcement machinery, as some contemporary deviance theorists would have it (Phillipson, 1971, Chapter 5), or to the persistence from one generation to another (perhaps as a result of long-standing deprivation and discrimination) of a structure of local values favourable to the growth of criminal behaviour (Mays, 1954; Miller, 1962). In either case, it would be difficult for anybody growing up and continuing to live in such an area to escape from such powerful and all-pervading pressures from his neighbours and friends. Indeed, as Shaw and McKay (1954) argued in their pioneering studies of these delinquency subcultures, the more socially well-adjusted and therefore obedient to the social mores of his own local community the resident of such an area, the more likely he probably is to become an offender.

Sex, age and area of upbringing and residence, then, greatly affect the statistical probability of his becoming an offender. We can take the following quantities as being non-controversial and indeed even conservative measures of the extent of the increased risk:

Being male rather than female	6 to 1
Being under 21 rather than over 21	5 to 1
Being brought up in a lower working-class rather than a middle-class area	4 to 1

This means that if you are male, under 21 and brought up in a delinquency area, you are 120 times more likely to be convicted as an offender than you would be if a woman, over 21 and raised and living in a middle-class area. To assume that criminality brings with it equal culpability in view of facts such as these is clearly untenable. Retributionists will often argue that the individual does not have to give in to adverse circumstances; that it is open to him to resist them; and that if he does not, he must accept the responsibility for his criminal behaviour. It sounds more reasonable to say that if he remains law-abiding in spite of such handicaps, he has proved himself not merely the moral equal but the moral superior of non-delinquents living in more favourable personal and social conditions.

Few criminologists nowadays are out-and-out determinists, contending that people should never be held responsible for their behaviour. That, it has been observed, is entering into an unnecessary quarrel. What can be asserted with some confidence, however, is that personal responsibility is limited by a variety of factors over which the individual has no control. As criminological research continues, more such factors will be discovered, causing the area attributable to free will to contract still further. For instance, cultural differences between races or other groups in plural societies are being shown to have a decisive effect upon both the amount and types of crime committed (Jones, 1981). Again, students of criminal careers have in recent years pointed to the way in which conviction, and the resultant stigmatization of a person, will cause his situation to change for the worse. Opportunities of all sorts are closed to him and people begin to look on him as a criminal, so that it becomes increasingly difficult for him to become anything else. In the end it also becomes increasingly difficult for him to see himself as anything else – a change in his self-image which is accelerated if his sentence, as is so often the case, leads to increased interaction between himself and other similarly stigmatized persons.

How can we, in the light of all this research, have any confidence in our ability to allocate blame to those convicted of crime? How can we know how much to place in that pan of the scales which is concerned with 'the degree of sin'? And, as we have seen, it is likely that our perplexities will increase as time passes and further research is undertaken. Nobody should suggest that the legal doctrine of mitigation could tackle problems of this magnitude.

But at least people will feel that they know where they are with the other pan of the scales. A punishment is a punishment is a punishment ... Fry again offers us the key to an examination of the validity of this belief; he refers in his dictum not to sentences of this kind or that but to the degree of 'suffering', a subjective criterion. There is no doubt that he is right to do this. Suffering is the reality of punishment; a given sentence, by contrast, is external to the individual, placing him in a situation which may have a very different significance for him according to his personality, his past experience and his expectations from life.

For the poor man even a small fine may cause severe privation, while for the rich man a large fine may involve no suffering at all. Imprisonment may cause little concern to the introverted person, whose social activities were minimal even before his incarceration.

The very dependent and inadequate person may actually welcome it, as offering him relief from the burden of making his own decisions and maintaining his own role-performance in society. On the other hand, to the gregarious, the timid, the urgently sexed or those who have status, a good name, a happy family or a good job to lose, it is a very heavy punishment indeed. In the long run, of course, it may do more damage to the introverted and the inadequate by encouraging these damaging tendencies in them. Old lags in every prison are proof that this happens, but this is a rehabilitative or correctional consideration and cannot be relevant to a discussion of retribution, where what matters is that the individual shall be aware of suffering punishment in proportion to his culpability, irrespective of the objective outcome of the punishment.

Physical punishment is experienced in even more obviously varied ways than fines or prison. It is not necessary to import masochism into the argument, though research on 'punishment-seekers' among criminals (Flugel, 1945, p.153; Jones, 1971, pp.65–6) suggests that they may not be all that uncommon. Literature and common experience alike bear testimony to differences between individuals in their ability to bear physical pain. One man will not only be able to endure it stoically but can even use it to increase his own self-regard and public reputation, while another is reduced to utter terror at the very thought of it. To call one a brave man and the other a coward does not in any way reduce the disparity in suffering between the two.

The only real measure of punishment is suffering. As with culpability, we cannot assess its severity without a knowledge of the inner workings of the mind which is not available to us. When the courts impose a punishment, however, most do so without taking into account what it means to the individual who is being punished.

In fact we no more know how much to put into the punishment pan than into the 'blame' pan. If the scales balance, it can only be by accident, and by the very definition of retribution, this means not justice, but injustice. What we must be getting is the appearance of justice, but because the concept seems so necessary to us, we are apparently content with that. It is sad that we should consider it so indispensable as a basis for social morality, in view of the moral strictures to which it is open.

Moral philosophers point to the fact that in responding to crime by punishment, society is not achieving any moral objective at all (Hobhouse, 1949, pp.125ff.). All that it does is to return suffering for suffering, thus increasing the amount of evil in the world. A more justifiable morality might be to see the aim of punishment as that of providing the offender with help, so that he may be freer to choose whether to conform with the laws of his society or not. This leads to the consideration of deterrence, and rehabilitation or correction, as possible alternatives to retributive punishment. This will be discussed later.

There appears to be a dilemma here, for retribution also acts sometimes as a moderating influence, where, for example, enthusiasm for deterrence or a lengthy period of rehabilitation would otherwise lead to excessive sentences. A safeguard of this sort is clearly required, but it does not necessarily have to be associated with the negative aspects of retributive punishment. Indeed even where punishment or the imposition of hardship is seen as necessary to reconcile the offender with society, recognition of the moral undesirability of such a means should be enough to ensure that it is limited to the absolute minimum required.

Although the administration of justice in the sense of just retribution is the traditional aim of the courts and still remains the principle to which all others are subservient in their sentencing practice, they are also very preoccupied with *the protection of the public*. Legislators also have often had this in mind, but the earliest British attempts (in the Prevention of Crime Act 1908) to impose longer preventive sentences of imprisonment in the case of persistent offenders ran foul of the judicial insistence on just retribution. A two-tier sentence was envisaged, the first tier being the appropriate tariff sentence for the crime committed and the second, an additional period of incarceration to protect the public by keeping the offender out of circulation for a while. This explicit separation of the two elements in the sentence made the breach of the principles of retributive justice only too obvious and judges used the new provisions very little.

The later re-enactment of preventive detention in the Criminal Justice Act 1948 did not draw this fatal line but permitted judges to impose longer sentences of between four and fourteen years upon offenders of 30 and over who had more than two previous imprisonable convictions, where the Court was satisfied that this was necessary for the protection of the public. Whether as a result of this obfuscation of the breach of retributive principle or because higher post-war crime rates had caused judges to become more punitive, they made energetic use of this new opportunity. It was, however, a somewhat indiscriminate use. As Dr W. H. Hammond showed in his study of preventive detainees (Hammond and Chayen, 1963), many of them, far from being the kind of public menace against whom the legislation was directed, were inadequates who had qualified for preventive detention by strings of petty offences. Dr Hammond's report spelt the end of preventive detention. It was abolished and replaced by still another version known as the extended sentence.

Judges nowadays, though, are prepared to pass longer sentences on preventive grounds and to impose custodial sentences rather than probation or a fine, not necessarily to satisfy the requirements of retribution, but because they believe it to be necessary for the safety of the public. Imprisonment is, of course, the essential component in any such sentence, and a close examination of the role fulfilled by prisons throughout their history shows that their primary task has always been the essentially preventive aim of containment – 'keeping them in, and keeping them quiet while they are in'. They occasionally profess the other objectives of sentencing: retribution, deterrence, rehabilitation – but these are always abrogated for the time being if the effectiveness of the containment aim is ever threatened. This could be seen very clearly when a number of escapes in the early sixties led to the setting up of the Mountbatten Committee on prison security, and eventually the cutting back of various developments such as hostels, group counselling and outside work programmes, which had been considered of rehabilitative value but were now adjudged security risks.

In at least one respect the preventive approach represents a significant shift of emphasis. Though it does not purport to do more than keep the dangerous criminal out of harm's way, it does at any rate have a practical purpose in view, in seeking to limit the impact of crime on the community. Deterrence and rehabilitation go beyond this, of course, in aiming to make criminals less likely to offend after their sentences are completed. All, however, set themselves to achieve objective improvements in the crime situation, and it is right, therefore, to evaluate them according to their success in doing this. This sets them apart from the aim of retribution, which is a wholly moral concept, seeking to do 'what is right' irrespective of whether crime is increased or reduced as a result. No doubt there are pragmatists who will argue that in deciding whether a particular course of action is morally right you cannot ignore its effects upon society and upon other people, but they are struggling against the age-old tradition of drawing a sharp distinction between what is right and what is expedient. We all recognize the tag 'honesty is the best policy' to be an argument from the standpoint of self-interest and not morality. If doing the right thing always paid off, being good would be much easier for all of us than we actually find it to be.

Because it is solely pragmatic, preventive sentencing, or incapacitation as it is sometimes called nowadays, must be subjected to moral criticism. There would seem to be no doubt about the propriety of protecting the public by a preventive sentence, so long as the absolute necessity for it can be demonstrated in the particular case. There is a precedent in the compulsory hospitalization of mentally ill persons, which is also limited these days to cases in which this is considered essential. Such discretion is, however, too dangerous to be left in the hands of fallible judges. The conditions under which a sentence of this kind can be passed must be carefully defined by statute and limited to cases in which 'dangerousness' can be demonstrated. The difficulty of defining the 'dangerous offender' is now becoming clear (Bottoms, 1977), but we have to do it as best we can. There is also a further problem: because the preventive element in the sentence is admittedly over and beyond what the crime would justify, there is no warrant for imposing on the offender the many other forms of privation – of autonomy, sex, standard of life, etc. – inseparable from conventional imprisonment.

This was recognized by the special privileges allowed at Parkhurst to preventive detainees sentenced under the 1908 legislation, but much more than this is needed. It will call for very much more imagination and courage on the part of our prison administrators than they have ever shown in the past.

But what about the intrinsic aim of the preventive sentence? There is no gainsaying its effectiveness so long as the criminal is under lock and key – and with the extreme security established in maximum-security prisons since Mountbatten (Jones and Cornes, 1977, p.26), his chances of escape are slight. Nevertheless, his term of imprisonment must end some time, and a purely preventive sentence does little to make him less of a criminal. On the contrary, the known deleterious effects of long periods in prison mean that he will probably be released as an even more dangerous person than when originally sentenced. So, by its own practical criterion of the protection of the public, the achievements of preventive sentences are at best very doubtful. They can be justified only in combination with a more active policy designed to reduce the adverse effects of 'prisonization' and even to equip the detainee to make a better social adjustment on his release.

With *deterrence* (Beyleveld, 1979), the further pragmatic aim of changing the offender's attitudes comes into view. In common language, deterrence is concerned with imposing sentences which will frighten people into good behaviour. There are two forms: individual deterrence, in which a convicted offender is punished in order to 'teach him a lesson', and general deterrence, in which his punishment is intended as an example to other people.

As already indicated, limits will and ought to be imposed on the severity of the punishments which might be imposed for such purposes. Experience suggests, in any case, that deterrent punishment which exceeds what the current climate of opinion considers justifiable often proves ineffective. People will not report crimes if they believe the likely punishment to be over-severe or (as occurred at the beginning of the nineteenth century, when even trivial crimes were met with the death penalty) juries will refuse to convict (Trevelyan, 1980, p.520). The intimidating effect of excessive terror on potential criminals themselves is also limited; when the prospect is very terrifying, people just do not believe that it could happen to them.

The acid test for deterrent punishment is whether it does deter. It is probably impossible to answer that question on any factual basis (Walker, 1979). This is most obvious in the case of general deterrence. To assess the effect of any particular penalty on the level of criminal behaviour in the community at large would require a knowledge of how people reacted both with it and in its absence. The simultaneous occurrence of both these possibilities could only be achieved by an act of the creative imagination – hardly a sound basis for policy-making or scientific generalization. It would be possible to set up an experiment in which the crime situation was assessed before and after the imposition of the penalty, but it would be hazardous to conclude that any difference (or lack of difference) was solely due to its deterrent (or non-deterrent) effect. Many other factors within society influence its level of criminality. The observed changes in the crime figures are more likely to be the result of these more profound social forces.

The nearest to a satisfactory experiment of this kind comes when police activity in a community ceases entirely for a while, the presumed deterrent effect of detection and punishment then being inoperative. Such a case occurred during the Second World War when the German occupation force in Denmark, for fear of armed resistance, deported the Danish police force. There was a steep increase in crimes against property, while crimes against the person remained more or less constant (Hurwitz, 1952, p.303). The broader social situation cannot, of course, be left out of account. In particular, reactions to occupation by an enemy army and the shortages of wartime are bound to have had their effect. But the episode does not give support to any strong deterrent effect outside the field of property crime. Police strikes, which would also remove the threat of punishment temporarily would provide a better test, uncontaminated by the effect of war and occupation. The only account of such a strike described the effects of one which occurred in Montreal in 1969 (Clark, 1975). The study was very impressionistic, but so far as such data can be relied upon, the effect on property crime far outstripped that on criminal violence.

There would at first sight appear to be more hope of success in the study of individual deterrence, because it is possible to compare the behaviour of a person before and after punishment. Unfortunately, individual circumstances change even more swiftly than those in the community at large. And if the punishment is a prison sentence, the post-punishment assessment may in any case have to take place a long time after that of the pre-punishment phase. So, a man may succeed because he now has a child, a house or a job, or because a friend or his after-care officer has got through to him, or he may fail because his wife has left him, he has got into debt or returned speedily to the bosom of his former criminal associates.

How too are we to separate the deterrent function of the sentence from its other effects? Prison again provides an example. There could, in spite of some current scepticism about this (Cross, 1971), be some rehabilitative influence, but this would be counteracted by the more generally acknowledged effects of those more adverse influences known as 'prisonization' (perhaps better broken down into the quite distinct processes of institutionalization and criminalization) (Jones and Cornes, 1977, p.6).

The problems encountered in carrying out empirical tests of the value of deterrence force us back to a more theoretical analysis, in which we look at what is involved in the process of deterring offenders. Deterrence assumes an act of calculation on the part of the potential criminal. He is supposed to set off the prospects of detection and punishment against the benefits he would expect to gain from the crime – stealing a sum of money, say, or attacking his enemy. If it seems worthwhile to him, he carries on; if not, he draws back from the brink. In the former case, argue the advocates of deterrence, it is necessary to increase the penalty to a level at which crime no longer seems profitable to him. Such requirements for effective deterrence are certainly not always met. Intelligent professional criminals probably plan their crimes in this way, but most other crime is a matter of impulse. That must be particularly true of crimes of violence, which the Danish experience shows to have been largely uninfluenced by the removal of the police. In the case of the disturbed offender, judgement is likely to be clouded by emotion, while cognitive problems would impair judgement in the case of many mentally ill, psychopathic or subnormal persons. Nor are young offenders very likely to approach their offences in the sophisticated manner required by deterrence theory.

A second consideration results from the fact that it is the prospect of punishment which is being contemplated by the potential criminal. He may or may not be caught; and if he thinks that the prospect is slight, his fear of ultimate punishment will be much reduced. The proportion of those 'crimes known to the police' which are cleared up is about 40 per cent in most Western countries – it was an unusually high 47 per cent in England and Wales in 1973 (Home Office, 1978, p.30). But this is not the whole story. Many more crimes are committed than are reported to the police: a recent assessment of the 'dark figure' estimated it at eleven times the number of crimes which find their way into police statistics (Sparks, Genn and Dodd, 1977, p.157). So only one crime in eleven is reported to the police, and of these, less than half end in a conviction or are otherwise cleared up. This means that the odds against crimes being cleared up are over 23 to 1.

Criminals, of course, do not make this kind of computation. The odds get through to them through the frequency or otherwise with which their criminal acquaintances are caught. This will often be so infrequent as to give them reason to believe that they too have every chance of escaping scot-free. This is why many authorities on the subject argue nowadays that deterrence is more likely to be increased by an improvement in the certainty of punishment than by an increase in its severity. On the other hand, the increased pressure of police activity on our lives which this would entail might not be very welcome. Low levels of reported crime and modest detection rates may be the price which we have to pay for our freedom.

Reporting and detection rates and therefore likelihood of punishment vary according to the type of crime. Table 2 (Home Office, 1978, p. 30) gives the detection percentages for cases of different indictable offences reported to the police in England and Wales in 1977. Table 3 gives a rough estimation of the proportion of crimes recorded by the police, according to the kind of offence. It is based on a victim study in three London areas by Sparks *et al.* (1977, p.157).

Table 2

	Percentage
Violence against the person	79
Sex offences	77
Burglary	31
Robbery	28
Theft and receiving	40
Fraud and Forgery	82
Criminal damage above £20	30
Other offences	94
All offences	*41*

Table 3

Number of criminal incidents recorded by the police as a percentage of numbers reported to researchers by victims – averages for three London areas

	Percentage
Assault, robbery and theft from the person	3.7
Burglary, theft in dwellings	20.3
Theft of and from motor vehicles	14.0
Other thefts	7.3
Other offences	14.3

The two tables are not comparable, but wide differences between types of crime in both detection and reporting rates clearly exist. It may be speculated that, other things being equal, those crimes with the highest rates in these respects are most likely to be deterrable. But other things are rarely equal, mainly because of the effect of the element of 'calculability' discussed above. What we ought therefore to be asking is not, as Professor Walker (1979) sometimes seems to be asking, 'Can crimes be deterred?' but, taking into account their different levels of calculability and certainty, '*Which* crimes are most likely to be deterred?'

A general point is probably also worth making. The theory of deterrence implies that people are only kept from crime by the fear of punishment. If this were so, we should be living in a very explosive social situation, with our pent-up antisocial drives not only, as we have seen, seeping out whenever a chink could be found in society's defences, but also erupting violently from time to time as the level of tension built up to intolerable heights.

Introspection by itself is enough to discredit crude deterrence. Most of us do not often think of committing crimes; our socialization experiences have conditioned us to be law-abiding, and these are reinforced by the way in which our behaviour is prescribed for us by the roles arising from our life-styles – our jobs, families, friendships, etc. Deterrence then, for most people, has only occasional scope. It is only for a minority of ill-socialized individuals that deterrence has more comprehensive relevance. For this minority it may be more rational as a general policy to think of trying to reduce criminal propensities than to try to hold back the flood by external coercion.

When discussing retribution, the question was asked why we cling so much to a negative and punitive social morality, when a more constructive one might be open to us. The same might be asked about our preference for deterrence as a means of changing the behaviour of criminals. There does seem to be a punitiveness in our nature which finds expression in these attitudes towards criminals. Psychoanalysts see the handling of innate human aggression, exacerbated as it is by the instinctual frustration which results from social training, as our main problem of personal and social adjustment. If we can find scapegoats on to whom this aggression can be displaced, our relationships with other people will be less conflict-ridden. Criminals provide us with plenty of justification for using them as such scapegoats (Flugel, 1945, p.168; Zilboorg, 1955). Sometimes, it has been suggested, even they do not provide us with enough outlets; the stage is then set for the use of others, such as, for example, ethnic minorities, whose skin pigmentation or social habits set them apart from the rest of us (Jones, 1963, pp.23–4).

The difference is that they have done nothing to justify our punishing them; they are merely targets for a resentment which is generated elsewhere, perhaps by our inability to find a job or a house (Phizacklea and Miles, 1979). So to vindicate our prejudiced attitude towards them, we invent racial and other myths about their inferiority and vice. The criminal being obviously 'bad' is a more straightforward target for rejection. There is nevertheless an element of fantasy even in our attitude to him, as is shown by the way in which his badness and dangerousness are exaggerated in the public imagination. The pathetic and inadequate men who constitute the greater part of the population of our prisons would not recognize themselves in this threatening figure.

Such a theory may seem to destroy any hope we might have of finding our way towards more constructive penal methods. Shall we not always need a punitive penal system to absorb our hostility? Fortunately, mother nature is not as biologically inflexible as early Freudian theory seemed to suggest. There are wide differences in the amount of aggression expressed in societies in different parts of the world (Mead, 1958). We ourselves are much more compassionate than our predecessors even a hundred years ago. This is reflected in our penal system which, with all its faults, has become steadily less cruel; at the cost, as some feel, of its deterrent function. If there is anything in the scapegoat theory, however, it does explain why we find retribution and deterrence so attractive. Even rehabilitation is not immune to this influence and certain correctional methods which have punitive overtones, such as aversive forms of behaviour modification (Eysenck, 1970, pp.163ff.), could prove to have much attraction for us.

Rehabilitation occasionally finds its way into the consideration of the courts, though always subordinate to the retributive tariff and the protection of the public, and often to deterrence too. It has been expounded more, at least as an ideology, by the institutions of the penal system, even where the reality of their methods is somewhat different. The prime example is the prison where 'training and treatment' is the order of the day, but where the underlying trend is for containment and the ultimate outcome, prisonization. Probation, by virtue of its history, has a more real commitment to rehabilitation, but even it has a deterrent threat at its heart. Probation in effect says: 'Behave yourself or else . . .', and it is the probation officer who has to make a reality of that threat by reporting the probationer back to the court if he breaches the conditions of his order.

Because it aims at changing people's motives rather than punishing them and is thus believed (often wrongly) to be a softer option, rehabilitation is usually treated as a privilege to be accorded to the criminal if he deserves it. This is how many judges see it. They will devote little time to considering the rehabilitation of an offender whose crimes are particularly reprehensible, whose long record suggests (to them) that he is incorrigible, who is truculent in court, etc.

If there is any possibility of rehabilitation at all, this must be a mistake. It is certainly to the advantage of the criminal himself that he should be rehabilitated, but it is even more to the advantage of society. What is at stake is whether we should attempt to apply to the improvement of our society the kind of rationality which has paid us such rich dividends in the fields of science and technology. It is acknowledged that human beings are a special case, less uniform and predictable, and more complex, than the forms of inanimate nature with which we have been so successful in the past. There are also fears that we may lose our freedom and autonomy if there is any substantial advance in the effective control by some over the motives and behaviour of others. The advent of behaviour-modification techniques shows that this is not an idle fear (Epstein, 1975). Methods of rehabilitation must be subject to the kind of professional ethics which operate in medicine and must in any case be subject to the willing cooperation and conscious participation of the person to be rehabilitated.

It is not this fear of the effectiveness of rehabilitation which holds the centre of the stage at the present time, however, but what is seen as its ineffectiveness. Study after study has been carried out to show that whatever punishment or correctional approach is adopted, the effect in terms of reconviction is much the same (Brody, 1976). Quite illegitimately, it is concluded from this that no correctional approach can be successful. Some, even more irrationally, believe that this justifies concentrating on deterrence, even though there is no evidence that this works either and quite good reason for assuming that in many cases it does not. Undiluted retribution is not acceptable either, especially at a time of normative uncertainty like the present, leaving 'incapacitation', based on the naked exercise of power, as the only way open to us for restraining our criminals. The loss to us in this would not only be in the possibility of reducing recidivism through effective correctional measures but also in the abandonment of reason and constructiveness and concern for others, even criminals, in our approach to this difficult social problem. This is probably the most serious loss of all, reflecting an attitude whose consequences must extend far beyond our behaviour towards criminals.

Not that the pessimism about what is called 'correctionalism' is all that soundly based. In spite of the methodological difficulties in evaluative research (Brody, 1976, p.41), there are a substantial number of studies which give positive results (Palmer, 1978). Palmer also raises a more fundamental point. In most cases, the effectiveness of correction (as, incidentally, with deterrence) is tested 'across the board', i.e. in its indiscriminate application to all kinds of criminals. This is crude and, because there are other possibilities, it is untenable. Experiments have been carried out by the California Youth Authority in developing a 'horses for courses' approach to sentencing (Warren, 1977; Palmer 1975, 1978), and that would seem to be preferable not only as a strategy for sentencing but also in the evaluation of correctional methods.

We have seen also that the results of the studies in question have been used as a basis for generalizations far wider than they could possibly justify. They have been carried out in what are, for the most part, unregenerate penal systems. Consider the studies of particular innovations, such as, say, social work, in prisons. The evidence from British research on this is somewhat contradictory (Shaw, 1974; Fowles, 1978), but this has not inhibited the more pessimistic of the researchers from seeing his research as yet another nail in the coffin of correctionalism (Fowles, 1978). However, the effect of social work on reconviction has been studied in the context of a large British local prison where it has to contend with all kinds of adverse influences, ranging from the criminalizing role of the inmate subculture to the psychologically deadening and institutionalizing effects of the vast tracts of unoccupied time and the rigidity of prison routine. To surmount such obstacles, social work would have to be more effective than anybody would ever imagine that it could be.

One cannot help but be impressed by the sheer durability of prison regimes; often they seem as indestructible as the massive buildings themselves. In Britain, fashions have come and gone: the 'separate system' of the nineteenth century, the 'training' philosophy developed by Alexander Paterson in the inter-war period (Fox, 1952, pp. 66ff.), the psychological emphasis of the immediate post-war period and the managerialism of the present day. Yet all of these have concealed an underlying continuity, in which rigid routine, a criminalizing inmate culture and a basic containment aim determine what really happens to prisoners. Parsons, doctors, psychologists, social workers, teachers, industrial managers, have all been introduced in turn, but their activities have proved to be no more than icing on a cake which underneath it all retains its old bitter taste. Sometimes these functionaries have themselves been taken over by the prison; as one long-service prison medical officer put it, 'Treatment and control (i.e. of prisoners) are two sides of the same coin' (Prewer, 1974, p.128). One might have been forgiven for believing that for a doctor, with a prior obligation to his patients rather than to the prison authorities, they would be very different things.

If rehabilitation is to be carried out in prisons, their basic structure will have to be reformed. This applies just as much to other components of the penal system. For instance, the probation system remains firmly tied to its original concept of individual supervision, in spite of the overwhelming evidence that crime is a social not an individual pathology (Bottoms and McWilliams, 1979, p.188). Given a whole-hearted attempt to apply what we know about crime in our rehabilitative efforts, it becomes reasonable to evaluate our success empirically. Until then, like gamblers with loaded dice, the pessimists will always win.

The courts are no exception to this need for root-and-branch change. It is probably because of them that our correctional efforts are not as successful as we would like – and often equally unsuccessful, whatever we do. As we have seen, they move in their sentencing decisions from deterrence to prevention and rehabilitation, while retribution sets the limits for all. As a result, when seen from the rehabilitative standpoint, sentences are probably more or less randomized. Statistically speaking, this is a prescription for a success rate based purely on chance, i.e. of 50 per cent success and 50 per cent failure irrespective of the punishment applied – which is more or less what we get.

We have had experience in, for example, the California Youth Authority of a sentencing procedure based predominantly on correctional considerations, but there has in recent years been a reaction against transferring the sentencing function in this way from the courts into the hands of lay experts on human and social affairs even in the case of children (Morris, 1978). In part, this reaction has been a result of the alleged lack of success of the correctional approach, but it has also reflected a return to favour of what might be called 'legality', or the preservation of strict rules of law and procedures to protect the individual's rights. A particular target is the discretion which is seen as indispensable for the sentencer who is going to make a rehabilitative decision. He may need to be untrammelled by formalities if he is to prescribe for each individual offender, and also be free to vary his prescription as the rehabilitative process progresses from stage to stage, but in plain language this means that he will have arbitrary power over the individual's life – to place him in custody or free him, or to keep him under control for a longer or shorter period than traditional retribution would dictate for his kind of offence.

It would be hypocritical to pretend that this kind of discretion does not always exist, though it is operated within the penal system rather than the judiciary. A decision as to who shall go to an open prison and who shall continue to experience the penned-up and more squalid life of a closed institution is made by prison administrators, not judges, and yet it makes all the difference to the nature of the punishment, the degree of 'suffering'. Many privileges granted by the prison authorities themselves or punishments imposed or remitted by them also have a great effect upon the sentence, the 'degree of suffering' experienced. Even the length of the sentence can depend on whether or not parole is granted; although this is the subject of a quasi-judicial inquiry, it is no more truly judicial than, say, the procedures of the California Youth Authority. The length of the borstal sentence, within fairly wide limits, is at the discretion of the administrators themselves. Similarly, the probation order gives wide powers over the probationer to his probation officer. He can require the probationer to notify his place of address, to keep in touch as instructed and to receive visits at home. And, of course, the power to report the probationer to the court if his performance is unsatisfactory makes the officer, informally, even more powerful in the life of his probationer.

Judicial decisions themselves are not free from arbitrariness. The foibles of particular judges are well-known, and there are biases shared by many of them, such as a backward-looking morality, a detestation of violent or sex offenders and a contempt for psychiatric or sociological explanation (these often being seen as special pleading or excuses for the criminal). There is often lack of uniformity in sentences passed by one court or another, especially in magistrates' courts. So it is not a case of giving up a perfect system for one entirely different.

Yet there is a genuine problem, calling for some attempt to wed correctional sentencing with appropriate safeguards for the individual. The substitution of a body of correctional precedents for the legal precedents on which courts rely would be one such possibility. Social diagnosis would in any case require the development and utilization of past experience in this way: if every case were unique, the sentencer would be starting out afresh in ignorance every time. Another safeguard would be to utilize within the new framework of 'law' the experience gained by judges in adhering to established procedures. This would necessitate the inclusion of a judge in the sentencing bench or rather the introduction of non-judicial sentencing expertise into the court's deliberations. In Britain we have experience of doing this in other branches of the law, notably in Admiralty cases, where an authority on shipping sits as an expert assessor with the judge.

In practice, both the judges and the public utilize whichever of retribution, prevention, deterrence and rehabilitation suits them at any particular time. If punitive feelings have been aroused in them, they can be prudently deterrent and then, if this is shown to be untenable, return to being righteously moral, saying: 'Well, he deserved it anyway.' If they are afraid, they can insist that the criminal be locked up for a long time, while if their sympathy is aroused they will want to do something to help him. This is a largely unconscious process and, if unchecked, can make the development of a correctional policy almost impossible. In particular, it has to be understood that if we try to combine more than one of these aims in a single sentence we usually achieve none of them.

It has been stated above that crime is a social and not an individual problem. As a result, its correction cannot be attempted in total isolation from the society out of which it emerged. This is a lesson which prisons, most obviously, but probation officers too have to learn if either are to realize their correctional potential. That correction in the past has not recognized this accounts for the belief of anti-correctionalists that it is based on a false analogy with medicine, in which criminality is seen as requiring the application of psychological methods of re-education, or even treatment, to the individual offender. Such an assumption is not necessary to the correctional position – indeed is not compatible with the broad social orientation which current knowledge in the field dictates. To criticize correction on the grounds that it can only be a form of individual treatment is to construct your own Aunt Sally in order to have something to aim at.

References

American Friends Service Committee, 1971: *Struggle for Justice*, Hill & Wang, New York

Aron, Raymond, 1968: *Main Currents in Sociological Thought*, vol.1, Penguin

Beyleveld, D., 1979: 'Deterrence Research as a Basis for Deterrence Policies', *Howard Journal of Penology*, vol. 18, no. 3, pp.135ff.

Bottoms, A. E., 1977; 'Reflections on the Renaissance of Dangerousness', *Howard Journal*, vol. XVI, no. 2, 1977, pp.70ff.

Bottoms, A. E., and McWilliams, W., 1979: 'A Non-Treatment Paradigm for Probation Practice', *British Journal of Social Work*, vol. 9, no. 2

Brody, S. R., 1976: *The Effectiveness of Sentencing,* Home Office Research Study No. 35, HMSO

Clark, G., 1975: 'What Happens When the Police Strike', in W. J. Chambliss, *Criminal Law in Action,* Hamish Hamilton, pp.440ff.

Cohen, Percy S., 1968: *Modern Social Theory,* Heinemann

Cross, Sir R., 1971: *Punishment, Prison and the Public,* Stevens

Epstein, Irwin, 1975: 'The Politics of Behaviour Therapy: The New Cool-out Casework', in Howard Jones (ed.), *Towards a New Social Work,* Routledge & Kegan Paul, pp.138ff.

Eysenck, H. J., 1970: *Crime and Personality,* Paladin

Flugel, J. C., 1945: *Man, Morals and Society,* Duckworth

Fox, Sir L., 1952: *English Prison and Borstal Systems,* Routledge & Kegan Paul

Fowles, A. J., 1978: *Prison Welfare: An Account of an Experiment in Liverpool,* HMSO

Gerth, H. J., and Mills, C. W., 1961: *From Max Weber,* Routledge & Kegan Paul

Hammond, W. H., and Chayen, E., 1963: *Persistent Criminals,* HMSO

Hobhouse, L. T., 1949: *Elements of Social Justice,* Allen & Unwin

Home Office, 1977: *Prisons and the Prisoner,* HMSO

Home Office, 1978: *Criminal Statistics, England and Wales, 1977,* HMSO

Hurwitz, S., 1952: *Criminology,* Allen & Unwin

Jones, Howard, 1963: 'Human Relationships and Group Behaviour', in Ted Dunn (ed.), *Alternatives to War and Violence,* James Clarke

Jones, Howard, 1971: *Crime in a Changing Society,* Penguin

Jones, Howard, 1981: *Crime, Race and Culture,* John Wiley, New York

Jones, Howard, and Cornes, Paul, 1977: *Open Prisons,* Routledge & Kegan Paul

Kenny, C. S., 1902: *Outlines of Criminal Law,* Cambridge University Press

Lenin, V. I., 1941: *State and Revolution,* Lawrence & Wishart

Mays, J. B., 1954: *Growing-up in the City,* Liverpool University Press

Mead, Margaret, 1958: *Sex and Temperament in Three Primitive Societies,* Mentor, New York

Miller, Walter B., 1962: 'Lower Class Culture as a Generating Milieu of Gang Delinquency', in M. E. Wolfgang, I. Savitz and N. Johnston (eds.) 19, *The Sociology of Crime and Delinquency,* John Wiley, New York, pp.267ff.

Morris, Allison M., 1978: 'Revolution in the Juvenile Court: The Juvenile Justice Standards Project', *Criminal Law Review,* pp.267ff.

Palmer, Ted, 1975: 'Martinson Revisited', *Research in Crime and Delinquency,* vol. 12, no. 2, pp.133ff.

Palmer, Ted, 1978: *Correctional Intervention and Research,* Lexington Books, Lexington, Massachusetts

Phillipson, Michael, 1971: *Sociological Aspects of Crime and Delinquency,* Routledge & Kegan Paul

Phizacklea, A., and Miles, R., 1979: 'Working-class Racist Beliefs in the Inner City' in A. Phizacklea and R. Miles (eds.), *Racism and Political Action in Britain,* Routledge & Kegan Paul, pp.93ff.

Prewer, R. R., 1974: 'Prison Medicine', in L. Blom-Cooper (ed.), *Progress in Penal Reform*, Oxford University Press

Shaw, C. R., and McKay, H. D., 1954: *Juvenile Delinquency and Urban Areas*, Chicago University Press

Shaw, Margaret, 1974: *Social Work in Prisons*, HMSO

Sparks, R. F., Genn, H. G., and Dodd, D. J., 1977: *Surveying Victims*, John Wiley, New York

Trevelyan, G. M., 1980: *English Social History*, reprint, Penguin

Vold, G. B., 1958: *Theoretical Criminology*, Oxford University Press

Walker, N., 1979: 'The Efficacy and Morality of Deterrents', *Criminal Law Review*, pp.125ff.

Warren, Marguerite Q., 1977: 'Correctional Treatment and Coercion', *Criminal Justice and Behaviour*, vol. 4, no. 4, pp.355ff.

Zilboorg, G., 1955: *Psychology of the Criminal Act and Punishment*, Hogarth

2. Juvenile Justice

Doreen Elliott

Socrates' complaint that the youth of his day were contemptuous of authority, disrespectful to their parents and elders and tyrannical to their teachers has been echoed by many similar complaints down through the ages. More than once in recent times, the way in which juvenile delinquents should be dealt with in our society has been a platform on which the political parties have fought a general election. It is a useful and emotive election issue: useful, if we recognize with W. B. Miller (1973) that 'Ideology is the permanent hidden agenda of criminal justice'; and emotive, since the heat of public opinion is fanned by the often distorted and sensational reports in the media.[1] Popular attitudes tend to polarize around two views: those who would seek to take a firm line and to punish offenders appropriately; and those who would seek to understand and help.

Just as the individual member of the public forms his or her own opinion from the information available to them, so society has to make decisions about how to deal with juveniles who offend the law from the information available; this will be reflected in legislation and social policy. Inevitably, the way in which we perceive delinquency will influence the choice of methods used to respond to its existence. It will be suggested that the way in which delinquency is currently defined in our society is unclear in three respects. First, there are difficulties in determining the extent of its incidence: there is evidence that more delinquency exists than the figures show; this would suggest that it is a more normal pattern of behaviour than is usually thought. Second, there are difficulties in defining its scope: not all children who come before the court are necessarily delinquent. Third, many theoretical explanations exist, none of which alone provides a satisfactory answer to the question: 'Why does it happen?' Unfortunately, this uncertainty is reflected in society's response, which is thus in turn open to accusations of being confused, unjust and inefficient. Confused, because it compromises between those who wish to punish and those who wish to understand – the difference between a criminal-justice approach and a welfare-oriented approach – and, in doing so, does justice to neither. Unjust, because in the course of the compromise, the individual loses important legal rights but, despite a welfare orientation, the stigma of delinquency remains. Inefficient, because it fails to deter or to 'cure' delinquency.

To test the validity of these and other criticisms, it is necessary to explore both the theoretical background and the historical context of the system of juvenile justice. The primary focus is England and Wales, but comparative references will be made to systems operating in other countries.

The 'normality' of delinquency

Various studies have been carried out which indicate that delinquent behaviour occurs more frequently than statistics recording delinquent activities known to the police would suggest. Hood and Sparks (1970) summarize various self-report studies carried out in Britain, the United States and Scandinavia. Analysis of these studies, in which samples of the population were asked to reveal in confidence whether they had committed certain offences, shows clearly that there is a high incidence of delinquency among the population which is never reported to the police. West and Farrington (1977) emphasized their confidence in the self-report method of investigation after having checked their study sample's admissions of delinquent acts with police records. This third report of their study, which was carried out on a sample of schoolboys in London over a period of ten years, showed that the differences between identified delinquents and non-delinquents in their sample were less significantly related to offences committed than to other factors of life-style, such as smoking, gambling, drinking, sexual activity, dress and aggression.

There is ample evidence from research studies to support the conclusion of Morris and Hawkins (1970) that 'delinquent behaviour of some kind among young people, if not universal, is at least far too widespread to be regarded as abnormal'. The knowledge that most juvenile delinquents do not become adult criminals adds strength to the argument that much juvenile delinquency is widespread, normal behaviour at a certain stage of development. Systems of juvenile justice which have set up a sophisticated 'treatment' approach, thus implying abnormality in the offender, may therefore be in danger of missing the point completely.

The normality of delinquency is, however, recognized to some extent in our present system of juvenile justice. The philosophy of the Government White Paper 'Children in Trouble' which formed the basis for the drafting of the 1969 Children and Young Persons Act suggests that

It is probably a minority of children who grow up without ever misbehaving in ways which may be contrary to the law. Frequently, such behaviour is no more than an incident in the pattern of a child's normal development.

Defining delinquency

If the commission of acts which transgress the law is not confined to the juveniles who become identified as delinquent, how then can we define a delinquent? Appearance before a juvenile court is no more reliable an indicator. The juvenile courts in England and Wales exercise criminal jurisdiction in respect of children and young persons between the age of criminal responsibility (ten years old) and seventeen years of age. The intention of the 1969 Children and Young Persons Act was that criminal jurisdiction should apply only to young people above fourteen years of age, except for cases of homicide. This section – Part 1, Section 4 – has not been implemented, and it is unlikely that it will be in the near future. But the juvenile courts also exercise civil jurisdiction in respect of children and young persons of any age up to seventeen who are the subject of care proceedings.

Parsloe (1978) has classified the types of situation which bring children and young persons before a juvenile court in Britain and the USA as follows:

(1) Acts which if committed by an adult would be criminal acts . . .

(2) Acts which are not illegal for adults but which society has made illegal for children and young persons . . . (e.g. certain kinds of sexual behaviour, truancy, consumption of alcohol).

(3) Being beyond the control of parents or guardians . . . a breakdown of the usual family controls in behaviour.

(4) Children who are physically or sexually abused or neglected, or treated in ways likely to impair their health.

(5) Children whose emotional development is neglected or impaired, including those who are in moral danger.

(6) Children to whom (4) or (5) might happen because they live in a house where other children have been found to suffer in these ways.

(7) Children who are deserted, deprived or abandoned.

The system of juvenile justice can therefore, for instance, be brought to bear in the case of a child or a young person who has committed homicide or in the case of a young person who has been the victim of a violent parent. Popular opinion finds it easy to identify the first as delinquent and may call for punishment. In the second case, it is more likely to extend pity, but it becomes confused if both situations are true of the same case. What, then, is the appropriate response?

One might restrict the application of the term 'delinquent' to children who appear before the court under criminal proceedings, but the research of Thorpe, Paley and Green (1979) suggests that this may be inappropriate. They discovered that practice in several local authorities has confused care proceedings under civil jurisdiction (1969 Children and Young Persons Act, Section 1 (2) (7)) with care proceedings under criminal jurisdiction (Section 7 (7)); in the latter case, the criteria for being in need of care and control proceedings in the cases studied by Thorpe *et al.* did not meet the criteria which would justify care orders under civil jurisdiction proceedings. One third of the sample studied received a care order in this way on their first court appearance. Caution must be exercised, therefore, in attempting to define as delinquent, juveniles who are the subject of criminal proceedings.

Work on police cautioning in England and Wales by Ditchfield (1976) subsequent to the passing of the 1969 Act, showed that

> for children aged 10–13, the police caution became the most important form of disposal – two thirds of offenders being officially cautioned instead of being sent to court. With one third of offenders in the 14–16 age group also being cautioned, this meant that the police appeared to play as large a part as the magistracy and social services in determining how juvenile offenders should be dealt with.

The work of Priestley, Fears and Fuller (1977) indicated similar conclusions. If a large proportion of 'delinquents' never reach the court, it is obviously inadvisable to seek a definition of delinquency which is related to court appearance.

These examples show the difficulty of arriving at any simple, clear-cut definition of delinquency.

Explanations of the causes of delinquency

Just as both the definition and frequency of incidence of delinquency are far from clear, so there is no easy way of determining its causes. Academic disciplines such as sociology and psychology have made particular contributions in an attempt to arrive at causal explanations of delinquency. Whilst many different views are put forward, it is as well to remember at the outset, as W. B. Miller (1973) has pointed out, that an ideological bias of some kind influences the ideas of all who try to explain crime or are responsible for the implementation of justice. Views on the causes of delinquency have largely polarized into two kinds: those which see individual pathology as a primary causative factor and those which blame the structure of the immediate environment and the wider society in which the delinquent lives. These two approaches correspond roughly to psychological/physiological and sociological explanations.

Individual explanations

Physiological explanations dominated early attempts in the nineteenth century to arrive at some explanation of criminal behaviour. The best-known is that of Cesare Lombroso, an Italian, whose published research in the late 1890s claimed that many criminals had clearly identifiable physical traits: a long arm span; a flattened nose and skull; a very prominent jaw; and low sensitivity to pain. The occurrence of these physical stigmata in varying degrees suggested the predisposition of the individual to crime. It did not, of course, explain it. These views were attacked in the early part of the twentieth century, and West (1967) summarizes briefly the studies which clearly refuted this approach.[2] Whilst Lombroso's explanation might seem ludicrous in the 1980s, physiological factors continued to be a serious area of investigation, albeit increasing in sophistication with the passing of time, and much effort and energy were put into identifying chromosome patterns in criminals even in the late sixties.[3] The research carried out by the Gluecks in the fifties, comparing, among other factors, body types – identified earlier by Sheldon – of known delinquents with non-delinquents suggests that this approach took a long time to die.

Other approaches have attempted to make a causal link between delinquency and low intelligence, but with little success, particularly since the recognition of cultural bias in the structure of intelligence tests. The association of delinquency with certain personality types has been suggested by Eysenck (1964), who focused particularly on an introvert/extrovert scale. Linked closely with learning theory, this kind of explanation ignores cultural differences, which were, however, taken into account to some extent in Trasler's (1962) work in the same area.

All these approaches are subject to the criticism that they deal only with reported crime; the above evidence that delinquency is both a widespread and normal part of development raises serious doubts about the validity of this kind of individualized approach in explaining all kinds of delinquency.

Psychoanalytic theories have played an important and influential part in forming both lay and professional views on delinquency. The early work of Bowlby (1953), linking stealing, among other factors, with maternal deprivation is one of the best-known of these approaches. Andry (1960) studied the family structure of a number of juveniles in a remand home and found that inadequacy in the father's role was a significant factor in these families, thus linking the concept of adolescent identity crisis with delinquency. The psychoanalytic view emphasizes the importance of the early history of the individual, as exemplified in the work of Healy and Bronner (1936), who stressed the importance of early family relationships, and Friedlander (1947),[4] who stressed that experiences before the age of seven are those which determine the likelihood of an individual becoming delinquent. Any subsequent experiences are considered of secondary importance.

The psychoanalytic and other individual explanations lead to a view of the delinquent as sick, neurotic or psychotic. They fail to take account of the significance of later experience or of social and organizational structures which influence the way in which we define and deal with delinquency. Anthropological studies of adolescence in other cultures[5] raise serious questions about the validity of the psychoanalytic view of adolescence as primarily the prolonged process of resolving a psycho-sexual identity.

The most obvious, but least studied, aspect of individually based approaches to delinquency is the sex factor. Most delinquents are male. In England and Wales the ratio of male to female delinquency is 14:1 (Cowie, Cowie and Slater, 1968, p.170). In America the ratio of males to females arrested is 8:1; of males to females imprisoned 20:1; and of males to females committed to prison establishments 15:1 (Sutherland and Cressey, 1974, p.126). It is apparent, therefore, that more leniency is shown towards the female offender. Whilst various theories can be offered as partial explanations for this significant difference in the criminal behaviour of the sexes, there is no fully satisfactory explanation; its existence challenges both individual and social approaches to the aetiology of delinquency.

Individual theories have been largely superseded by social explanations of delinquency. The fact that, despite this, the debate continues is evident from the conclusion of a study reported in 1977. West and Farrington (1977, p.160) were at pains to point out that they had not expected the identified delinquents in their sample of schoolboys studied over a period of ten years to be much different from the rest, and they conclude:

Without in any way contradicting the importance of social and cultural factors in determining the incidence of delinquency, the results of the present study demonstrate, unfashionably, but irrefutably, that the individual characteristics of the offender also play a large part ... These findings vindicate the concept of the delinquent character.

A cautionary note about research methodology may be helpful at this point. In a day-to-day conversation or interview between two people, choice of questions and the way in which they are phrased, the implications contained in the nuances of voice tone and non-verbal communication, all affect the content of the answers given. Similarly, the way in which a research study is constructed, the decisions about which areas will be explored and which factors will be measured can reflect the researcher's predisposition towards a particular point of view.

Recognition of the factors affecting research studies serves as a reminder that social problems such as juvenile delinquency have no easy, straightforward explanations in our present state of theoretical knowledge; nor does our system of juvenile justice produce simple answers in response.

Social explanations

Durkheim's concept of *anomie* formulated in the late nineteenth century has had an important influence on subsequent work. He suggested that in the process of social change and development a state of normlessness occurs when man's aspirations become unlimited and rise beyond any possibility of fulfilment. This theoretical concept is described succinctly and in more concrete and recognizable terms by Hood and Sparks (1970, p.81) as

... a product of social disorganization and lack of cohesion in the slum. A general breakdown of social controls, the concentration of persons with few social ties – such as immigrants, the mentally ill and the destitute – and a consequent lack of parental control over the young.

Merton (1938) adapted this idea by suggesting that anomie represents a situation in which there is a breakdown in the relationship between culturally approved goals and legitimate access to them. It therefore applies to certain groups in society rather than to society as a whole and leads on to the idea of the delinquent subculture articulated by Cohen (1955), who suggested as a result of his study of delinquent gangs that the subculture legitimizes behaviour which rejects the established values in society. This view to some extent explains delinquent acts not resulting in material gain, e.g. hooliganism and vandalism. W. Miller (1958) takes the argument further by suggesting that the established norms in society are middle-class values and that the working-class values of toughness, making easy money, risk-taking, and anti-authority views can thus easily be seen as 'delinquent'. Cloward and Ohlin (1961) link the anomie-based theories with that of Sutherland's differential association (Sutherland and Cressey, 1974, p.76ff.), suggesting that criminal behaviour is learned and attempt to explain why few juvenile delinquents become adult professional criminals. They suggest that three groups exist: the *criminal subculture* (found in areas where the young are apprenticed by older delinquents and become adult criminals. However, access to these illegitimate means of achieving desired goals is limited by social and psychological factors just as legitimate means are limited), the *conflict subculture* (which exists where both legitimate and illegitimate routes are closed. The result is petty crime, vandalism and violence. It represents resistance to the established system) and the *retreatist subculture* (which represents alienation of a different kind. The individual questions his own adequacy and drops out, as in for example, the case of drug-takers).

Subcultural explanations of delinquency fail, however, to recognize the great diversity of cultures within a culture. English working-class culture, for example, can hardly be regarded as a whole. Regional differences, among others, ensure that the working-class culture of the Cornish fisherman is different from that of a car factory worker in the Midlands. Further, subcultural theory accounts for too much crime: on the basis of this explanation one might expect all members of the working class to be delinquents, whilst in fact only a proportion become identified as such. It fails, too, to account for the fact that norms are frequently broken in sections of society other than the working class – it does not explain the existence of white-collar crime – and, clearly, the view of the retreatist subculture as that of a double failure to achieve goals by either legitimate or illegitimate means is open to question when the difficulty of defining common goals is recognized. The so-called 'retreatist' may well be playing a different game altogether, pursuing different objectives with a different set of rules.

Some of these criticisms have been reinforced by challenges to the subcultural approach from other theorists: early research on the internal dynamics of delinquent gangs by Thrasher (1927) has been continued by Yablonsky (1962) and Short and Strodbeck (1965), who conclude that the values of the gang are not always delinquent values; that the gang is not a cohesive group but a 'near-group'; that the characteristics of the leader do not suggest that they would be 'successes' if only they had appropriate opportunities. Along with the work of Matza (1964), who suggested that delinquency is a role which is taken on fortuitously from time to time, these views move towards a social-psychological approach which takes the view that human behaviour arises out of a complex set of processes of social interaction. It is closely linked in its criticisms of subcultural theory with those who emphasize 'labelling' theory. Developing the early work of Lemert (1951), labelling theorists such as Becker (1963) and Cicourel (1968) have attempted to shift the emphasis in the definition of delinquency from the characteristics of the delinquent to the way in which society attributes deviancy to certain acts and individuals and groups.[6] The results of West and Farrington's study (1977) also lent support to the theory of deviancy-amplification – the idea that once a person is labelled, his delinquency tends to increase. The study showed that, when compared with equally badly-behaved youngsters who were not convicted (but whose offences were known to the study through the self-report assessment), the convicted youngsters became more delinquent. However, further research is needed to identify more clearly the process by which this happens.

This broad and necessarily brief overview shows some of the difficulties in ascertaining clearly the causes of delinquency, in determining its incidence in our society and in defining its scope. The result is that individualist approaches have tended to lead to a treatment-oriented approach; subcultural theories lead to opportunity-creating programmes; and labelling/interactionist theories lead to diversion programmes, aimed to keep the delinquent out of the stigmatizing process of the juvenile justice system, or to radical social action. These variations in theoretical approach are to some extent represented in the realities of the system of juvenile justice, which consequently reflects the tensions and conflicts that these differing approaches might be expected to produce.

The conflict between welfare and justice

The development of juvenile justice has tended to reflect changing attitudes to the role of children in society. Plumb (1950, p.87) writing on the social consequences of the industrial revolution points out:

> . . . a rapidly expanding population means a world of children. The children of the poor had always worked as soon as they could walk, but now their work was exceptionally valuable to factory owners.

The horrors of the child chimney-sweeps and of child labour in the factories and mines are well-known (see, for example, Heywood, 1959). The horrors of a harsh penal code were the product of a fear of what the great social and economic upheavals might produce and, ironically, a product of the so-called 'age of enlightenment'. Parsloe (1978) quotes documentary evidence suggesting that by the early nineteenth century, while children were not sentenced to the death penalty by the courts, they were still imprisoned in appalling conditions with adult offenders and transported for minor offences.

The 'Liberal Awakening'[7] of the early nineteenth century was followed by a series of reforms regulating child labour and introducing compulsory education. Heywood (1959) notes that between the Accession and Diamond Jubilee of Queen Victoria over a hundred acts for the welfare of children had been passed. The creation of a separate prison for children at Parkhurst in 1838 and the setting up of reformatory schools (1854) and industrial schools (1857)[8] marked the fragile beginning of changing attitudes to juveniles who offended and the beginning of state responsibility for the welfare of children.

The changes in attitudes and practice evident throughout the nineteenth century were given statutory expression in the Children

Act of 1908, but it also included more radical innovations. Imprisonment for children was abolished; the age of criminal responsibility remained at seven, but juvenile courts were set up to deal with young offenders, though their status was clearly that of a criminal court. The new responsibility accepted by the state for the welfare of children was seen in the power of the juvenile court to send a child in need of care, and who had not offended, to an industrial school.

This new state concern for juveniles was reflected in developments in other countries too; many had already put a juvenile court system into operation by the time of the Children Act. In 1899, the State of Illinois, U.S.A., put the first juvenile court into operation,[9] though Nyquist (1960) suggests that the state of South Australia was operating such a system ten years previously, albeit not using the name 'juvenile court'. He also points out that the movement to create separate juvenile courts spread rapidly through America, so that all but two states were operating them by 1917. Canada, parts of Germany and Russia set up such a system along with Britain in 1908, though juvenile courts never developed in Scotland to the same extent as they did in England, Wales, Northern Ireland and Eire. Hungary and some parts of Switzerland followed suit the following year. In view of the fact that so many countries followed this pattern, the setting up of the Child Welfare Boards in Norway (1896), followed by Sweden (1902), Denmark (1905) and much later by Finland (1936) and Iceland (1946),[10] which operated outside the criminal-justice system, is all the more remarkable. It illustrates clearly that in the conflict between justice and welfare the Scandinavian countries alone, from the beginning, opted for a welfare approach. Their system also incorporated a higher age of criminal responsibility, fourteen in Norway, fifteen in other Scandinavian countries. Young offenders over this age would, in theory, come under the jurisdiction of the courts, but, in practice, prosecution is waived and the majority of cases are dealt with by the Child Welfare Boards. The age of criminal responsibility in Britain has remained one of the lowest in Europe.

Thus the development of the welfare principle was in its embryonic stage in Britain at the turn of the century, gradually developing until the Children and Young Persons Act 1933, when the juvenile courts were required to have 'regard to the welfare of the child or young person' (Section 44.i.). The distinction between industrial schools (for the younger and more deprived) and reformatory schools (for the older and more delinquent) was abolished, and they became instead schools 'approved' by the Home Office to receive children dealt with by the courts. However, the tension between welfare and punishment was to surface again and again in the next decade, the welfare principle still being far from established in Britain. It was extended in some measure in the Children Act 1948, which introduced the obligation of local authorities to accept responsibility for children in need at the wish of the parents. At the same time, however, the Criminal Justice Act 1948 introduced detention centres whose philosophy of the 'short, sharp shock' and administrative links with the prison system made apparent their association with a justice as opposed to a welfare model. This tension was apparent in the events which led to the passing of the 1969 Children and Young Persons Act (England and Wales) and the Social Work (Scotland) Act 1968 and resulted in a difference of emphasis in the system in each country, Scotland adopting a system of children's hearings, more closely related to the Scandinavian system, whilst England and Wales retained the juvenile courts. In Ireland the 1908 Act remained operative.[11] In both England and Wales and in Scotland, committees were set up to recommend possible improvements prior to the new legislation.

Developments in England and Wales

The Ingleby Committee reported in 1960 after four years' deliberations, but its main recommendation to replace criminal proceedings with welfare-oriented care and protection proceedings for all children under twelve, irrespective of the offence committed, was not subsequently adopted in law. However, the influence of an individualistic approach to the causes of delinquency described earlier, and represented especially by the work of Bowlby (1953), was clearly reflected in this report; its position has been summarized by Morris and McIsaac (1978, p.17):

It singled out the lack of a satisfactory home as a major cause of juvenile crime as well as of child neglect and, as a result, supported the provision of housing, health, education and other welfare services to families at risk.

Yet it also recognized very clearly the conflict between the justice and welfare approaches apparent in the juvenile court:[12]

> The court remains a criminal court ... Yet the requirement to have regard to the welfare of the child and the various ways in which the court may deal with an offender, suggests a jurisdiction that is not criminal. It is not easy to see how the two principles can be reconciled.

The influence of social approaches to delinquency were beginning to have their effect, however, and this is clearly reflected in the assumptions made about delinquency by a committee chaired by Lord Longford in 1964:[13]

> Chronic or serious delinquency in a child is, in the main, we believe, evidence of lack of the care, the guidance and the opportunities to which every child is entitled. There are very few children who do not behave badly at times; but the children of parents with ample means rarely appear before juvenile courts. The machinery of the law is reserved mainly for working class children ...

The recommendations of this committee were incorporated in a Government White Paper the following year (Home Office, 1965) which advocated the abolition of the juvenile courts in favour of family courts. These, it was hoped, would remove the stigma of criminal proceedings. The recommendations stimulated much discussion and criticism, and in 1968 modified proposals were put forward (Home Office, 1968), attempting to create more of a compromise between the justice and welfare approaches by retaining the juvenile courts. It was this document which was to provide the basis for the Children and Young Persons Act 1969.

The Children and Young Persons Act 1969

If, as was suggested earlier, the influence of underlying political ideology needs to be taken into account in relation to academic theories about juvenile delinquency, even more evident is its importance in the creation and implementation of the 1969 Children and Young Persons Act. The Longford Committee proposals were initially published by the Labour Party, which, once in office, used them as the basis of the Government White Paper, which in turn profoundly influenced the final structure of the bill. The Conservative Government returned in 1970 had opposed some parts of the Act whilst in opposition and used the discretion which the terms of the Act allowed not to implement certain sections. One of the most important of these illustrates clearly the unresolved tension produced by the conflict of the welfare and justice approaches. Part 1, Section 4 of the 1969 Act states: 'A person shall not be charged with an offence except homicide, by reasons of anything done or committed whilst he was a child.' Implementation of this section would have brought about a more complete welfare orientation to juvenile justice in England and Wales. As it was, this section, along with the linked Section 5, was not implemented. Crucial to both sections was the intention of the Labour government slowly to increase the age of criminal responsibility to fourteen. It has remained unchanged at ten. The sacrifice of ideology to expediency is not unknown in politics, and the clauses and intentions which were so vital to the welfare orientation of the Act have not been implemented by a subsequent Labour Government on return to office. In fact it stated quite clearly, (Home Office, 1976, p.2, para. 5), on a related issue of custodial sentences, that there was to be no change: 'The provisions in [the 1969 Act] which do most to shift the balance away from custodial sentences have not been implemented and, for the most part, must for the present remain so.'

Various factors had contributed to the fact that the Act was already widely questioned by the time Labour were returned to power in 1974. The basis of this questioning is examined in more detail in a later section of this chapter.

Although the important section dealing with criminal responsibility has not been implemented, other important changes were brought about by the 1969 Act. One of these was the transfer of responsibility for delinquents from central government under the Home Office to local government in the guise of the newly created social services departments.

Part 1 of the Act gave local authorities more responsibility and discretion in dealing with offenders. The juvenile courts lost their power to make an approved school order or a fit person order, these being replaced by the more general care order, where the forms of care were to remain unspecified by the court and decided as appropriate by the local authority.

Twelve regional planning committees were set up in England and Wales, to have responsibility for planning community homes in the area. These were created out of the approved schools system, and responsibility for these institutions was removed from central government under the Home Office to the local authorities. In addition, the new supervision order, which replaced the probation order, was a responsibility to be shared initially between local authorities and the probation service. Linked with the operation of the supervision order was the idea of intermediate treatment, which was also to involve local authorities in setting up schemes for its administration.

At the same time – 1971 – as these new areas of responsibility were being transferred to local authorities, the Seebohm recommendations embraced in the 1970 Local Authority Social Services Act were being implemented. The creation of a generic basis for social services departments, which replaced the previous specialist services for welfare, child care and mental welfare, led to a redistribution of personnel and, in the course of this, a diffusion of expertise as experienced workers were promoted to the increased number of middle-management posts, involving no contact with clients. Further changes, brought about by the alteration of local authority boundaries in the Local Government Act 1972 and by the demands on limited social-work resources of additional statutory obligations with regard to the chronically sick and disabled, were hardly the backcloth for success in implementing the complex provisions of the 1969 Children and Young Persons Act.

Criticisms of the 1969 Children and Young Persons Act

These organizational factors, which ensured such a shaky beginning for the Act and which militated against its successful implementation, provided little encouragement for any government to step further along the road to a welfare model. At the same time, other criticisms of the Act have been brought forward from various groups in society. Representations from these various interests were made to the Expenditure Committee of the House of Commons and are summarized in their Report (House of Commons, 1975).

One group of criticisms suggested that the Act was based on a philosophy founded on erroneous assumptions about the nature of delinquency. The National Council for Civil Liberties argued (p.14, para. 20) that as the Act was

> based upon suspect and already superseded notions about delinquency stemming from family disorder and legalizing a range of 'treatments' which have relevance only for the minority of psychiatrically disturbed children among child offenders, [it] was doomed from the outset . . .

That view was supported by the Royal College of Psychiatrists and by the British Association of Social Workers who suggested (p.VIII, para. 14) that

> juvenile crime is more closely related to social and material factors than to emotional and family disturbance.

There is no doubt that any system of juvenile justice relying so heavily on the assumptions of one particular theoretical approach is likely to be unsatisfactory, given that delinquency is a complex social problem requiring multi-causal explanations and solutions.

Organizational factors concerned with the implementation of the Act were the subject of another group of criticisms. The lack of resources was a particular area of concern. There had been a substantial increase in the amounts of money available for social services' expenditure: as the DHSS put it (p.XX, para. 55):

> the object of the Act was to provide a statutory framework for the development of an admittedly *under-developed* service. [My italics]

However, they felt that the funds were still insufficient after the passing of the Act, as did the Association of Directors of Social Services, who indicated (p.XXI, para. 56) that there remained a whole area of identified but unmet need.

The national economic position during the seventies must also be taken into account: the effect of widespread inflation and the consequent limits imposed on public spending are important. Reference is made in the Report (House of Commons, 1975) to the intention to increase community home provision from 1,109 places to 2,326 places with an expenditure of £24 million in 1975–6 (p.XXI, para. 56). But, as the Government White Paper (Home Office 1976 p.15, para. 49) records, 'In the event, the changed economic conditions necessitated a reduction in this programme.' As well as economic factors, this view probably represented a change in policy away from residential to community care. (Some of the issues involved are discussed in Chapter 3.) For the individual juvenile, the lack of resources could mean that decisions might be influenced primarily by financial factors rather than by considerations of either welfare or justice. This is particularly important in relation to the provision of specialized residential accommodation, which is very expensive in both capital and outgoing costs, whereas accommodation within the penal system – remand centres or borstals – is available at no cost to the local authority.

Other organizational factors, arising out of the legislative changes mentioned earlier, are given little emphasis in the Report of the Expenditure Committee. The importance of these emerged more clearly as the new system settled down and developed in the second half of the decade.

Criticism is made of the limitations of the regional planning committees set up by the Act, in terms of both their composition and their ability to carry out their prescribed function. Schedule 2, Section 35, of the 1969 Act gives wide discretion to local authorities to appoint to these committees. It was felt that the various agencies involved should have had representation by right rather than by invitation. The role of the regional planning committees in coordinating existing provision and planning new provision is backed by no statutory authority (House of Commons, 1975, p.XX, para. 53):

> They have neither the power to compel a local authority to construct accommodation of any kind, nor to share accommodation with its neighbours, nor to compel the head of any institution to accept a particular child.

Twelve years after 1969, over the country as a whole, there is little evidence of imaginative work done by the regional planning committees. There has been no published research which has monitored their function or the results of their work, and, since these committees would appear to be a crucial component for the satisfactory working of the system, their evaluation should be a matter of priority.

Another group of criticisms of the 1969 Act arises out of widely differing concerns about its punitive aspects, intentional or otherwise. They are concerned with sanctions for non-payment of fines; custodial sentences; and the issue of unruly certificates. Concern was expressed to the committee by the Magistrates' Association and by the Justices' Clerks' Society that the courts were no longer able to impose sanctions for the non-payment of fines (p.xx, para. 53). One result was that magistrates used fines less than before. A recommendation was made by the Committee suggesting an attendance-centre order in the case of non-payment of fines. This was resisted by the government on the grounds that these centres were not available in all parts of the country and that nowhere were they available for girls (Home Office, 1976, p.10, para. 32). Concern was also expressed about the number of unruly certificates (about 3,000) issued annually on young people who become unmanageable whilst in the care of the local authority – to authorize the young person's being held in a prison establishment. The issue is clearly linked with concern about custodial sentences; an unintended consequence of the Act was that, even allowing for the general rise in numbers appearing before the courts, a greater proportion of young people have been received into prison establishments. It is a matter of particular concern when considered alongside the fact that the number of supervision orders was greater than the equivalent number of probation orders issued under the previous system. It is ironic, therefore, that one consequence of the welfare-oriented 1969 Act is that treatment of juveniles by the courts unintentionally became more punitive.

The erosion of the legal rights of the child as a result of the welfare orientation of the 1969 Act is another important area for concern and centres on the right to representation and trial by jury;

loss of liberty by administrative decision; and variations in police practice. Parsloe (1978) points out that a child or young person who is brought before the juvenile court either as the subject of care proceedings in which an offence is alleged, or as the subject of criminal proceedings, does not have the rights accorded to an adult in that situation with regard to trial by jury, unless the young person is charged with murder. It is Parsloe's contention that this situation has arisen out of the problem of balancing needs and rights: a high court takes great care in reaching a verdict, whereupon sentencing takes a comparatively minor and routine role. In the case of a young person appearing before the juvenile court, his welfare depends on the exercise of discretion by various interests represented in the court in order to achieve this fine balance of needs and rights. What happens to him might be considered more important than a finding of guilt or innocence. The intended welfare orientation of the 1969 Act implicitly contained recognition of 'the best interests of the child'. Subsequently, however, with the emergence of awareness that one of the unintentional results of the Act has been an increase in custodial sentences and a reduction in supervision orders, the issue of representation of the juvenile's interests has become an important one.

Anderson's (1978) study of representation in the juvenile court shows clearly some of the reasons why this role is an inappropriate one for the social worker, on whom it often falls at present. The social worker's training and experience includes a knowledge of the law, but not the necessary skills of legal practice to act as legal representative to the client. Furthermore, Anderson suggests, the court is likely to find such a role unacceptable, requiring the social worker's professional judgement of the the client's situation to be as objective as possible. The social worker's assessment is rarely questioned and, because it is often compiled from the worker's judgement of the client's situation without the client having the opportunity to influence its content, an independent legal representative would be better suited to represent the client's interests. Lemert (1976) suggests that there is evidence of a move to more frequent legal representation of the juvenile in the courts.

An area of concern expressed to the Expenditure Committee

(p. XXXI, para. 30) was that once a care order is made the juvenile might lose his liberty merely by an administrative decision in a local authority social services department. Given a certain kind of unstable, unsupportive and probably poor (in the economic sense) family background, a young person may well find himself being sent away to a community home school without necessarily having committed serious offences. Should he object to the apparent injustice that his 'mate', who lives two streets away and was involved in the same incidents, is allowed to remain at home by running away persistently from the community home school, committing further offences and becoming difficult to manage, there is a likelihood he could end up losing his liberty as the result of placement in a secure unit. These units are usually capable of accommodating about half a dozen boys or girls, with a higher staff ratio than the community home schools to which they are attached. There are, in addition, larger 'special units' attached to the large regional establishments for assessment and training in County Durham, Lancashire, Avon and Surrey geared to longer-stay boys and girls. But the fact remains that a young person can lose his or her liberty without being committed to a prison establishment by a court. Whilst there is legal machinery for an appeal against the care order, there is no appeal against the decision to remove from home a child who is the subject of a care order. Jones (1979) has pointed to a linked area of concern – the granting of bail for juvenile offenders. He reports a decision where a juvenile was refused bail and which has important implications for legal rights.

The increased use of the police caution resulting from the 1969 Act, whilst, as the Expenditure Committee's Report suggests (p.XXXI, para. 31), 'in complete conformity with the spirit of the Act', yet also provides the irony indicated by Priestley, Fears and Fuller (1977) that the police were the only agency to emerge with increased – albeit unsolicited – powers after the passing of the 1969 Act. Their research showed clearly the wide variations in action taken by two different police forces. Of most concern, however, is the evidence which came to light that the under-twelves are hardly ever prosecuted and the over-fifteens are the age group most often prosecuted, so only approximately half the children dealt with by the juvenile justice system, those in the middle age range, are treated with the blend of welfare and justice intended by the Act. They conclude (p.99) that their research

> depicts more clearly than might be expected a system in which major decisions about children are made primarily on the basis of how old they are, and what they have done, rather than on some assessment of their personal needs

– a conclusion evident also from the report of a Home Office study on police cautioning by Ditchfield (1976). Morris and McIsaac (1978) suggest that the existence of police warnings is incompatible with a welfare approach: because police issue cautions after checking with social services departments as to whether juveniles are known to them, this adds to the labelling effect on 'problem families' and reinforces the view that all delinquents come from these families, since the police are less likely to issue cautions in these circumstances than to bring the child before the court.

Thus the 1969 Act has proved open to criticism in many respects – from criticisms of its underlying philosophy and treatment approach to criticisms about the way in which it has been implemented and the unintentional consequences of a more punitive system on the one hand and more children being dealt with out of court by the police on the other.

Developments in Scotland

Despite the fact that in the changed legislation Scotland opted more clearly for a welfare model of juvenile justice, this system has not escaped criticism either. In 1964 the Report of the Kilbrandon Committee was published. Its emphasis on the inappropriateness of the distinction made between children who come before the court as offenders and those who appear in need of care and control led to important changes, embodied in the Social Work (Scotland) Act 1968. Since 1908 juvenile courts had been established in only four areas in Scotland and so it was perhaps easier than in England and Wales to initiate a system which removed most juveniles under the age of sixteen from the processes of the criminal law.

As a result of this Act, as in England and Wales, social services departments were created, coordinating social work functions involving a variety of client groups which had previously been carried out by several different departments. In Scotland, however, the changes differed in a vital way: the work of the probation service was also incorporated into the new departments, whereas in England and Wales it has so far retained its function as a body separate from the social services departments.

Responsibility was laid on the new departments for dealing with juvenile offenders, though a suitable time lapse of two years was allowed for the new departments to establish themselves before the system which replaced the juvenile courts was put into operation in 1971.

A key figure in the operation of the new system is that of the Reporter, since he is the person to whom referrals about children in trouble are initially made, normally by the police. He is appointed by the local authority and exercises a good deal of discretion in that his role involves making decisions as to which children and young persons should be dealt with directly by social services departments and which should be referred to the system of children's hearings. He may also decide that no further action is required. In practice, those children and young persons in need of compulsory measures of care are referred to the hearings.

Children's hearings are the name given to the process by which the children's panel, consisting of three members, amongst whom both sexes must be represented, along with the child or young person and his family, meet informally, in buildings not associated with the courts or police, to discuss what action is to be taken. The child may have a representative, if required. Only if the child and his parents accept the grounds for referral can the hearing proceed. If the facts are disputed, then the case is referred to the Sheriff. This separation of judicial and disposition functions is an important principle of the system, as is the deliberate introduction as panel members of men and women who do not belong to the legal profession. The decisions which a hearing may make with regard to an individual child are: that no further action is required; that the child be supervised in the community; that the child be sent to a residential establishment. The local authority social worker is always present at the hearings and carries out the decisions made as well as providing information in the form of reports. Martin and Murray (1976) have indicated that the decisions for 1974 included 42 per cent of children appearing before the hearings being discharged, 47 per cent required to be supervised in the community and 11 per cent removed from home to a residential establishment.

The system has been open to criticism on various counts: some of these are general criticisms which are made of any welfare approach incorporating a 'treatment' ideology and which have been articulated by May (1971) and, with special reference to the Scottish system, by Morris and McIsaac (1978) and Martin and Murray (1976). Other criticisms are concerned with the role of the Reporter, in whom much power is vested – the operation of the system will depend on how he interprets his role within the discretion allowed; with the role of the panel and the way appointments to the panel are carried out; and to the structure of the hearings, in that they have less flexibility in disposition than the court system they replaced.

Conclusion

It appears that the welfare approach to juvenile justice, which has been established in Scandinavia since the turn of the century, has been increasingly prevalent during the century in the varying state practices in the USA and has more recently been adopted in Scotland, is increasingly under criticism. Indeed Lemert (1976) reports a recent and distinct move towards a return to a justice approach in America. Even in the half-hearted form in which the welfare approach exists in England and Wales it is attacked on all sides: by conservatives, because it insufficiently encompasses punishment and social control; by liberals, because the legal rights of the individual are threatened; and by radicals, because it is based upon false assumptions about the nature of delinquency, paying too little attention to causes to be found in the social structure. There are, however, some encouraging indications that wider societal problems are now more fully recognized by government policy

– an important first step to resources being made available and ultimately to a move away from the treatment model. The 1976 White Paper (Home Office, 1976, p.1, para. 1) states that

> other aspects of social and economic policy must play an important part – even though it may not be an easily demonstrated or measured part – in making or marring the adjustments of young people to the demands made on them, and the opportunities created for them – or more importantly not created for them by society.

Changes such as these are long term; meanwhile the system has to deal with juveniles who offend. A system of juvenile justice which protects the legal rights of the young person; which does not pass indeterminate sentences under the guise of 'treatment'; which does justice to the idea that some form of social control is necessary; and which avoids the stigmatizing and labelling effects of the criminal process is yet to be found.

Most commentators seem to point towards a need to separate the justice and welfare roles, thus abandoning in England and Wales the present system of juvenile courts. Priestley, Fears and Fuller (1977) suggest that older offenders might be dealt with by the adult criminal justice system, whilst care proceedings cases should come solely under the auspices of the welfare system. For the remainder of those who commit first-time and minor offences, no action should be taken, along the lines advocated by Schur (1973), when he coined the phrase 'radical non-intervention', or Lemert's (1976) less trendy version, 'judicious non-intervention'. Fox (1971) argues for the return of the concept of punishment involved in the return to a purely justice approach, for some offenders, on the grounds that it deals with the major criticisms of the welfare approach, i.e. the individualization of justice; the indeterminate sentence; and the extent of official discretion. Morris and McIsaac (1978) similarly propose a system involving the idea of separation of functions into 'formal' action (which brings the child into the judicial system) and 'informal' action. Formal action would be taken by juvenile tribunals, whilst the remainder, informal action, are 'diverted' from the criminal process. The difficulty, they recognize, is in deciding whom to divert, as well as the possibility that in the process of diversion many of the pitfalls of the welfare ideology may arise.

What is clear is that the juvenile justice system needs reform to take account of the state of recent knowledge about delinquency. Whilst interactionist/labelling theories, like any other, provide neither a total nor a fully satisfactory explanation for delinquency, they do point clearly to defects in the system which cannot be ignored. The system needs to take account of individual rights and needs but also to recognize that delinquency is a social problem and that in some cases some form of social control will be necessary. A system which is more sensitive to the different kinds of delinquency and which is able to respond in a greater variety of ways than the present one might be envisaged. This might entail the separation of the welfare approach – for the majority of offenders who are neither more 'sick' nor more 'delinquent' than youngsters who happen not to get caught – from the adult criminal-justice system which would deal with serious and persistent offenders in a way which reasonably safeguards their rights. A modified form of the Scottish system would have much to offer if it could be combined with more juveniles completely diverted from the system. Government social and economic policy in support of such a system would be vital, and its operation would present a challenge to the imagination of the education services, which at present too readily off-load delinquency problems to social service departments.

Much further discussion and research is clearly required. So is reform.

Notes

1. For a discussion of the influence of the media in one area of delinquency see Chapter 1 by S. Hall, 'The Treatment of Football Hooliganism in the Press', in Ingham (ed., 1978).
2. See West (1967), Chapter 5, 'The Bad Seed'; also Sutherland and Cressey (1974), Chapter 6, 'Physical and Physiological Conditions'. For a useful, wider, discussion of both individual and social explanations, see Trojanowicz (1973).
3. Recent research studies in this area and their political and ideological implications are discussed by Fox (1971).

4. See West (1967) for a brief summary of Friedlander's views and Sutherland and Cressey (1974) for a more detailed critical discussion of psychoanalytic concepts and their relationship to crime and useful references for further reading.
5. See Laycock (1970) for a useful summary of theories about adolescence.
6. For discussions of this approach, see Schur (1973) and Short (1976).
7. The title given by Halevy to Volume 2 (1926) of his classic history of the English People in the 19th century, Ernest Benn.
8. For an account of this, see Carlebach (1970).
9. For a more detailed discussion see Parsloe (1978), Chapter 3, 'United States: From the First Juvenile Court to the Present'.
10. See Nyquist (1960), Chapter V, 'Juvenile Justice in Retrospect'.
11. For discussion on the possible implementation of the Scottish System in Ireland see CARE (1974).
12. Report of the Ingleby Committee on Children and Young Persons, 1960, HMSO, quoted in Morris and McIsaac (1978), p.17.
13. Extract from *Crime, A Challenge to Us All*, 1964, Labour Party Publications, in Berlins and Wansell (1974), p.22.

References

Anderson, R., 1978: *Representation in the Juvenile Court*, Routledge & Kegan Paul

Andry, R. G., 1960: *Delinquency and Parental Pathology*, Methuen

Becker, H. S., 1963: *The Outsiders*, Free Press

Berlins, M., and Wansell, G., 1974: *Caught in the Act: Children, Society and the Law*, Penguin

Bowlby, J., 1953: *Child Care and the Growth of Love*, Penguin

CARE, 1974: *Discussion Paper No. 2: Justice for Children: The Scottish System and its Application to Ireland*, CARE, Dublin

Carlebach, J., 1970: *Caring for Children in Trouble*, Routledge & Kegan Paul

Cicourel, A. V., 1968: *The Social Organisation of Juvenile Justice*, John Wiley, New York

Cloward, R. A., and Ohlin, L. E., 1961: *Delinquency and Opportunity*, Routledge & Kegan Paul

Cohen, A., 1955: *Delinquent Boys, The Culture of the Gang*, Free Press

Cowie, J., Cowie, V., and Slater, E., 1968: *Delinquency in Girls*, Cambridge Studies in Criminology, vol. XXIII, Heinemann
Ditchfield, J. A., 1976: *Police Cautioning in England and Wales*, A Home Office Research Unit Report, HMSO
Eysenck, H. J., 1964: *Crime and Personality*, Routledge & Kegan Paul
Fox, R. G., 1971: 'The XYY Offender, A Modern Myth?' *Journal of Criminal Law, Criminology and Police Science*, vol. 62, no. 1
Friedlander, K., 1947: *The Psychoanalytic Approach to Juvenile Delinquency*, Routledge & Kegan Paul
Healy, W., and Bronner, A. F., 1936: *New Light on Delinquency and its Treatment*, Yale University Press
Heywood, J., 1959: *Children in Care*, Chapter 2, 'Industrial Society and the Child', Routledge & Kegan Paul
Home Office, 1965: *The Child, the Family and the Young Offender*, Government White Paper, HMSO
Home Office, 1968: *Children in Trouble*, Government White Paper, HMSO
Home Office, 1976: *Observations on the Eleventh Report to the Expenditure Committee*, HMSO
Hood, R., and Sparks, R., 1970: *Key Issues in Criminology*, World University Library
House of Commons, 1975: *Eleventh Report from the Expenditure Committee: The Children and Young Persons Act 1969*, vol. 1 (Report), HMSO
Ingham, R. (ed.), 1978: *Football Hooliganism: The Wider Context*, Inter-Action Reprint
Jones, R., 1979: 'Bail for Juvenile Offenders', *Social Work Today*, vol. 10, no. 34, 1 May 1979
Laycock, A., 1970: *Adolescence and Social Work*, Routledge & Kegan Paul
Lemert, E., 1951: *Social Pathology*, McGraw-Hill, New York
Lemert, E., 1976: 'Choice and Change in Juvenile Justice', *British Journal of Law and Society*, vol. 3, no. 1, summer 1976
Martin, F. M., and Murray, K. (eds.), 1976: *Children's Hearings*, Scottish Academic Press
Matza, D., 1964: *Delinquency and Drift*, John Wiley, New York
May, D., 1971: 'Delinquency Control and the Treatment Model: Some Implications of Recent Legislation', *British Journal of Criminology*, vol. 11
Merton, R. K., 1938: 'Social Structure and Anomie', *American Sociological Review*, vol. 13 (reprinted in Wolfgang, Savitz and Johnston, 1962)
Miller, W., 1958: 'Lower Class Culture as a Generating Milieu of Gang Delinquency', *Journal of Social Issues*, vol. 14 (reprinted in Wolfgang, Savitz and Johnston, 1962)
Miller, W. B., 1973: 'Ideology and Criminal Justice Policy: Some Current Issues', *Journal of Criminal Law, Criminology and Police Science*, vol. 64. part 2
Morris, N., and Hawkins, G., 1970: *The Honest Politician's Guide to Crime Control*, University of Chicago Press

Morris, A., and McIsaac, M., 1978: *Juvenile Justice?* Cambridge Studies in Criminology, vol. XXXIX, Heinemann

Nyquist, O., 1960: *Juvenile Justice*, Cambridge Studies in Criminology, vol. XII, Macmillan

Parsloe, P., 1978: *Juvenile Justice in Britain and the United States: The Balance of Needs and Rights*, Routledge & Kegan Paul

Plumb, J. H., 1950: *England in the Eighteenth Century*, Penguin

Priestley, P., Fears, D., and Fuller, R., 1977: *Justice for Juveniles; The 1969 Children and Young Persons Act – A Case for Reform?* Routledge & Kegan Paul

Schur, E. M., 1973: *Radical Non-Intervention; Re-thinking the Delinquency Problem*, Prentice-Hall, Englewood Cliffs, New Jersey

Short, J. F., and Strodbeck, F. L., 1965: *Group Process and Gang Delinquency*, University of Chicago Press

Short, J. F. (ed.), 1976: *Delinquency, Crime and Society*, University of Chicago Press

Sutherland, E. H., and Cressey, D. R., 1974: *Criminology*, ninth edition, Lippincott, Philadelphia

Thrasher, F. M., 1927: *The Gang*, University of Chicago Press

Thorpe, D., Paley, J., and Green, C., 1979: 'The Making of a Delinquent', *Community Care*, no. 261, 26 April 1979

Trasler, G. B., 1962: *The Explanation of Criminality*, Routledge & Kegan Paul

Trojanowicz, R., 1973: *Juvenile Delinquency: Concepts and Control*, Prentice-Hall, Englewood Cliffs, New Jersey

West, D. J., 1967: *The Young Offender*, Penguin

West, D. J., and Farrington, D. P., 1977: *The Delinquent Way of Life*, Cambridge Studies in Criminology, vol. XXXV, Heinemann

Wolfgang, M. E., Savitz, I., and Johnston, N., 1962: *The Sociology of Crime and Delinquency*, John Wiley, New York

Yablonsky, L., 1962: *The Violent Gang*, Macmillan

3. Dealing with Delinquents

Doreen Elliott

What provision does the law make for correcting young offenders? The options range from absolute discharge to detention for an unspecified period of time 'at Her Majesty's pleasure'.[1] Some involve sending the young person away from home and some do not. In some cases it is even considered best to do nothing at all. But first, what about residential forms of correction?

Institutional placements

Community Home Schools

Schemes which register so many of their children as doubtful or criminal in after-life leave something yet to be desired, and one queries whether an examination of their features will not reveal some points open to improvement . . . There is a growing feeling that confinement in these Schools is, in itself, a drastic measure to be employed in the case of extremely depraved or insubordinate children alone, and then if possible only for the probationary term required to fit them for family life . . . It is difficult to see what many of those children have done to fit them to come under Home Office jurisdiction; they seem to be proper subjects for the Local Government Board; and one would like to see them restored to some sort of family life by being included in the Boarding-out recommendations for orphan and deserted children . . .

So wrote G. M. Tuckwell in 1894. Three quarters of a century later, Norman Tutt (1978a) was expressing a similar view:

Opposition to institutional provision for delinquency is well founded: institutions reinforce the delinquent subculture, deprive the developing adolescent of important experiences of personal relationships, and create a host of secondary problems, e.g. readjusting to family, peer group, obtaining employment, etc.

During this period the reform and industrial schools had become known first as approved schools and then, as recently as 1971, community homes with education on the premises (often now referred to as CHEs). The most significant change was the passing of the Children and Young Persons Act 1933. A distinction was no longer to be made between neglected children (who had previously been sent to industrial schools) and delinquent children (who had been sent to reformatory schools). The new schools now 'approved' by the Home Office were to take both categories of children. In practice, of the boys sent to approved schools, most had been found guilty of offences (usually larceny or breaking and entering) after one or more appearances in court, often having previously been on probation. 'In fact much of their crime is casual, unrewarding, ineptly performed, and of little more than nuisance value' (Millham, Bullock and Cherrett, 1975, p.17). Boys in the South, South-West, North-West and North-East were at that time studied and allocated to the 'most suitable' schools by regional assessment centres.

The proportion of girls in approved schools was always small and a larger proportion of them were non-offenders. The *Handbook for Managers of Approved Schools* (1961), quoted in Dunlop (1975, p.vii), suggests:

> About 5 per cent of the boys and 64 per cent of the girls received in the schools have been committed by the courts as: being in need of care or protection; beyond control; on account of truancy or otherwise as non-offenders.

The schools were not co-educational. Approved schools for girls usually accommodated 35–50 girls, with one or two bigger exceptions. The boys schools normally accommodated up to 120 boys. The schools were 'open' establishments and absconding from them was the subject of a Home Office research study (Clarke and Martin, 1971).

The schools were often built in country areas and had private grounds. In many cases they were isolated by their geographical position from taking an active part in the local community. Many were administered by voluntary agencies: religious orders, or children's or other charities, who appointed boards of managers to oversee them. The *Handbook for Managers* (1961), quoted in Dunlop (1975, p.vii), summarizes their aims:

> The main ingredients of approved school training are education (in the formal sense), religious education and guidance, practical or vocational training, attention to health and to the use of recreation and leisure, social training (how to live with others) and personal casework (help with personal problems).

The means by which these objectives were achieved varied greatly from one school to another. Many emphasized training for boys; instructors – skilled tradesmen and craftsmen who usually had no formal teaching qualifications – taught a variety of trades: electrical, painting, decorating, building, farming and catering. Two schools were nautical schools, though not all the boys who passed through them would join the Navy. Other specialized schools were farm schools with emphasis given to agricultural skills. Trade training was particularly important in the senior and intermediate schools catering for older boys. The junior schools, for younger boys, stressed traditional classroom subjects, though the educational function of the schools, which were outside the mainstream of the educational system, was often not exploited to the full. Little progress has taken place in this respect with the development of the CHEs. Criticisms concerning lack of curriculum development and specialist training for teachers are included in a recent report on their educational function – Community Homes with Education (1980).

In the early years, most operated on a block system involving mass living, with large dining-room, dormitories, etc., giving little opportunity for the expression of individuality. Later, small family-style groups replaced the blocks, encouraging a more homely atmosphere and greater freedom of expression for the boys. Jones (1968) draws attention to the parallel development in adult correction towards the 'individualization of treatment'. He points out, however, that the role of the adult in determining the environment remained central in the schools. Nevertheless, a few schools developed regimes where the boys were able to take a greater part in decision-making and where attitudes to behaviour were more permissive, external controls less important. The term 'therapeutic community' is often given to this kind of regime.

It will be apparent that the approved school system contained a wide variety of schools, the character and atmosphere in each being heavily dependent on the philosophy and outlook of the staff who worked in them.

The 1969 Children and Young Persons Act brought about the change from approved school to community home school, the relevant section of the Act being implemented in 1971. Administration and finance of the schools was transferred from the voluntary organizations and the Home Office to the newly formed local authority social services departments; it was intended that the approved school service would now be more fully integrated into the child-care system. This change was completed in most cases by 1974. Although two recently published research studies (Dunlop, 1975; Millham *et al.*, 1975) describe and analyse life in the schools, much of the work for each study was carried out prior to these changes. It is to be hoped that studies will be forthcoming which document clearly the changes which took place during the seventies.

Although the Children and Young Persons Acts of 1933 and 1969 represent legislative landmarks, the process of change within the schools has been slow and the criticisms represented by the quotation at the beginning of this section have been prevalent throughout. But although the issues are long-standing, the debate about the effectiveness of institutions in dealing with delinquents gained momentum during the sixties.

It is important to see this debate in the context of a wider challenge to other institutions dealing with groups of people. The value of children's homes and residential nurseries, psychiatric hospitals, prisons and institutions for the physically and mentally handicapped and for the elderly have all been seriously questioned. Perhaps one factor contributing to the challenge to all such institutions is that in a time of rapid social change, such as the fifties and sixties, institutions which may have been slower to change attitudes and practices stood out clearly as representatives of outmoded values. There were also more specific factors influencing attitudes:

Bowlby's (1965) conclusions on the effects of maternal deprivation on children were first presented to the World Health Organization in 1951. He suggested that deprived children find their ability to make other than superficial relationships impaired; that they show 'inaccessibility' in relation to others; that their social relationships are characterized by deceit and stealing and their intellectual development impaired. Subsequent work by both Bowlby (1971, 1975) and others (Rutter, 1972), modifying the original conclusion, have had less influence and impact than the initial ideas, which led to a growth in negative attitudes to the residential care of children. Sociological studies of institutions, of which the most influential was that of Goffman (1961), highlighting the loss of individual identity, lack of privacy and severe restriction in areas of personal choice also had considerable impact on attitudes to the role of institutions. Psychologically based criticisms of the effects of institutions on individuals, such as that of Barton (1959), draw attention to the loss of contact with the outside world; the loss of role, responsibility, and personal friends; and the often unsympathetic and sometimes brutal treatment by the staff experienced by patients in psychiatric hospitals, which leads to a secondary condition caused by the institution itself which Barton called 'institutional neurosis'.

Academic research on institutions has often been focused on their negative effects, as Dinnage and Pringle (1967) pointed out in their review of research on children's homes. Prosser (1976), bringing the survey up to date, indicated that this situation had still not been remedied. Jones's (1979) discussion of the development of institutions and the anti-institution movement as well as the effects of different regimes, and Smith's (1970) critical appraisal of Goffman's ideas, offer more detailed summaries of work on institutions to date.

The impact of changing attitudes about institutional care in general has been reflected in legislation: the Mental Health Act 1959 encouraged the treatment of the mentally ill in the community; the 1969 Children and Young Persons Act similarly encouraged community approaches to delinquency; and the introduction of these methods for adult offenders was reflected in the creation of the suspended sentence in the Criminal Justice Act 1967 and the community service order in 1972.

The cost of maintaining individuals in institutions has featured as an important factor in the debate. More specialized provision such as special units attached to community home schools and intended for unruly children or runaways, or youth treatment centres for emotionally maladjusted offenders, are especially expensive because of the high ratio of staff to residents necessary to individualize care as far as possible and to ensure maximum supervision. In an inflationary age such as ours, figures quickly become meaningless, but in 1977 it cost upwards of £10,000 per year to keep a young person in a secure unit and up to £400 per week in a youth treatment centre (Howard League for Penal Reform, 1977) of which at present there are only two operating in the country. Although these represent the extreme end of the scale in terms of cost, even the maintenance of an ordinary community home school, because of high capital investment and running costs, is an expensive item in a local authority budget, leading inevitably to the question: are the public getting their money's worth?

Figures relating to the effectiveness of institutional care for delinquents have added further to the arguments of the anti-institutional lobby. Success rates measured by the crude criterion of whether a young person was found guilty of an offence within three years of leaving the institution are far from encouraging. In 1938 69 per cent were 'successful' on these criteria; by 1956 the figure had fallen to 51 per cent; and by 1967 to 34 per cent (HMSO, 1972). Tutt (1976b) examined departures from community home schools and found that the discharge rate on completion of treatment was 58 per cent for boys and 63.3 per cent for girls. The remainder ended their institutional careers in a variety of ways such as failure to return after absconding: boys 18 per cent, girls 16.9 per cent; or removal by social workers against the wishes of the community home: boys 1.5 per cent, girls 8.3 per cent. Jones (1973, p.156) reporting on a study of four schools concludes:

> So far then as one can generalize from this very varied sample of four schools, the approved school system is not yet tackling successfully its main task: that of strengthening the judgement and self-restraint of the delinquents committed to its care.

Cornish and Clarke (1975), reporting on their research into the effectiveness of two different kinds of regime – a 'therapeutic community' and a regime with a more traditional 'training' approach – found them both equally ineffective in reducing delinquency in the boys concerned.

A formidable argument indeed to marshal against the use of institutions in dealing with delinquents. Less often these arguments are challenged and a case made for the positive aspects of community home schools. However, in a general survey of research on approved schools, Walter (1977) suggests that much of the work done so far has not been influenced by recent developments in the sociology of deviance and delinquency, and by implication, therefore, calls into question the validity of its findings. Burns (1976) sets out a detailed criticism of the Cornish and Clarke study and challenges its credibility on the grounds that '[the report] consists of 74 pages and only 3½ pages are devoted to the actual results of the comparisons of long-term effectiveness'. He further calls into question the research methodology of the study. In general, one important flaw in the research on institutions which deal with delinquents is that so far the studies have not compared them with control groups of young offenders in which non-institutional methods of correction have been used. And there is little hard evidence that community-based interventions are any more successful than institutions in reducing delinquent behaviour.

Studies which show positive results of residential treatment have received less attention. One such study is described by Jones (1979). The Youth Center Research Project took place in California from 1968–72. Like the Cornish and Clarke study, it aimed to compare the results of different types of institutional treatment. One was a behaviour-modification regime, where the aim was to bring about changes in behaviour patterns by rewarding acceptable behaviour. This method of intervention derives from the view of experimental psychologists that human beings learn by being conditioned; it stands in contrast to the other method of intervention with which it was compared, that of transactional analysis. Based on the ideas of Eric Berne, transactional analysis aims to help the individual understand the reasons for his behaviour; the implied assumption is that behaviour change will ensue. The results of the Youth Center Project showed that the attitudes, behaviour, and educational performance of both groups of boys improved whilst they were resident in the institutions and also that the improvement was maintained once they were on parole. The study showed clearly that institutional treatment can be successful; Jones (1979) discusses in more detail the differences between the two forms of intervention as well as the ethical considerations raised by the behaviour-modification programme.

That some kinds of residential treatment have value for some offenders was shown in the results of the third phase of another American research project. A combination of institutional and community treatment was also found to be successful for certain types of offender (Brody, 1976); the results have important implications for attempting to match offenders with types of treatment.

There are drawbacks associated with the use by researchers of recidivism as the criteria of success: many of the studies have not been sophisticated enough to distinguish between serious and trivial offences. No research has considered the vulnerability of a boy recently discharged from a community home school when an offence is committed in his neighbourhood and he is therefore an obvious candidate for questioning by the police. He is much less likely than boys who have not been to such a school to 'get away' with the offence or even receive a police caution.

Some of the criteria of success which staff of community home schools themselves apply to the work they do are even less easy to measure. Education is received which might otherwise have been lost through persistent truancy; it varies from the inculcating of basic literacy skills to preparation for CSE and GCE Experiences are gained and horizons widened in terms of both activities and attitudes; the positive effects of relationships built there may become apparent only in later years when the boys or girls rear their own families. Trade training has often provided the basis for stable employment after release. A case example of an official 'failure' illustrates some of the problems of choosing criteria on which to base a judgement of 'success':

An intelligent girl was committed to an Approved School as a result of a combination of various stealing offences, persistent truancy, and associating on the fringe of the hippie drug culture prevalent at that time. She stayed at the school for a time where she took one or two subjects at 'O' level. She failed to return from leave and could not be traced. As far as is known, she received no further institutional care or social work help.

Several years later, happily married and the mother of three children, she contacted a member of staff of the school, partly for advice as to whether or not she had a criminal record which should be declared on official documents; and partly for advice about suitable 'A' levels to take at the evening classes where she had already taken further 'O' levels.

The interpretation of the figures relating to recidivism which implies that the schools are failing needs to be seriously questioned. An equally naïve interpretation of the same figures would be to say that, since the offences are committed after discharge, the responsibility lies with the follow-up work in the community, which is usually carried out by social services departments for children discharged from CHEs, or by the probation service for young people discharged from borstals and detention centres.

Recent research studies have produced results which link factors in family background with success or failure on discharge from institutions. Kohen-Raz and Jonas (1976), in a post-residential follow-up of socially and emotionally deviant adolescents in Israel, point out the importance of taking into account such factors. McMichael's (1974) study of boys released from a school in Scotland concludes that after-care in relation to the sample studied was inadequate; that

> boys tend to fail on release if they return to the poor family relationships that existed at their committal

and that

> it is possible that care continued from such a school after a boy's release might be more successful in terms of reconviction rates than immediate return to the care of supervisors (i.e. social workers or probation officers) who, though acquainted with the boy and his family, are not perceived to be so committed to him.

Oxley's (1977) account of two projects in America where agreement by parents to participate in treatment was a condition of the children's residence reports that 'positive findings from a follow-up study suggest that such parental involvement is directly related to children's treatment gains'. The results of these studies would support a view of residential work with a more flexible role – where boundaries between institutional and community care are less rigidly defined than at present.

The continued polarization between community and institutional care is not a helpful one, as Murphy (1978) has pointed out in her review of alternatives to residential care in North America:

> it presupposes that there are only two alternative approaches to children in trouble and furthermore that there is incompatibility between them. This distorts the real intentions and goals of the de-institutional movement.

Some alternatives to institutional care which claim to be community treatment involve an element of residential care – intermediate treatment is an example from our own system – and this confusion is even more apparent in the title of an account of developments in America by Warner (1978), viz. 'Community-based Alternatives to Juvenile Institutions in U.S.A.: Group Homes'.

Murphy (1978) also points to a further issue which has received little attention: the identification of the differences between 'institutional' and 'residential' care. The differences lie in the nature of the regime: in an institutional approach, things are done 'to', 'at' and 'for' people with or without their consent. Thus an institutional approach to the care of the elderly or handicapped would be that they are washed, fed and clothed and sometimes even entertained in such a way that their role becomes increasingly passive. Good residential care should enable the resident to do as much as possible for himself, to exercise choice and make decisions on both personal and policy issues in the home.

Objections to the placement of delinquents in community home schools are based on the fact that their regimes still seem to represent an 'institutional' rather than a 'residential' model of care, despite the progress towards a 'residential' model in the last decade. Work has been done on identifying differences in other aspects of regimes and the implications for the standard of care of different organizational patterns (Jones, 1965; 1968; 1973). Clarke and Martin (1971) suggest that absconding patterns are closely related to regimes. Dunlop (1975) suggested that schools emphasizing trade training appeared to be more successful than other regimes. Millham *et al.* (1975), in a survey of a number of approved schools, examined a wide range of factors in comparing different regimes.

Other objections to the placement of delinquents in a residential setting rest on the assumption that the youngster will be deprived of the benefits of family life, but objections on these grounds fail to recognize the damage done by the paucity of family experience of many delinquent young people. A placement away from family relationships which are rejecting, tense, sometimes violent or – perhaps even worse – merely indifferent can offer welcome relief for an adolescent seeking to develop an individual identity. That some adolescents value the opportunity for independence from their family, along with the support provided by the home, is illustrated in a report by Righton (1979) of a conversation he had with a boy living in residential care. The youngster liked the opportunity of relating to a larger number of adults offering a wider variety of relationships than was possible in his own family setting. He liked sharing with a large peer group, whom, unlike his brothers and sisters, he was not expected to love. He enjoyed the activities available, often having been bored at home. He liked the unaccustomed privacy of the large rambling building and the increased freedom and lack of restriction he experienced in residential care.

It is clear that there are serious flaws in the *institutional care* of delinquents, but the case against good *residential care* is by no means proven. There does, however, need to be greater coordination with other approaches; we shall then be less likely to fall into the trap of recognizing that some causes of delinquency have their origins in social situations but continuing to withdraw the delinquent youngster from such situations, i.e. treating him according to an individual pathology model and doing nothing to alleviate the wider causes of the problem. It should be no surprise that youngsters treated in this way become delinquent again when they return home.

Much more flexibility of provision is required if residential care is to contribute more fully to the problem of delinquency. Until prejudice about its value is overcome, the motivation to explore new possibilities will not be there and the institutional versus community care debate will continue to be an unhelpful polarization of the issues.

Secure accommodation

One aspect of the institutional treatment of delinquents deserves consideration as a separate issue: that of secure accommodation or 'locking up children', as Millham, Bullock and Hosie (1978) more starkly, but perhaps more honestly, describe it.

Modern approved schools were normally 'open' institutions, but a concern over high absconding rates, along with the anxiety raised by such incidents as the Carlton School disturbances in 1959, led to a working party which recommended the addition of 'closed blocks' to some schools. It was intended that these blocks should provide both greater security for persistent absconders and more individual treatment. The recommendation was endorsed by the Ingleby Committee, also meeting at that time, and in 1964 the first 'closed block' was established at Kingswood School, a regional classifying school in Bristol. By now the term used for these closed blocks was 'special units' and more were opened at other classifying centres, in Redhill in 1965 and Newton-le-Willows in 1966. The units operated largely independently of the school to which they had been attached and boys might be admitted to a unit and discharged from it without spending time in the open section of the school. They accommodated up to twenty boys and developed a treatment, rather than the customary trade training, approach.

A further need was to provide special accommodation for very disturbed children for whom, it was felt, neither the special hospitals for psychiatrically disturbed offenders, nor the approved schools, were appropriate. The much publicized case of Mary Bell no doubt speeded up the establishment of a new kind of secure unit for this purpose, to be known as 'youth treatment centres' and open to girls as well as boys. The first was opened in 1971 at Brentwood in

Essex, followed in 1978 by another, Glenthorne in Birmingham. Unlike the special units which, along with the approved schools to which they were attached, came under the control of local authorities after the implementation of the 1969 Act, the youth treatment centres remained under the control of central government through the Department of Health and Social Services.

Apart from these two types of specialized secure units, many of the former approved schools had one or perhaps two detention rooms; strict conditions regulated the length of time and conditions under which a boy or girl might be detained in them. As an advance on the special units, 'intensive care units' were added to a number of community home schools (formerly approved schools) during the seventies. These are purpose-built units accommodating a small number of young people – e.g. up to six – with a higher staff ratio than the open school to which they are attached. They usually consist of single bedrooms, which can be locked, and living spaces for recreation, meals and education. The outer doors of the building are kept locked and special design features, e.g. strengthened doors and glass, ensure a degree of security. Most units would emphasize the value of constant supervision and a high staff ratio in order to facilitate closer relationships with the children. An intensive care unit usually admits children only from its parent school, to which it usually returns them after their short period of confinement. Its use is at the discretion of the officer in charge of the community home for periods of up to twenty-four hours, but not more than forty-eight hours in any seven days. The length of time spent by a young person in such a unit can be extended to a maximum of fourteen days by the board of managers or by the local authority financing the unit. The local authority to whom the child is in care may extend permission for an indefinite continuous period subject to the length of the care order (Bye, 1979).

Intensive care units are used when young people are hysterical, behave violently so as to endanger others or are likely to injure themselves. Sometimes they are used for persistent absconders.

A further group of establishments to be considered under the general term 'secure accommodation' are observation and assessment centres. Young people may be sent to these for assessment when first placed in the care of a local authority or while remanded for the preparation of reports pending further court appearances. The amount of secure accommodation available for use in these centres varies from one or two rooms to small purpose-built intensive care units. Hoghughi (1978a) describes the work of a larger, totally secure assessment centre. Most youngsters who are assessed in secure conditions are sent on to community home schools, where only a small proportion of them will be placed in a specialist unit or an intensive care unit.

While we have been hearing criticism directed at the institutional treatment of delinquents, there has also been a paradoxical demand for additional secure accommodation. This has shown itself in various ways. For instance, of all the bodies giving evidence to the Expenditure Committee (1975) of the House of Commons investigating the working of the 1969 Act, only Radical Alternatives to Prison argued against the principle of providing a greater number of secure places for young people.

This demand for more secure accommodation represents an unholy alliance of very different interests. The general public demand 'protection', despite research which indicates that violence associated with placement in a secure unit is more likely to occur within an institutional setting than against a member of the public (Cawson and Martell, 1979). The media stress sensational cases and help to harden punitive attitudes among the general population. Lack of resources, training incentives and opportunities for residential workers (only 12 per cent are professionally qualified and they have worked for many years in poor conditions for very low pay) may also play a part since they often lack the very training which would enable them to see that more secure accommodation is not the answer to their difficulties.

There have been proposals that the courts should be able to issue a 'secure care order', which would ensure that the young person concerned is detained in secure accommodation. At present this is an administrative decision often made at a case conference where neither the child nor the parents are present. The introduction of a 'secure care order' would have the advantage over the present system, of introducing a court hearing, which would allow public scrutiny of the case for and against, with legal representation of the child or young person. One important disadvantage, however, might lie in the doubt as to whether the court would be able to distinguish which children can best respond in that setting or whether it would simply be responding to the public demand for secure containment for certain offences such as arson with little regard to the individual needs of the child.

In addition to the factors already mentioned, proposals such as this arise out of concern about the increasing numbers of what are called 'unruly certificates' issued each year since the passing of the 1969 Act. Such a certificate is issued by magistrates when a child or young person cannot be contained within the child-care system; it authorizes his detention in a prison. The hope is that more secure accommodation will keep more young people out of prison. It is a debate which has not excited much public interest: discussion has tended to be confined to the professions involved. Hoghughi (1978b) comments:

> The fact that there are now more children locked up or otherwise deprived of their liberty than at any other time in our history, does not seem to cause much fundamental concern.

That it *should* be a matter for concern is clear from the results of two recent research projects. Both show up features of the current use of secure accommodation which are disturbing. Cawson and Martell (1979) point out that boys now being referred to closed units are considerably less delinquent than those placed in them prior to the 1969 Act and that girls currently being admitted to secure provision are less delinquent than girls who were formerly admitted to ordinary Approved Schools. Their results also indicate that although a 'large minority' of the youngsters studied were described as violent, most of this violence had occurred within an institutional setting; very few of them had been involved in physical violence outside the institution or were convicted of violent offences. Millham *et al.* (1978) concluded from their study that the backgrounds of boys in secure units 'do not differ markedly from those of other boys in the system' and that 'The boys in the units differ from other very deprived children in care so far as we can see only by the repeated and rapid transfers thay have experienced from various placements.'

Bearing in mind the total number of children in the care of local authorities, the few secure places available in 1975 may seem of little significance: 59 secure assessment places and 134 for secure long-term accommodation (House of Commons, 1977, p.xxvi). But the numbers are less important than the legal and moral issues involved: for what reasons and in what conditions do we as a society wish to lock up children?

Demands for the increase of secure places to a total of 2,500 (House of Commons, 1977, p.xxvi) must be resisted in the light of research which suggests that it is the flaws in the system itself which generate the demand for them. Whilst society will still require that children and young people who commit very serious offences should be deprived of their liberty, attempts to improve the quality of care, by offering greater flexibility and by diverting resources into improved training for staff, are likely to be far more successful in dealing with the kind of behaviour for which secure accommodation has been offered as a panacea.

Borstals and Detention Centres

Although the 1969 Children and Young Persons Act aimed to raise the lowest age at which a juvenile may be sentenced to borstal training from fifteen to seventeen years of age, this was one of the provisions which has never been implemented. In fact, despite the intention of the Act, increasing numbers of juveniles (people under sixteen years old) have been received into the borstal institutions and detention centres operated by the prison department of the Home Office. In 1965, 1,953 juvenile offenders received custodial sentences, representing 14 per cent of the total number of offenders aged 14–21. By 1977, the numbers receiving custodial sentences had risen to 7,078, i.e. 28 per cent of the total number of offenders (Home Office, 1978a, p.42).

As things are, a juvenile aged 14 and over may be committed to one of the 11 senior and 6 junior detention centres for a period of between 3 and 6 months. On release he is supervised, usually by a probation officer, for up to a year. The original philosophy of the 'short sharp shock' to deter youngsters who were mildly delinquent from embarking on a delinquent career has been modified in the direction of training over the years, though the Home Office is currently, in a number of centres, reverting experimentally to the earlier, more rigorous pattern. The day's routine is in any case highly structured and supervised and there is a military flavour to the emphasis on drill, parole and inspections. Millham *et al.* (1978) report an unpublished Home Office study (1977) of boys in detention centres which shows that only a small proportion have no previous offences. This substantiates the trend already apparent in an earlier study by Dunlop and McCabe (1965) of increasingly delinquent boys being detained. This, of course, is in complete opposition to the original aims of detention centres and raises questions about the appropriateness of the methods used.

Cases where 'borstal training' is seen as the appropriate disposal are transferred from the Juvenile Court to the Crown Court. Sentences are of an indeterminate length between 6 months and 2 years; in practice, most stay about 9 months. Supervision by a probation officer is carried out after release for a period of up to a year. The majority of places (3,828) are in 14 closed borstals, whilst 10 'open' borstals provide 1,927 places. For female offenders, 3 borstals are located within the purlieu of women's prisons and 2 are separate institutions. They provide 200 closed and 50 open places (Home Office, 1978, p.4).

The experience of a young person in a closed borstal is likely to differ very little from that of an adult in prison (Lowson, 1975). Work tends to be boring and uncreative, in contrast to open borstals where campuses or former stately homes with grounds offer opportunities for more imaginative activities. Attempts are made to provide educational opportunities and tutors employed by local education authorities are responsible for planning programmes. Stratta's (1970) study shows clearly the problems of restricted resources and opportunities within which they operate.

The day begins early for borstal trainees – usually around 6.30 a.m. Work takes up most of the morning and afternoon, but parades take place at various points throughout the day as an aid to staff in checking any illegitimate absences. Opportunity for physical recreation and a variety of sports and hobbies are provided in the evenings and at weekends. Throughout the day, the emphasis is on routine, order and control.

The placement of 14–17-year-olds in penal establishments like borstals clearly creates difficulties for the prison service, especially in providing adequate full-time education for those below the school leaving age. The substantial increase in their numbers subsequent to the implementation of the 1969 Act, the fact that the younger boys mix with the more sophisticated, older offenders, often being placed in borstal establishments located in adult prison-buildings, and the fact that 79 per cent of the boys under seventeen are reconvicted within two years, are all matters for concern.

The main proposal discussed by the Green Paper 'Youth Custody and Supervision' (Home Office, 1978a) suggests a single youth custody order for older juvenile offenders. Until such time as responsibility for the 14–17-year-olds can be passed entirely to local authorities, a junior custodial sentence is proposed, thus abolishing the difference between borstal and detention centre training. The success of such a scheme would be dependent upon the nature of the 'training' given, but much further discussion and thought is required about the way in which our society deals with its older juvenile offenders. The last decade has seen much attention given to younger juvenile offenders; perhaps the next decade holds hope for a better deal for the older boy or girl who receives a custodial sentence.

Community approaches

The increased questioning of the role of institutions has led to a greater emphasis in recent years on providing non-institutional alternatives for young offenders. Of these alternatives, intermediate treatment is the one which has been most widely adopted so far.

Intermediate Treatment

The term 'intermediate treatment' was coined in the Government White Paper 'Children in Trouble' (Home Office, 1968, para. 25, p.9):

> Existing forms of treatment available to the juvenile courts distinguish sharply between those which involve complete removal from home and those which do not. The juvenile courts have very difficult decisions to make in judging whether circumstances require the drastic step of taking a child away from his parents and his home. The view has often been expressed that some form or forms of intermediate treatment should be available to the courts, allowing the child to remain in his own home but bringing him also into contact with a different environment.

These ideas were incorporated in the Children and Young Persons Act 1969; although the term 'intermediate treatment' is now widely used and accepted, it does not appear, oddly enough, in the wording of the Act. The statutory basis for the practice of intermediate treatment is to be found in the sections of the 1969 Act dealing with supervision (Chapter 54, Part 1, Sections 12–19). These clauses imply two separate kinds of supervision. The first requires the young person to 'live for a single period at a specified place' for a time not exceeding 3 months (Section 12, 2a). These powers clearly imply short-term residential treatment for a period up to three months, and although there are some intermediate treatment programmes operating on this basis,[2] the more flexible powers associated with the second set of requirements have come to be used more widely. According to this, the young person may be required 'to reside at one or more places specified from time to time for one or more periods of time'. He may also be required to report for supervision at given times and to participate in certain activities (Section 12, 2b).

A further section of the 1969 Act requires that a regional planning committee in each area should make available facilities for the carrying out of supervision requirements, subject to the approval of the Secretary of State.

The statutory basis in the 1969 Act, and the policy as outlined in the White Paper, provide only the broadest outline of what intermediate treatment is, and, inevitably, ideas and attitudes have changed and developed as schemes get under way and the reactions of successive generations of young people experiencing them and staff operating them are recorded. The Personal Social Services Council (PSSC) Study Group on intermediate treatment (1977, p.37) suggested the following definition:

> Intermediate Treatment is action through a range of community-based programmes planned to meet identified needs of children and young persons who are at risk of appearing or who have appeared before the courts.

These community-based programmes take many different forms, since local authority responsibility is defined by statute in the broadest possible terms and therefore open to a large measure of discretion and regional variation. Schemes in the early days were experimental: objectives were not always clear and many projects were centred on the outward-bound type of activities. Subsequently, the range of activities offered to young people has varied greatly to include falconry and discos, as reported by Beresford (1979), remedial education, community service, work training schemes, photography, garage mechanics, drama, cookery, sewing, sport, discussion groups, expeditions, all being carried out in a number of local authorities studied by Vincent (1979). Paley and Thorpe (1974) also describe a number of projects.

The PSSC study group received information from a sample of local authorities in England and Wales and they suggested that the provision of intermediate treatment appears to fall into two broad categories: groups and centres. The dominant trend, they suggest, is for small activity-based groups run by area teams in social services departments. Social workers tend to play a major role in the organization of these groups, although there is involvement in their leadership from other professional groups. The study group reported, however, a wide variation in the degree to which these groups are developed on a systematic basis. Some authorities make available resources and actively encourage the setting up of these groups, whilst in others it may depend on the commitment and enthusiasm of individual social workers, some getting little or no reduction in their caseloads in recognition of the extra responsibility taken on in running the groups.

Intermediate treatment centres are provided by some local authorities and some voluntary organizations. They act as bases from which a variety of activities take place, some being integrated with day centres for other client groups, some acting also as residential centres. Most intermediate treatment is carried out in groups, with casework or individual approaches little used. Terms used to describe the activities offered are 'treatment', the provision of 'creative, exciting and socially accepted outlets for boredom and misdirected energies' and an 'experiment in liberal education' (Cooper, 1969 and PSSC, 1977, p.23).

Having attempted to describe what intermediate treatment is, the question must be asked: how far is it successful in achieving its aims? The PSSC report (1977, p.38) provides a clear statement of the objectives of intermediate treatment:

(1) A preventative role, helping to provide greater facilities for play and a variety of social and educational experience for those living in disadvantaged situations.

(2) A provision for those 'at risk' of coming before the courts who are 'known' to social services departments.

(3) A provision for children in trouble who have been before the courts and placed on a supervision order.

(4) A provision for those in the care of the local authority . . . (including those in foster and community home placements).

(5) A provision for the more difficult and persistently delinquent young person who can be contained within the community and who is able to live with his family.

These represent fairly the 'spirit' of intermediate treatment as expressed in the White Paper 'Children in Trouble' (Home Office, 1968), in the legislation, in the DHSS (1972) Guide and in the practice, which many projects have adopted, of deliberately trying not to separate the offenders and non-offenders and thus minimizing the distinction between prevention and treatment. This has many advantages. It overcomes some of the dangers (discussed in the previous chapter) of stigmatizing delinquents.

It was also recommended that intermediate treatment schemes

should operate in the locality of the young person's home in order to overcome criticisms of residential forms of treatment that they isolate a youngster from his home environment and peer group. It was further hoped that if intermediate treatment schemes were not made up solely of identified delinquents, a young person might well continue to attend on a voluntary basis even after the expiry of his supervision order.

However, this policy has had unintentionally adverse consequences for some young people. A report by Draper (1979) on Thorpe's research at Lancaster University describes how youngsters who have attended IT projects on a preventative basis and subsequently committed offences are seen by the court as being unsuitable for supervision orders. It is assumed that since they have already experienced this kind of contact on an informal basis, apparently to no avail, they are now only suitable for care orders. It is reported that in one local authority 60 per cent of children appearing in court for the first time had been placed in care. Because of the labelling process at work in situations such as this, some would argue for a much clearer distinction between youth work and intermediate treatment, asserting that the latter should be regarded as solely for offenders. This kind of approach would correspond to that mentioned in the previous chapter, calling for a clear separation of the justice and welfare elements in the system.

Recognition that intermediate treatment is a method of dealing with delinquents only might well encourage the further development of skills and resources which are required for the implementation of the fifth objective defined in the PSSC report (1977, p.61) – that of intermediate treatment for the persistently delinquent young person. The report states that

> Some projects do provide programmes for those more heavily engaged in delinquent activity. Overall, however, the indication is that the opportunities provided by this legal and administrative framework to develop a form of intervention for the more difficult and persistently delinquent have, for the most part, not been fully taken up.

Other, less objective comments have said that intermediate treatment is for everyone except delinquents,[3] and that intermediate treatment schemes have had no impact in reducing the number of youngsters in care or in borstals and detention centres. The PSSC report (1977) recommends that there should be two components: an initial residential placement of approximately two weeks, following immediately after the court appearance, and an intensive daily programme with an educational component. The report stresses, however, that this should not be confused with alternative education projects ('free schools' or 'truancy centres') for the persistent truant.

The fourth objective defined by the PSSC study group – that of providing intermediate treatment for those in the care of the local authority, in foster homes and in community homes – illustrates how it has become the container into which many conflicts, much confusion and a myriad of misconceptions about the treatment of delinquents have been poured. Many children in local authority care already feel stigmatized by virtue of being 'in care'. To add to this by imposing intermediate treatment schemes on the present structure seems insensitive at the very least.

Intermediate treatment, as it has developed, has failed to fulfil the expectations of the seventies that it would provide a radical alternative to the institutional treatment of delinquents. Beresford (1979) has suggested that it was deemed to have links with the labelling, interactionist view of delinquency and seen by young social workers influenced by the 'new criminology' as one of the few ways of being a radical social worker. If this was so, they were bound to be disappointed. If the concept of intermediate treatment was influenced by any theoretical base, it is much more likely to be subcultural theories: those schemes which have been set up are clearly geared to the creation of compensatory opportunities for individual delinquents.

Tutt (1976a), in summarizing the kind of experiences intermediate treatment schemes should offer, highlights 'control, relationship, excitement and achievement'. All of these focus on the 'treatment' approach to the young person. Rarely do intermediate treatment programmes involve the family or the school, although one welcome exception to this criticism is reported by Barritt (1978). He describes a small project which was set up in Derbyshire, involving the creation of a 'triangle of care' around each young person, consisting of the school, the home and the social worker. Even more rarely do intermediate treatment schemes have any impact on the system or the social structure, but that criticism may be equally applied to many other methods of dealing with delinquents.

What is in fact needed is a much more fundamental change in the kind of care we provide. More flexibility between the branches of care – residential care, foster care, day care, intermediate treatment – could provide a continuum of care facilities for a wide variety of individual needs. Closer links between residential provision and intermediate treatment schemes (where the skills of the workers involved are similar) could make more effective use of the positive elements in each. Paley and Thorpe (1974) put forward one such plan as follows:

Stages 1 and 2 – use of youth facilities available to all children

Stage 3 – specialist youth club catering only for disadvantaged and delinquent children

Stages 4, 5, 6 – small local treatment groups. Weekly meetings with increasing periods of residential care towards stage 6

Stage 7 – local treatment groups. Several nights per week. Family casework and intensive supervision

Stage 8 – short-term care up to three months

Stage 9 – day care. Including educational provision and family casework

Stage 10 – full-time residential care

A young person might enter this sequence at the point most appropriate to his needs at the time. Many other models are possible along these lines and a similar variety of types of provision for young people based on a local community residential centre has been proposed by Ward (1977). Whether the model is a community-based one involving short periods of residential care, as in the Paley and Thorpe proposals, or a more flexible form of residential provision, as illustrated by Ward (1977), it is clear that the rigid boundaries between residential and community provision need to be broken down in order to provide the most appropriate 'mix' for different kinds of young person.

Crucial to the success of any such system would be: clarification of its objectives and a clear statement of the philosophy on which it is based; individual assessment to decide the most appropriate point of entry; continued and even increased cooperation between the probation service, social services, education and youth services, the police and magistrates. The provision of generous resources and evaluation by research would be important factors too.

Whilst recognizing that there are many people working with a high degree of skill and integrity in challenging and difficult circumstances with delinquent youngsters, it is as well to recognize also that they might do an even better job if we continue to improve the framework in which they have to work.

Family placements

In Britain, the idea of finding foster homes for delinquent adolescents is a recent development of the community approach; however, it has been long established in some European countries such as Sweden where 80 per cent of young people who come to the notice of the authorities as offenders are placed with families. In Britain, a pilot scheme was started by Kent County Council in 1975: a number of adolescents were placed in families, who were paid a salary for providing 'treatment'. The scheme has a research officer linked with the University of Kent and its development has been well documented (Hazel and Cox, 1976; Hazel, 1978), receiving much publicity in both the popular press and professional journals. Several other local authorities quickly followed suit and established schemes of their own, though often without the built-in evaluation scheme of the Kent project, so little evidence of the progress of these schemes has been published. From data produced by the Kent project it would appear that it has met with some success in helping young people with quite severe problems. However, its claim that it is a more cost-effective approach to the problem of delinquency is open to question when the amount of social-work hours expended in the finding, preparing, assessing and supporting of the families is recognized. Like most of our methods of dealing with delinquents, intervention is focused on the individual offender, who is seen as difficult or disturbed, and very little attention is paid to work with his natural family, his neighbourhood peer group, his school or to the wider social factors which may have contributed to his delinquency.

The Massachusetts Scheme

More radical community methods of dealing with delinquents have been undertaken in countries other than Britain. The most notable is that of the State of Massachusetts, USA. After unsuccessful attempts in the late sixties to introduce more treatment to replace the penal orientation of the training schools, all the existing schools were closed. A programme of community alternatives evolved, many of them privately managed, of which some are profit-making schemes run on business lines. Rutherford (1978) describes how this radical move happened and suggests that the programmes can be divided into three types: a number of small, secure residential establishments, some non-secure residential establishments, including hostels and boarding schools, and a range of non-residential programmes where more innovation has taken place. Rutherford mentions, for instance, the Proctor Programme where students are paired with delinquent youngsters and financed for an 'expedition', perhaps from coast to coast by bus. He suggests that this makes available to the children of the poor an opportunity that has sometimes been used as a response to a crisis in wealthier families. Ohlin (1979) mentions briefly the Key Programme, a voluntary agency which nominates a 'youth advocate' to be in daily contact with the youngster. He should be always accessible, and he is responsible for negotiating and planning on a contract basis a programme to be undertaken. The Key Programme also makes use of the residential setting from time to time as appropriate.

What happened in Massachusetts was a desperate attempt to create change, though the new system still recognizes the need for some young people to stay away from their families, using residential care as a means of supporting them. Those who use the cost-effectiveness argument against residential provision should note that there was little saving in the cost of operating this new and intensive system in Massachusetts. It is interesting to note, too, that the debate about secure accommodation has taken a similar course to the British one, centring on whether courts should be able to place a young person directly in a secure setting. Whilst criticism of the residential treatment of delinquents has been persistent in Britain, there has so far been no strong lobby here for the closure of community home schools, detention centres and borstals. Cuts in public expenditure are already leading to a rationalization of provision in many areas. The extent to which closures continue beyond this remains to be seen.

Non-intervention

Despite all the schemes, sophisticated or otherwise, for dealing with delinquents, their numbers continue to rise dramatically: in 1955, 41,069 were found guilty or cautioned for indictable offences, and in 1975 there were 148,865 (Morris, 1978). Despite the rise in numbers, the large majority of delinquent juveniles do not become criminal adults. This apparently high success rate cannot be attributed to the efficiency of the system since a large number of offenders are already 'diverted' from it. Police cautioning and conditional discharges, for instance, account for approximately half of the dispositions of juvenile offenders. The question which needs to be asked, therefore, is how far this diversion can be extended, thus reducing stigmatization and the contamination of younger offenders by older and more sophisticated offenders. Morris (1978) summarizes some of the advantages and the disadvantages of diversion. Disadvantages tend to focus on issues of legal rights, e.g. that pressure might be put on the accused to admit guilt rather than plead not guilty in court; that diversion programmes, because they are treatment-orientated, involve greater interference with liberty over a longer period of time than legal interventions. The loss of the deterrent value of a court appearance is also pointed out. One problem with diversion is that it can only ever be used for a proportion of offenders, since, by its very nature, it depends on the existence of the system from which diversion takes place. However, Lemert's (1976) concept of 'judicious non-intervention' is one which merits more considered application in our present system.

Summary

In Britain, whilst there is some evidence that attempts are being made to develop a more flexible system of responses to juvenile delinquency, it would be disastrous to be complacent. Advisory services for young people are woefully inadequate (Tyler, 1978; World Health Organisation, 1978). The educational system, the one social agency through whose hands all young people pass and which has therefore great potential for both prevention and 'cure', tends rather to create delinquency, as Reynolds and Jones (1978) point out. Much more cooperation is needed between education and social services to create a more effective response.

If there is such a thing as a national character trait, the art of compromise may, as is often claimed, be a particular strength of the British. Compromise is certainly reflected in our treatment of our delinquents. In the previous chapter, it was suggested that individualist theoretical explanations of delinquency lead to treatment-orientated programmes; that subcultural theories lead to opportunity-creating programmes; and that interactionist theories lead to diversion programmes. There is evidence of each of these elements in the present system. But compromise can be the product of uncertainty and confusion, and, as long as our understanding of delinquency remains unsatisfactory, our responses as a society will continue to be confused and in some cases inappropriate. What is clear is that there is growing dissatisfaction with the present system on the part of various interest-groups: lawyers question the lack of safeguards of legal rights; social workers resent the untimely aborting of the welfare approach; the 'law and order' lobby of public opinion questions its effectiveness, and police and magistrates remain on the whole critical of its philosophy and operation. A substantial case (Tutt, 1979) has been made for a new initiative by calling for a Royal Commission on Juveniles. This has been supported by social workers through their professional associations. The outcome of any such moves, by the very nature of the subject matter, cannot fail to be contentious.

Notes

1. The disposals available are listed in this extract from *The Sentence of the Court. A Handbook for Courts on the Treatment of Offenders* (Home Office, 1978, pp.58–9).

A Juvenile offender may not be sentenced to imprisonment or made the subject of an order for probation, community service, or criminal bankruptcy, or of a recommendation for deportation. The court may defer sentence . . . or decide upon one or more of the sentences and orders listed below:

(1)* Absolute or conditional discharge . . .
(2) Binding over the offender or his parent guardian . . .
(3)* Disqualification from driving . . .
(4)* Forfeiture of property used for criminal purposes . . .
(5) Compensation order of a maximum of £1,000 (£100 in Care Proceedings).
(6) Restitution Order.
(7) Hospital or guardianship order under the Mental Health Act 1959.
(8)* Fine. The maximum fine is £50 for a child and £200 for a young person.
(9)* Attendance Centre Order . . .
(10) Supervision Order . . .
(11) Care Order.
(12)* Detention Centre Order if the offender is a boy aged 14 or over.
(13)*† Borstal Training, if the offender has attained the age of 15 years . . .
(14)*† Detention during Her Majesty's pleasure (a mandatory sentence for offenders convicted of murder committed under the age of 18) or in such place as the Secretary of State may direct . . . for a term ordered by the Court.

2. Two such schemes which have been described are:
(i) The Coach House, Farringdon House, Devon Social Services

*Disposals available only in Criminal Proceedings.
†Disposals available only to the Crown Court.

Department – see *Social Work Service*, no. 11, DHSS
(ii) Starnthwaite Ghyll, Lancashire C. C. Social Services Department, – see *Community Care*, no. 62, 4 June 1975

3. Panel speaker (reported by D. Thorpe) summarizing DHSS conference on IT, 1979, in *Social Work Today*, vol. 10, no. 45, p.1, DHSS

References

Barritt, Adrian, 1978: 'IT as Social Policy', *Social Work Today*, vol. 9, no. 40

Barton, R., 1959: *Institutional Neurosis*, John Wright

Beresford, Peter, 1979: 'Is IT Missing the Point?' *Community Care*, no. 269

Bowlby, J., 1965: *Child Care and the Growth of Love*, Penguin

Bowlby, J., 1971: *Attachment*, Penguin

Bowlby, J., 1975: *Loss*, Penguin

Brody, S. R., 1976: *The Effectiveness of Sentencing*, Home Office Research Study no. 35, HMSO

Burns, J. L., 1976: 'The Evaluation of Research Data and the Orientation of Results Papers: A Commentary on "Residential Treatment and its Effects on Delinquency"', *Community Homes Schools Gazette*, vol. 70, no. 9

Bye, P. (ed.), 1979: *Securicare: A Guide for Staff Working with Children in Secure Units*, Denbyshire Social Services

Cawson, P., and Martell, M., 1979: *Children Referred to Closed Units*, DHSS Statistics and Research Division Report no. 5, HMSO

Clarke, R. V. G., and Martin, D. N., 1971: *Absconding from Approved Schools*, Home Office Research Study no. 12, HMSO

Cooper, J. D., 1969: 'Social Care and Social Control', *Child Care Quarterly Review*, October

Cornish, D. B., and Clarke, R. V. G., 1975: *Residential Treatment and its Effects on Delinquency*, Home Office Research Studies, no. 32, HMSO

D.E.S., 1980: *Community Homes with Education*, HMI Series, Matters for Discussion 10, HMSO

DHSS, 1972: *Intermediate Treatment: A Guide for the Regional Planning of New Forms of Treatment for Children in Trouble*, HMSO

Dinnage, R., and Pringle, K., 1967: *Residential Care: Facts and Fallacies*, Longman

Draper, John, 1979: 'IT: An Offer We Ought to Refuse?' *Community Care*, no. 260, 19 April 1979

Dunlop, A. B., 1975: '*The Approved School Experience: An Account of Boy's Experiences of Training under Differing Regimes of Approved Schools, with an Attempt to Evaluate the Effectiveness of that Training*, Home Office Research Study no. 25, HMSO

Dunlop, A., and McCabe, S., 1965: *Young Men in Detention Centres*, Routledge & Kegan Paul

Goffman, E., 1961: *Asylums*, Anchor Books New York; Penguin, 1968
Hazel, N., 1978: 'The Use of Family Placements in the Treatment of Delinquency', Chapter 5 in Tutt (ed.), 1978b
Hazel, N., and Cox, R., 1976: 'The Special Family Placement Project in Kent', *Social Work Service*, no. 12, December 1976, DHSS
Hoghughi, M., 1978a: *Troubled and Troublesome: Coping with Severely Disordered Children*, André Deutsch
Hoghughi, M., 1978b: 'Democracy and Delinquency: A Note on Increasing Demand for Secure Accommodation for Persistent Delinquents', *British Journal of Criminology*, vol. 18, no. 4, pp.391–5
Home Office, 1961: *Handbook for Managers of Approved Schools*, HMSO
Home Office, 1968: *Children in Trouble*, Government White Paper, HMSO
Home Office, 1972: *Statistics relating to Approved Schools, Remand Homes and Attendance Centres in England and Wales for the Year 1970*, HMSO
Home Office, 1978a: *Youth Custody and Supervision: A New Sentence*, HMSO
Home Office, 1978b: *The Sentence of the Courts, A Handbook for Courts on the Treatment of Offenders*, (first edition, 1964), HMSO
House of Commons, 1975: *Eleventh Report from the Expenditure Committee: The Children and Young Persons Act 1969*, HMSO
Howard League for Penal Reform, 1977: *Unruly Children in a Human Context*, Barry Rose
Jones, H., 1965: *The Approved School: A Theoretical Model*, Sociological Review Monograph no. 9; reprinted in Mays (ed.), 1975
Jones, H., 1968: 'Organisational and Group Factors in Approved School Training' in Sparks and Hood (eds.), 1968
Jones, H., 1973: 'Approved Schools and Attitude Change', *British Journal of Criminology*, vol. 13, no. 2
Jones, H., 1979: *The Residential Community*, Routledge & Kegan Paul
Kohen-Raz, R., and Jonas, B., 1976: 'A Post-residential Treatment Follow-up of Socially and Emotionally Deviant Adolescents in Israel', *Journal of Youth and Adolescence*, vol. 5, no. 3
Lemert, E., 1976: 'Choice and Change in Juvenile Justice', *British Journal of Law and Society*, vol. 3., no. 1, Summer 1976
Lowson, D., 1975: 'Borstal Training: Its History, Achievements and Prospects' in Mays (ed.), 1975
Mays, J. B., (ed.), 1975: *The Social Treatment of Young Offenders*, Longman
McMichael, P., 1974: 'After-care, Family Relationships and Reconviction in a Scottish Approved School', *British Journal of Criminology*, vol. 14, no. 3, pp.236–47
Millham, S., Bullock, R., and Cherrett, P., 1975: *After Grace, Teeth: A Comparative Study of the Residential Experience of Boys in Approved Schools*, Chaucer Publishing
Millham, S., Bullock, R., and Hosie, K., 1978: *Locking Up Children: Secure Provision within the Child Care System*, Saxon House

Morris, A., 1978: 'Diversion of Juvenile Offenders from the Criminal Justice System', Chapter Three in Tutt (ed.), 1978b

Murphy, J., 1978: 'Alternatives to Residential Care: A Review of Developments in North America this Decade', *Community Home Schools Gazette*, vol 72, no. 9

Ohlin, L., and Tutt, N., 1979: 'Children in Trouble: An American View', *Community Care*, no. 275, 2 August 1979, pp.18–21

Oxley, G. B., 1977: 'A Modified Form of Residential Treatment', *Social Work*, vol. 22, no. 6

Paley, J., and Thorpe, D., 1974: *Children: Handle with Care. A Critical Analysis of the Development of IT*, National Youth Bureau

PSSC, 1977: *A Future for Intermediate Treatment*, Report of the IT Study Group, Personal Social Services Council

Prosser, H., 1976: *Perspectives on Residential Child Care*, National Foundation for Educational Research/National Children's Bureau

Reynolds, D., and Jones, D., 1978: 'Education and the Prevention of Delinquency' in Tutt (ed.), 1978b

Righton, P., 1979: 'Home Life', *Social Work Today*, vol. 10, no. 30

Rutherford, A., 1978: 'Decarceration of Young Offenders in Massachusetts: The Events and their Aftermath', Chapter Six in Tutt (ed.), 1978

Rutter, M., 1972: *Maternal Deprivation Re-assessed*, Penguin

Sanders, W. B., 1970: *Juvenile Offenders for a Thousand Years*, University of North Carolina Press

Smith, G., 1970: *Social Work and the Sociology of Organisations*, Routledge & Kegan Paul

Sparks, R. F., and Hood, R. G., 1968: *The Residential Treatment of Disturbed and Delinquent Boys*, Cropwood Conference Papers, Cambridge Institute of Criminology, University of Cambridge

Stratta, E., 1970: *The Education of Borstal Boys*, Routledge & Kegan Paul

Tuckwell, G. M., 1894: *The State and its Children*, quoted in Sanders, 1970

Tutt, N. S., 1976a: 'Intermediate Treatment', *Social Work Service*, no. 11, DHSS

Tutt, N., 1976b: 'Recommittals of Juvenile Offenders', *British Journal of Criminology*, vol. 16, no. 4

Tutt, N., 1978a: 'Working with Children in Trouble: Delinquency – Social Work's Changing Role', *Social Work Today*, vol. 19, no. 3

Tutt, N., 1978b: *Alternative Strategies for Coping with Crime*, Basil Blackwell and Martin Robertson

Tutt, N., 1979: 'There must Be a Better Way', *Community Care*, no. 284, 4 October 1979, pp.20–23

Tyler, M., 1978: *Advisory and Counselling Services for Young People*, Research Report No. 1, HMSO

Vincent, J., 1979: *New Initiatives in Intermediate Treatment*, Social Policy Research Ltd

Walter, J. A., 1977: 'A Critique of Sociological Studies of Approved Schools', *British Journal of Criminology*, vol. 17, no. 4

Ward, E., 1977: 'The Centre Way to Caring', *Community Care*, no. 182

Warner, J. R. 1978: 'Community-based Alternatives to Juvenile Institutions in USA: Group Homes', *Social Work Service*, no. 17, DHSS

World Health Organisation, 1978: *Objectives of Youth Advisory Services*, Report on a Working Group

4. The Courts as Sentencers

Eric Stockdale

Not a little of the criticism directed at the courts as sentencers comes from those who see simple answers to particular cases without appreciating what a South Australian committee (1973, pp. 6, 8) called 'the inevitable complexity of sentencing'. The committee pointed out that

> It is too little realized that in a modern developed community it is impossible to have a simple sentencing system. Failure to appreciate this fact explains the sterility and oversimplification of much public discussion in sentencing . . . We make this seemingly obvious point with emphasis because it has become apparent to us that, obvious though it may be once stated, and obvious though it may be to many who are professionally concerned with sentencing, it is not at all obvious to the general public, to the press and to most politicians until pointed out to them.

The context was Australian, but the cap fits in England.

In the present chapter the writer does not intend to give a description of the complex sentencing process in England and Wales, but rather, at the express request of the editor of this volume, to consider some of the main criticisms which have been made of the courts as sentencers.

Sentencers 'out of touch'

It is often said that sentencers are out of touch with life as it is lived. Some of the critics, who object strongly to offenders being stereotyped, have a stereotyped sentencer in mind when they make this sort of comment; others may have a different one. Some think only of the High Court judges they see on their occasional visits to the local Crown Court centre; others think of their local magistrates. In fact, there are six different classes of sentencers, each requiring separate consideration.

Since 1972, when the Courts Act 1971 merged the jurisdiction of assizes and quarter sessions in the new Crown Court, created the new rank of circuit judge and restyled the recorder system, we have had the following sentencers:
(1) the High Court judge; (2) the circuit judge; (3) the recorder; (4) the deputy circuit judge; (5) the stipendiary magistrate; and last, and by far the largest in numbers, (6) the lay magistrate.

(1) The High Court judge tries a smaller proportion of the cases in the higher criminal court, the Crown Court, than he used to in the days of assizes. Before 1972, there were many offences such as rape, robbery and grievous bodily harm with intent, which were triable only at assizes by the High Court judges. Nowadays, many such cases are tried by circuit judges, whilst the High Court judges increasingly confine their attention to cases of murder and other matters of grave public concern. One result of this change is that the High Court judge as a sentencer in the trial court is now a little less important than he used to be in the days of assizes. However, his influence over sentencing is still great because of his important work as a member of the Court of Appeal, Criminal Division.

(2) The circuit judge hears criminal cases in the Crown Court, including appeals from the magistrates' court. Most circuit judges practised for many years as barristers before their appointment, but it is now possible for solicitors to be appointed to the post, and the first such appointments have recently been made. To be considered for appointment to the circuit bench, a solicitor must first serve as a recorder for at least three years. The circuit judges try a large proportion of the Crown Court cases, and their sentences constitute a large proportion of those passed on offenders.

(3) The recorder also sits in the Crown Court, with all the powers of the circuit judge, but there is one important distinction between the two. The recorder is a senior barrister or solicitor who will sit as a judge for, say, six weeks in the year only. For the rest of the year he will be a practising lawyer, which provides him with opportunities denied to the full-time judges. The recorder will, in the

course of his practice, have the chance to see many different judges in action in different parts of the country. He will also have the opportunity of discussing their sentences with his colleagues and of debating whether a particular sentence is lenient, appealable or just about right. The recorder, therefore, has a much better opportunity of knowing the range of sentences passed by different courts than the circuit judge, who *never* sees another professional judge in action.

(4) The deputy circuit judge does not have an appointment like the recorder; he is usually a senior practising lawyer who is asked by the Lord Chancellor to sit for a day or for a week. However, he must be taken into consideration, as, owing to the pressures on the courts, deputies have recently dealt with a large number of cases. Their position might be more clearly understood if they were called deputy or assistant recorder when sitting.

(5) The stipendiary magistrates are full-time professional magistrates who are also lawyers; they sit in the busy London courts (where they are known as metropolitan magistrates) and in a small number of other urban courts. As they are lawyers, there are two principal differences between them and their lay colleagues. The first is that they adjudicate and sentence on their own, and the second is that they do not require the advice of a qualified clerk, as the lay benches do on occasion.

(6) The lay magistrates deal with most of the criminal cases coming before the courts, as only a small proportion find their way to the Crown Court. The lay magistrates sit only part-time and are not paid for their services – unlike all the other sentencers mentioned so far. They usually sit in threes and are bound to follow the advice of their clerk on matters of law, including questions of sentencing law.

Magistrates occasionally sit in the Crown Court with a circuit judge, recorder or deputy, to hear appeals, offenders committed for sentences and some other cases. When in the Crown Court, the lay magistrate is a full member of the court with an equal vote. At the sentencing stage, two magistrates can outvote the judge who is presiding in their court, and they sometimes do so. In a survey conducted by the Institute of Judicial Administration of Birmingham

University, magistrates were asked, 'Do you think that you and your magisterial colleagues have ever effectively determined, against the expressed opinions of the judge/recorder, the *sentence* in any case on which you have sat?' Of the 1,675 approached, as many as 435 (26 per cent) replied in the affirmative (Hawker, 1974). What the research could not show was whether the results in those cases were better than they would otherwise have been, rather than merely different.

We have seen, therefore, that the sentencer will be either a very experienced lawyer or a layman. The lay sentencer will usually have two fellow-sentencers to share the decision with him and will always have access to legal advice. As there are over twenty thousand magistrates and several hundred legally qualified judges, it is clearly nonsense to claim that they are all out of touch and lack experience of life as it is lived. It is true that they are not truly representative of the community as a whole, for the Lord Chancellor has found it difficult over the years to persuade enough men from the factory floor to come forward to volunteer for the magistrates' tasks. It must be added that there is no warrant for supposing that the working man on the magistrates' bench would be more tender towards the offender than the middle-class businessman, teacher or housewife (who may have been a nurse or probation officer before marriage).

Obviously the judges are even less of a true cross-section of the public than the magistrates, but their backgrounds are far more diverse than they used to be. They have nearly all had a good school and university education, but they are no longer so often from public school and Oxbridge backgrounds. The present-day judiciary also includes men and women with experience in many different occupations, including those of probation officer, police officer, teacher, journalist and engineer. It is also overlooked sometimes that even judges can have experience of being husbands, parents, motorists, customers, neighbours and so on. They do not live in isolation, and the practice of law for many years also gives them a very practical insight into mankind's problems.

Lack of penological experience

A more valid criticism of newly appointed sentencers in particular is that they have had relatively little experience of penal institutions and that few of them have studied penology.

It was to meet such shortcomings that the Lord Chancellor initiated some elementary training in penology for new magistrates some years ago and, a little later, sentencing seminars for the judiciary. The training of magistrates is now fairly well established in a regular pattern, but judicial training schemes have recently been the subject of considerable discussion. The Lord Chancellor's Department (1978) handbook on *The Training of Magistrates* states that one of the purposes of basic training for magistrates is to enable them

> To learn about the various courses which may be taken in dealing with offenders so that they understand the nature and purpose of the sentences they impose, the other methods of treatment which they may use, and the orders they may make, and their effects.

Perhaps 'some of their *apparent* effects' would have been a more apt wording.

Most laymen who are prepared to give their time to being magistrates are happy to undergo instruction on matters relating to sentence. They are conscious of their own lack of experience on appointment and are anxious to supplement their stock of knowledge (Baldwin, 1975). The same cannot be said of all newly appointed judges. Some appointees will arrive on the bench armed with knowledge acquired over many years in the criminal courts; of these, a number will feel adequately prepared for their new sentencing tasks. They will not feel unduly handicapped by the lack of 'theoretical' reading or by the fact that their only experience of prison has been gained from visits to clients in interview rooms. Other new judges will be keen to supplement what they themselves regard as only a very limited experience of the penal system. In particular, such lawyers as are appointed to the bench because of their distinction in the civil courts are often anxious to learn about all matters relating to the criminal process, matters which they may not have considered much since their early days at the Bar, if at all.

In 1975, the Home Secretary, the Lord Chancellor and the Lord Chief Justice set up a working party under the chairmanship of Lord Justice Bridge 'to review the machinery for disseminating information about the penal system and matters related to the treatment of offenders; to review the scope and content of training, and the methods whereby it is provided'. The use of the word 'training' should be noted. In the following year the Home Office circulated a document with an accurate title: *Working Party on Judicial Training and Information: Consultative Working Paper*. Some judges were displeased with the word 'training', so the final report (Bridge Working Party, 1976) appeared with the watered-down title, *Judicial Studies and Information: Report of the Working Party*. Fortunately, the report had as its cornerstone the proposition that

> the judge called on to pass sentence in the Crown Court needs not only to be thoroughly well-versed in the law and practice directly relevant to any sentencing problem which may confront him but also to be thoroughly well informed on the extremely wide range of topics which are in different degrees indirectly relevant to his choice of sentencing options. Newly appointed judges certainly do not in all, and perhaps not in many, cases bring with them to the bench the full measure of these desirable qualifications derived either from their previous forensic experience or from their own private investigations and studies.

In the circumstances, the working party recommended an extension, albeit fairly minor, of the present limited 'judicial studies' scheme, and also that the judiciary should be supplied regularly and adequately with information on sentencing matters. The Lord Chancellor accepted the recommendations made in principle and set up a Judicial Studies Board under the chairmanship of a High Court judge.

Sentencers' failure to pay sufficient regard to others

Sentencers are criticized from time to time for not paying sufficient regard to the views of Parliament, of the Court of Appeal, of public opinion or of probation officers. Each of these criticisms must be considered separately.

It is *Parliament* which fixes the maximum penalties for offences and can change them whenever it considers they no longer reflect the true seriousness of the offence. Statutes often raise the maximum fine permissible for particular offences, as in the Criminal Justice Act 1967 and the Criminal Law Act ten years later.

Clearly, no court can pass a sentence in excess of the statutory maximum, so Parliament's wishes are, perforce, implicitly obeyed on this point. Indeed, the Advisory Council on the Penal System (Home Office, 1978) drew attention to the fact that the courts pass the maximum possible sentence comparatively rarely.

The legislature's views on the maximum term influence sentences in another way. Judges have been encouraged by the Court of Appeal to reserve the maximum sentence for 'the worst kind of offence' – except where the legal maximum is a low one, such as two years' imprisonment. The Court of Appeal will reduce a maximum possible sentence where it has been passed in circumstances which do not justify such a drastic step. The Court's attitude is that something has to be kept in reserve, as it were, for the most serious set of circumstances (D. A. Thomas, 1979).

Many of the sentencing powers of the courts are set out in the Powers of Criminal Courts Act 1973, but this statute contains provisions of varying effectiveness. Just as the courts must obey Parliament on the issue of maxima, so they have no option but to obey *mandatory* rules contained in the Act. For example, Section 19(1) provides, 'Neither the Crown Court nor a magistrates' court shall impose imprisonment on a person under seventeen years of age'. However, the Act also provides *discretionary* powers. Section 19(2) commences with the words, 'No court shall impose imprisonment on a person under twenty-one years unless the court is of opinion that no other method of dealing with him is appropriate', and Section 20(1) provides similarly for the offender over twenty-one who has not previously had a sentence of imprisonment passed upon him. The words 'unless the court is of opinion that no other method of dealing with him is appropriate', contained in both sections, obviously give a large element of discretion to the sentencer. Whether a sentencer decides in a given case one way or the other, he cannot fairly be accused of disregarding the legislature's wishes, for it gave him a choice. Inevitably, some judges would take one view of a case, and others a different one. It follows that disparity of sentences cannot be ruled out altogether. If Parliament wished to restrict the choices of the courts still further, as is happening in some American jurisdictions, then it could do so – but there would be a heavy price to pay in terms of rigidity and a retreat from the principle of individualization of sentences.

A clear distinction must be made between Acts of Parliament and other pronouncements emanating from the general direction of Westminster. From time to time a Home Office minister will make a statement in the House of Commons about the overcrowding of prisons and his concern about the number of persons being imprisoned. That is a perfectly proper exercise of his powers as a member of the executive and the legislature, but it does not bind the courts. Similarly, the courts are not bound to follow – any more than the Home Secretary is – the views expressed by bodies such as his recently abolished Advisory Council, despite the presence of distinguished judges on it.

In its 1977 Interim Report (Home Office, 1977) on *The Length of Prison Sentences*, which was circulated to the judiciary, the Council called for a reduction in the length of sentences passed.

> Given, however, that there is no reason to suppose that longer sentences have a greater impact upon the prisoner than shorter ones, the general rule which we advocate for all courts to follow is to stop at the point where a sentence has been decided upon and consider whether a shorter one would not do just as well.

Most sentencers will be prepared to consider that last suggestion; how many of them will feel able to respond by reducing the sentence they had in mind cannot be measured. Some sentencers may also take into account the views of those critics who complain that the courts are passing sentences which are too short. Insofar as criticisms are directed at sentencers for not automatically following the views of a minister or of the Advisory Council, they are misplaced. Whilst only an arrogant man would fail to consider carefully the views expressed by a body of distinguished experts, no criticism can fairly be made of the sentencer who considers those views, disagrees with them and thereafter continues to follow his own inclinations in applying the law. The House of Commons (1979) Expenditure Committee, when it considered the problem of overcrowded prisons, was certainly aware of the constitutional position of the judiciary and of the distinction between legislation and mere suggestions.

The *Court of Appeal* hears appeals against sentences passed in the Crown Court, but only those brought by the sentenced offender. The prosecution has no right to appeal against a sentence which is considered to be too low; this fact inevitably limits the amount of guidance which the Court can give on the correctness of sentences generally. The Court essentially hears appeals against sentences which are complained of as being too high; it rarely has the opportunity of considering the 'ordinary' sentences being passed. One of the shortcomings of this practice is that the members of the Court may be getting a wrong impression of what is happening in the Crown Court generally. In allowing or dismissing an appeal against sentence, the Court of Appeal will give detailed reasons, which will be transmitted to the sentencing judge. In the past, the judiciary generally became aware of appeal decisions from the very limited reports of such cases, but the new Judicial Studies Board should be able to ensure that courts are better informed in future. The combined effect of all recent appeal decisions has been brilliantly set out by D. A. Thomas (1979) in his *Principles of Sentencing*, a copy of which is provided to the judges, and his notes on sentencing appeals in the Criminal Appeal Reports (Sentencing) and in the *Criminal Law Review*, which have also helped to narrow the information gap. The Court of Appeal complains from time to time that one or other of its decisions has been ignored by a particular judge, but there is no ground for supposing that the judiciary generally fails to follow the guidelines of the higher court.

The guidelines laid down by the Court of Appeal may also include references to considerations such as the overcrowding of prisons. Whilst a sentencer could not be faulted for choosing to ignore a politician's statement on the subject (even that of the minister concerned with prisons), he may be fairly criticized for failing to follow the directions of a higher court. On 24 April 1980, Lord Lane, the new Lord Chief Justice, made an important announcement in the Court of Appeal in the case of *Upton* (see *The Times*, 25 April 1980): the time had come to appreciate that non-violent petty offenders should not be allowed to take up what had become valuable space in prison. If there really was no alternative to an immediate prison sentence, then it should be as short as possible. Sentencing judges should appreciate that overcrowding in many of the penal establishments in this country was such that a prison sentence, however short, was a very unpleasant experience indeed for inmates. These guidelines should – and doubtless will – carry considerably more weight with sentencers than a similar plea from Westminster.

Appeals from the magistrates' court against sentence are heard by the Crown Court, where the sentence will be considered afresh by a judge and two magistrates. This participation by the magistrates is very useful, apart from anything else, in that it provides a ready communications link between the two courts. The Crown Court appeal decisions are not reported, save by the local press, but the magistrates can bring to their local benches any lessons to be learned from the appellate work of the Crown Court. Once again, there is no reason to suppose that magistrates do not try to follow such guidelines as are provided by their local Crown Court.

Public opinion is often said to be ignored by sentencers. Such comments sometimes appear in letters claiming, with dubious authority, to speak for the silent majority. One of the major problems is that it is extremely difficult for the mere sentencer – never mind the social scientist – to ascertain what public opinion is. It is not difficult for the sentencer to gather that the public is basically against bank robbery and rape. It is not so easy to discover what the public at large, or even a majority of the public, feels is an appropriate sentence for a baby snatcher. If the judge imprisons the disturbed female offender, he is liable to be called heartless and unnecessarily harsh by some. If he does not imprison her, he may well be attacked by others for 'putting all our babies at risk'. The judge will be able to comfort himself with the thought that he had considerably more information to go on than the ten-line summary of the case by a newspaper reporter. One of the unfortunate results of the provision – for the sentencer's use – of a large amount of information about the offender in written social inquiry, medical and other reports is that the public now obtains a smaller proportion of the total information than formerly.

A few years ago an apparently lenient sentence in two rape cases caused a certain amount of indignation – although what proportion of the public was indignant cannot be ascertained. Some of the more angry critics called for the dismissal of the judges in question, overlooking the constitutional implications of their call. A judiciary liable to be dismissed if it offends some Members of Parliament or of the public is scarcely in a better position to serve the public properly than a judiciary subject to removal at the whim of a Stuart monarch. Lord Hailsham pointed out the dangers at the time (Hailsham, 1975):

> My main object in writing, however, is to warn against the encroachment on the independence of the judiciary implicit in some actions by some Members of Parliament and some press comment. Modern practice does not inhibit, indeed encourages, criticism of individual sentences, and this is wholly healthy. But nearly four years as Lord Chancellor leads me to believe that it is seldom profitable to discuss sentences on the basis of press reports alone without, at least, a full transcript of the proceedings. When criticisms amount to demands for the removal of a Crown Court judge by political pressure brought on a Lord Chancellor, and are founded on the supposed inadequacy of a single sentence, they begin to constitute a serious danger to judicial independence.

Reference has already been made to the difficulty of measuring public opinion, but even if a sentencer could find a satisfactory test, he would still have to decide how much notice to take of such opinion. In 1975 the European Committee on Crime Problems (1975, p.31) made the following comments in its report on *Sentencing*:

> A number of participants at the judicial seminar recognized that public opinion had a strong influence on sentencing . . . It was thought right not only that judges (who were, after all, members of the public) should follow public opinion in some cases, but should also try to lead it in others.

Unfortunately the Committee did not go on to suggest how the judges should distinguish those cases in which they were to lead from those in which they ought to be followers of public opinion. The truth, perhaps, is that most judges are influenced but not ruled by what they consider to be the views of the majority of the law-abiding section of the community.

The Probation and After-care Service provides the courts with about a quarter of a million social inquiry or pre-sentence reports annually. A little over a quarter of them are for the Crown Court, the remainder for the magistrates' courts, including juvenile courts. Inevitably, with so many probation officers and so many sentencers being involved, the latter have on occasion been criticized by the former for not taking enough notice of the reports or for commenting adversely on their contents. Difficulties have arisen from time to time over the propriety of the probation officer making a recommendation in his report. As long ago as 1961, the Streatfeild Committee considered the problem (Streatfeild, 1961). In an oft-quoted passage, the committee stated that

> The first function of a probation report is to provide information about the offender and his background ... Secondly, probation officers have been encouraged at some courts to express an opinion about the likely response of the offender to probation and other forms of sentence. We endorse these aspects of the probation report.

Whilst many courts were prepared from then on to receive a recommendation about both 'probation and other forms of sentence', some courts were still only prepared to entertain an opinion on the prospects of success of a probation order, if made. One of the reasons for the reluctance of those courts to hear further opinions was that, as Martin Davies (1974, p.24) has pointed out, 'Probation officers are trained as social workers and not as correctional agents.' Their experience is principally in the community, even though the service has in recent years taken over welfare work in penal institutions as well as after-care work. In 1974, the Home Secretary, with the approval of the Lord Chief Justice, wrote to all chief probation officers:

> If an experienced probation officer feels able to make a specific recommendation in favour of (or against) any particular form of decision being reached, he should state it clearly in his report.

The courts were notified accordingly, so one can understand experienced probation officers feeling offended if they are rebuked for making a specific recommendation.

A recent case causing some adverse comment in probation circles was that of *Blowers* (reported in the *Criminal Law Review*, 1977, p.71ff. See also Harris, 1979). Blowers had pleaded guilty to two assaults with intent to rob and had been sentenced to four years' imprisonment. He and a companion had assaulted an elderly couple in the street. He had three previous convictions: for assault, possessing an offensive weapon and criminal damage, but had only been fined before. The Court of Appeal, in rejecting his appeal against sentence, commented that it was surprised to note the probation officer's recommendation that a community service order might be tried. The court added that such unrealistic recommendations created difficulties.

Helen Napier (1978, p.122), writing in the *Probation Journal*, criticized the court's strictures on three grounds:

> Firstly it invites probation officers to offer their own prejudgment of the sentence by considering the whole range of factors which are relevant to the court's decision . . . Secondly these comments suggest that probation officers should have in mind, at the time of writing their reports, what a court is likely to do and should keep their recommendations within a 'realistic' (i.e. acceptable to the court) amount of deviation from this . . . Thirdly it blurs the distinction between the role of the probation officer and that of the sentencer.

Roy Barr, the liaison probation officer on duty in the Court of Appeal when the case was heard, in a letter responding to Helen Napier, suggested that the problem was more apparent than real (Barr, 1979, p.26):

> The problem of 'realism' in recommendations to the court can be resolved quite simply. Colleagues in the expression of their professional opinion as to disposal adhere to a formula in which they make their suggestion coupled with an acknowledgement that they 'realize' the court, having other factors to consider, may not be able to accept it; e.g. 'it is suggested with respect the imposition of a suspended sentence of imprisonment (or whatever) would be an appropriate and constructive disposal in this case. I

do however realize the court might be unable to accept this in the light of its responsibility to protect the public.'

This suggestion would seem to be eminently sensible and, if put into practice, should help to end the discussion, which after all these years is becoming a bit of a bore!

Plea bargaining

The practice of plea bargaining, or plea discussion, is a topic which has only fairly recently come up for regular discussion in England, although in the United States it has caused major concern for some years. The issue arises, for example, when a defendant receives an indication from his lawyer that he has discussed the case with his opponent and that it might be wise to plead guilty to some of the various charges. Any defendant in a criminal court is under pressure; what causes concern is improper pressure, whether applied by a lawyer or, worse, by a sentencer. A patient in hospital for an operation is under similar pressure – important decisions have to be made and he cannot be sure how sound the advice of his professional advisers is. The defendant has the advantage over the patient that he knows the truth about the basic fact. The patient will not know whether his appendix ought to come out or not, but the defendant will know whether he is guilty or not (save in the rare case where there is a tricky point of law).

A frequent instance of a discussion of pleas between counsel for the prosecution and the defence is in the case of wounding or causing grievous bodily harm with intent – a more serious offence than one committed without that specific intent. Juries will very often acquit of the more serious offence and convict on the lesser alternative charge, despite the fact that the use of a knife, say, points to the existence of the serious intent at the material time. In such circumstances it is perfectly proper for counsel for one side or the other to suggest that a plea of guilty to the lesser charge should suffice. If the defendant agrees to such a course, the judge's approval will usually be obtained and a trial averted. The defendant will be advised by his counsel that he must not plead guilty even to the lesser charge unless he is in truth guilty.

The writer raised the question of plea bargaining in such cases in an article in the *Criminal Law Review* in 1958, and discussed it in a book in 1967 (Stockdale, 1958 and 1967). In the book (pp.22, 23) the writer commented that 'provided that everything that is done is done in the best interests of the public and of the accused, this procedure seems to have several advantages to commend it', but added that the matter 'ought to be discussed properly'. It was not until 1970, when the Court of Appeal decided the case of *Turner* (reported in the *Criminal Appeal Reports*, vol. 54, p.352), that a serious discussion began, although Paul Thomas (1969) had written a useful initial article a short while earlier. Turner, the Court decided, might have got the impression from his counsel that the judge had indicated that there would be a more lenient sentence if he were to change his plea to guilty. The Court laid down some guidelines for courts:

(1) Counsel must be free to advise his client, in strong terms if necessary, and his advice may properly include the statement that a plea of guilty can be regarded as a mitigating factor.

(2) The defendant must have a freedom of choice after receiving advice.

(3) Both counsel must be able to speak to the judge, but such exchanges should preferably take place in open court.

(4) The judge should never indicate the exact sentence he may impose, save that he may indicate that, whether the defendant pleads guilty or is found guilty by the jury at the end of a trial, the sentence will be the same either way, e.g. probation.

Much of the pressure on the defendant arises from the fact that a court may properly consider giving him a lesser sentence for pleading guilty. He may well feel that it would pay him to admit his guilt in those circumstances. If he is in truth guilty and pleads guilty, no harm will have been done by such a plea as far as the public interest is concerned: all that will have happened is that the defendant will have foregone his chance of an acquittal by the jury despite his guilt. The decision in *Turner* seemed at the time to provide adequate safeguards against improper pressures being applied, and a number of commentators were satisfied that all was well. For example, Anthony Davis (1971, p.228) wrote, 'Such discussions as go on informally . . . are not, apparently, harmful.' Similarly, Sarah McCabe and Robert Purves (1972) concluded:

It is difficult to see how the practice of plea bargaining *as it exists in England* operates to deny the defendant his 'right to put the prosecution to its proof'. Rather, it clearly operates to provide the defendant with the opportunity to confess under conditions of tactical advantage calculated to secure the best possible terms, particularly if the defendant waits to change his plea.

Unfortunately, one or two cases since then and the research of John Baldwin and Michael McConville (1977) show that there is cause for concern, despite the Court of Appeal guidelines. Baldwin and McConville relied heavily on answers from defendants themselves, but it would be a mistake to disregard all the evidence from such sources, especially where confirmation was available from others. One defendant who changed his plea to guilty at the last moment maintained:

In the end, I just pleaded guilty to get it over and done with, really. I am still innocent, but what can you do? I'd got no choice but to plead guilty – that's how I saw it, anyway. If your barrister comes up to you and tells you you've got a 50–50 chance that if you plead guilty you'll get off with less than if you plead innocent, well, what would you do?

Many readers will answer the question by saying, 'If I was really not guilty, then I would not plead guilty, even though the sentence after a conviction by the jury – which might never happen – could be longer.'

Another defendant told the researchers:

The barrister wanted to get it over with. He went to see the judge with the other barrister and told me that if I pleaded guilty, I would get a suspended sentence, but if I fought the case, I'd be done for wasting the court's time and would get three years' imprisonment or, if I was lucky, a suspended sentence. He left it up to me – so I pleaded guilty and got a suspended sentence.

There would seem to be three alternative explanations for this statement: (i) If it was true that the judge threatened a three-year sentence (which could not in law be suspended) when the proper sentence was a suspended one of two years or less, then he was behaving outrageously and both counsel should have reported him to the Lord Chancellor. (ii) If counsel lied to his client about what the judge had said, then he acted most improperly. (iii) Alternatively, the defendant may have misled the researchers, either deliberately or because he had completely misunderstood what counsel had told him. There were, however, other cases recounted which were more disturbing than these two.

Baldwin and McConville concluded their important work with the suggestion that much of the difficulty would be removed if the courts were to stop giving lesser sentences for pleas of guilty – as they quite often do: 'The operation of the discount system has in our view little to do with justice; it exists primarily because of administrative expedience.' It is certainly difficult to see why a professional burglar, who has been caught red-handed in the middle of the night in someone else's house, should be given any credit for admitting his guilt.

In view of the importance of the issues raised by Baldwin and McConville, it is most unfortunate that the legal profession should have resented their report as much as it did. If ever there was a discussion topic which called for the close cooperation of judiciary, legal profession and academics, the future of pleas of guilty is one.

Disparity

Recurring criticisms of judges and magistrates are that their sentences do not always match those passed on similar offenders in other courts and that it is difficult to see the justification for the different sentences passed on co-defendants in the same case. It is far easier for a sentencer to arrive at a fair balance between different offenders in the same case than for him to fit those sentences in with others passed in different courts. So, too, it is easier for the Court of Appeal to correct disparity where it exists in a single case with a number of defendants. In considering such appeals the Court is handicapped to some extent by its inability to increase a sentence which it considers to be too low. The only way it can correct any disparity which is thought to be serious enough to warrant appellate correction is to reduce the sentence of the aggrieved appellant. However, this will normally only be done where there is 'such a glaring difference between the treatment of one man as compared with another that a real sense of grievance would be engendered' (D. A. Thomas, 1979, p.32).

Difficulties sometimes arise because co-defendants are sentenced at different times; for example, one may fail to surrender to his bail until months after his companion has been sentenced. It has sometimes happened that the latecomer has had to be dealt with by another judge, as the first was no longer available. This has increased the difficulties, but the courts administrators now have instructions to try and avert such problems by ensuring that the same sentencer is available whenever possible.

Sentencers generally are very conscious of the need to try to do justice as between co-defendants, and they strive to assess fairly the relative degrees of culpability and to give the appropriate weight to the differing mitigating circumstances and previous histories. In doing so, courts must be careful to avoid any suggestion that they are applying one law for the rich and another for the poor. The problem of co-defendants with differing abilities to pay a fine is as old as fines themselves. Often one defendant has savings and earnings, while the other is penniless and unemployed. The more prosperous of the two offenders obviously cannot be allowed to 'buy' his way out of prison, if that be the correct sentence. This particular problem of differing abilities to pay has increased in recent years, not only because of increased unemployment, but also because of the introduction of the attractive idea of the compensation order. The idea of the victim being compensated by the offender has great appeal, but it is often bedevilled by the inability of one of two defendants to pay, a matter which the court must bear in mind, as the Powers of Criminal Courts Act 1973, Section 35(4) makes clear.

The inevitability of some degree of sentencing disparity emerged from the earlier discussion of public opinion. Just as members of the public will have differing views about the gravity of particular offences, so will the sentencers, who number over twenty thousand. Some of the earlier studies of disparities were considered by Roger Hood and Richard Sparks in their useful 1970 book, *Key Issues in Criminology*, but the most detailed study of the subject appeared in the following year. This was John Hogarth's (1971, p.299) monumental study of Canadian sentencers, with the significant title, *Sentencing as a Human Process*. Hogarth considered the many factors which contribute to inconsistencies, and made the point that they exist

> not only in sentencing practices but also in the principles that the courts apply. These differences not only reflect divisions among judges and magistrates as to the principles of sentencing, but also deep contradictions within society as to what the proper basis should be for dealing with crime ... Until these fundamental contradictions in principle are resolved, differences are bound to exist in the kinds of information different judges and magistrates consider relevant to the cases before them.

When one bears in mind that some of the problems are caused, as Hogarth demonstrated, by society generally having differing views about sentencing objectives, then one can see that merely transferring the sentencing powers from the courts to some other sentencing authority would be unlikely to make the problem of disparity disappear. A broad training and a constant supply of useful information for sentencers, coupled with a satisfactory appeal system, would seem to provide the best safeguard against disparities being too great.

Alternative sentencing tribunals

Granted that some of the criticisms of the present system may be justified, the question which arises is, What alternative individuals, or groups of individuals, would produce better sentences? There are three classes of person who can contribute to a sentencing decision: (i) the judges and magistrates; (ii) the experts in different fields, such as psychiatrists and psychologists, probation officers and other social workers, research and academic criminologists, prison and police service representatives; (iii) representatives of the general public other than the above. A sentencing body could be made up from each of the three classes or from any two of them. Whilst sentencing is now undertaken by members of the first class alone and could be done by the second class, it is unlikely that satisfactory results would be obtained by resorting to the third class on its own. There might be a role for members of the public alone in minor cases, such as litter-dropping, but it is unlikely that this country would welcome the introduction of the 'comrade' courts tried in some countries. It would be far more sensible for us to take such minor offences out of the sphere of the criminal courts altogether.

For many years, we have had sentencing in important cases by a single judge. One way of reducing disparity might be to have three professional judges jointly determining sentences. There is no guarantee that such a course would improve sentencing markedly; more important, we could not find sufficient additional judges in the foreseeable future to make such a provision possible – even though continental jurisdictions, with a professional judiciary running into many thousands, can apparently afford to have more than one judge involved in serious cases. Many judges sitting in the Crown Court welcome the help of magistrates in those cases in which they sit to sentence, but, once again, it is difficult to see how we could obtain enough extra magistrates to increase the number of occasions when a composite bench of lawyer and two laymen could adjudicate jointly. The only large pool of laymen available to the courts is the pool from which jurors are drawn. If we were to restrict the right to jury trial further, we might be able to use 'spared' jurors to sit with the judge for sentencing purposes. Once again, this solution is only theoretical, as it is unlikely that the use of the jury will be substantially curtailed, even though the implementation of more recommendations of the James Committee (1975) (on the trial of minor offences) may be forced on us by the pressure of numbers in the Crown Court.

As many Crown Court judges have found discussion with their magisterial colleagues helpful, it might be thought worthwhile to consider the system tried in some American jurisdictions, in which the trial judge discusses his sentence with two of his colleagues before passing it. It is unlikely that such a system would prove acceptable in England, where we appreciate the general rule that all judges contributing to the decision should be present throughout the material stage of the process. A more attractive idea, perhaps, is the use of formal sentencing guidelines as tried by some American courts. These guidelines, based on a large number of actual sentences, have been devised by Professor Leslie Wilkins, formerly of the Home Office Research Unit, together with some colleagues and with the active cooperation of the judiciary (Wilkins, 1980).

One suggestion which has been made on numerous occasions is that a panel of experts should be responsible for sentencing, with or without the trial judge's participation. At the moment, the sentencer may receive reports from various experts, but the decision must be his alone – or theirs alone, if there are three magistrates. If the sentence is one of eighteen months' imprisonment or more, a panel of experts, in the shape of members of the Parole Board, may well decide whether the offender should be released early on licence, but that is another matter. Roger Hood (1974) has pointed out that switching sentencing from the judiciary would not guarantee the avoidance of bad decisions. 'Just as one meets insensitive and punitive judges, one meets insensitive and punitive psychologists, psychiatrists and social workers.' In favour of the courts, he added, 'The point is that judicial decisions made with reasons are open to review and debate, whereas decisions based upon "clinical" diagnosis and which have the status of "professional expertise" are difficult to attack and hard to appeal against.' Clive Davies (1974) made a similar point: 'For all their faults, magistrates and judges have the great merit of doing their work in open court, where the defendant's family and friends have a right to be present at the proceedings, and the press to report and criticize.'

Despite the ability of various experts, including judges, to work well together on the Parole Board, there is still no satisfactory evidence that a panel would produce better sentences than a court. At the risk of being accused of complacency, and fortified by the support of Hogarth, the writer has come across no compelling reason for changing the opinion he expressed in 1967 (Stockdale, 1967, p.200):

One proposal sometimes put forward for better sentencing is to have the sentence decided by a sentencing tribunal or panel of experts, but this has found little support in England, where the courts are respected and experts are distrusted by many. Probably the more satisfactory solution is to continue to have sentencing decisions made by the courts, but to ensure that those courts are properly trained, and that they are prepared to listen to the advice of experts.

Hogarth (1971, p.389) expressed a similar view:

If decision-making in sentencing must involve an inevitable balancing of competing values, then it would appear that training in law and experience at the Bar and bench are valuable assets to the decision-maker ... The solution does not appear to be to replace lawyers with behavioural scientists, but rather to provide lawyers with the training and knowledge required to make the best use of information derived from the behavioural sciences.

Some of the critics who are concerned about the extent of the discretion vested in sentencers look across the Atlantic for solutions. One method of curbing judicial disparity which is being tried in the United States is the legislative one of limiting judicial discretion for any given offence to a choice of one of three sentences – normal, mitigated and aggravated – with a fixed term for each. How successful such a scheme turns out to be depends largely on the wisdom and humanity of the legislature in question. If *every* robber is given a mandatory twenty, thirty or forty years' sentence, then no single robber can complain of sentencing disparity. However, there is one thing which is far more disturbing than a sentence which is disparate, and that is the sentence which is downright unjust, in the broadest sense of that term.

Looking to the future some years ago, that formidable critic of the judiciary, Howard Jones (1965, p.104), wrote,

Yet the final decision would probably remain with the judge and the magistrate. Whether the decision is wise or not will depend less upon the competence of his advisers than on his own ability to understand and to sympathize with the advice which has been given to him.

Although we had not yet set up the Parole Board at that time, and although much ink has flowed since those comments were made, they provide an appropriate last word for the present discussion of the courts as sentencers.

References

Baldwin, John, 1975: 'The Compulsory Training of the Magistracy', *Criminal Law Review*, 634ff.

Baldwin, John and McConville, Michael, 1977: *Negotiated Justice*, Martin Robertson

Barr, Roy, 1979: *Probation Journal*, vol. 26

Bridge Working Party, 1976: *Working Party on Judicial Training and Information: Report of the Working Party*, HMSO

Davies, Clive, 1974: Letter to *The Times*, 16 October 1974

Davies, Martin, 1974: 'Social Inquiry for the Courts', *British Journal of Criminology*, vol. 14, 18ff.

Davis, Anthony, 1971: 'Sentences for Sale: Plea Bargaining', *Criminal Law Review*, 218ff.

European Committee on Crime Problems, 1975: *Sentencing*, (obtainable from) HMSO

Hailsham, Lord, 1975: Letter to *The Times*, 26 June 1975

Harris, Brian, 1979: 'Recommendations in Social Inquiry Reports', *Criminal Law Review*, 73ff.

Hawker, Geoffrey, 1974: *Magistrates in the Crown Court*, University of Birmingham Institute of Judicial Administration pamphlet

Hogarth, John, 1971: *Sentencing as a Human Process*, University of Toronto Press

Home Office, 1977: *The Length of Prison Sentences*, Interim Report of the Advisory Council on the Penal System, HMSO

Home Office, 1978: *Sentences of Imprisonment: A Review of Maximum Penalties*, Report of the Advisory Council on the Penal System, HMSO

Hood, Roger, 1974: *Tolerance and the Tariff*, NACRO Reprint no. 11, National Association for the Care and Resettlement of Offenders

Hood, Roger, and Sparks, Richard, 1970: *Key Issues in Criminology*, Weidenfeld and Nicolson

House of Commons, 1979: Fifteenth Report from the Expenditure Committee: *The Reduction of Pressure on the Prison System*, HMSO

James Committee, 1975: *The Distribution of Criminal Business between the Crown Court and Magistrates' Courts*, HMSO

Jones, Howard, 1965: *Crime in a Changing Society*, Penguin

McCabe, Sarah and Purves, Robert, 1972: *By-passing the Jury*, Basil Blackwell

Napier, Helen, 1978: *Probation Journal*. vol. 25

South Australian committee, 1973: First Report of the Criminal Law and Penal Methods Reform Committee

Stockdale, Eric, 1958: 'The Problem of Wounding with Intent', *Criminal Law Review*, 675ff.

Stockdale, Eric, 1967: *The Court and the Offender*, Gollancz

Streatfeild Committee, 1961: *Report of the Interdepartmental Committee on the Business of the Criminal Courts*, HMSO

Thomas, David A., 1979: *Principles of Sentencing*, second edition, Heinemann Educational

Thomas, Paul, 1969: 'An Exploration of Plea Bargaining', *Criminal Law Review*, 69ff.

Wilkins, Leslie, 1980: 'Sentencing Guidelines to Reduce Disparity?', *Criminal Law Review*, 201ff.

5. The Modern Prison

John McCarthy

The opinions expressed in this paper are those of the author, and should not be taken to represent the official policy or views of the Home Office.

Past and present

The basic reason for the existence of imprisonment in modern society is our desire to punish, the need to reject and to hurt those who hurt us. Institutionalized punishment, through the courts, organizes and standardizes the method, if not the degree, of retaliation. The heart of the punishment method used by the prison is the isolation of a person in a cell. The use of a cell (and the word itself) stems from the medieval monastic orders. Hermits looked for isolation in order not to be distracted by the world in their search for God. This custom was institutionalized in monasteries and nunneries, where each member had a personal cell in which to pray and meditate, away from community life. This isolation was a voluntary act. The Victorians introduced from Quaker Pennsylvania the 'separate and silent' prison system, which used compulsory isolation and silence for the same reason (Teeters, 1957). It deliberately and compulsorily depersonalized prisoners, as the monks deliberately but voluntarily depersonalized themselves. The system linked state religion and state justice, to produce redemption through penitence and deterrence through punishment.

The similarities between the monastic routine and the 'separate and silent' system were many (Goffman, 1968). It is possible to argue that the only difference was the element of compulsion. It may help to list some of the resemblances. The reception procedures for new inmates in some orders were identical to those in prison; there were common methods of depersonalization such as haircuts, uniform and deprivation of personal property; there was the uniform cell layout; prisoners in some institutions had to wear hoods over their faces when not in isolation (the comparison with religious hoods is obvious). In some establishments prisoners faced the wall when the governor walked past (out of humility) in the same way as the religious keep to the side of the corridor. There were periods in some prisons when the usual rule of silence was allowed to be broken. Mirrors were forbidden; the communities were single sex; and contacts with the outside world were severely restricted if not forbidden. This kind of life, if adopted voluntarily, can be an act of love; if imposed compulsorily, it is a punishment which engenders hostility in the majority of inmates. This hostility is inimical to the original purpose of penitence through meditation. The central figure in the process of spiritual reformation was the prison chaplain, who was the only person, apart from the governor and surgeon, who was allowed to talk to the inmates. He was of great importance. The large chapel was the only place in the prison with any pretension to significant decoration and was at the centre of the prison in the metaphorical as well as literal sense. The chaplain had the advantages of not having to be concerned with success rates or criteria, as victory in the religious sense is not assessable.

It is now worthwhile examining the organization of a prison today. As will be seen from the diagram overleaf, the prison now has departments of education, industry, administration, psychology, probation and a hospital. The role of the chaplain has been largely superseded by other professionals. Spiritual reform changed to treatment and training in the sixties. Chapel attendances became voluntary: in many prisons the chapel began to be used for association, films and concerts as well as services. Much penal philosophy started to emphasize 'breaking down the prison wall' in order to link up more with the outside community. Local prisons had to have three inmates in a cell because of overcrowding, and more personal property became permissible, so prisons became much less like monasteries. After a period of scepticism about the effect of state religion, then one of disillusionment with treatment because of its apparent failure, the prison service has now become agnostic. The 'penitent' became a 'patient' but still awaits encouragement to be a 'person'.

The daily prison routine has in essence changed little since its religious origins. Traditionally, the responsibility for the smooth running of the prison belongs to the chief officer and is executed

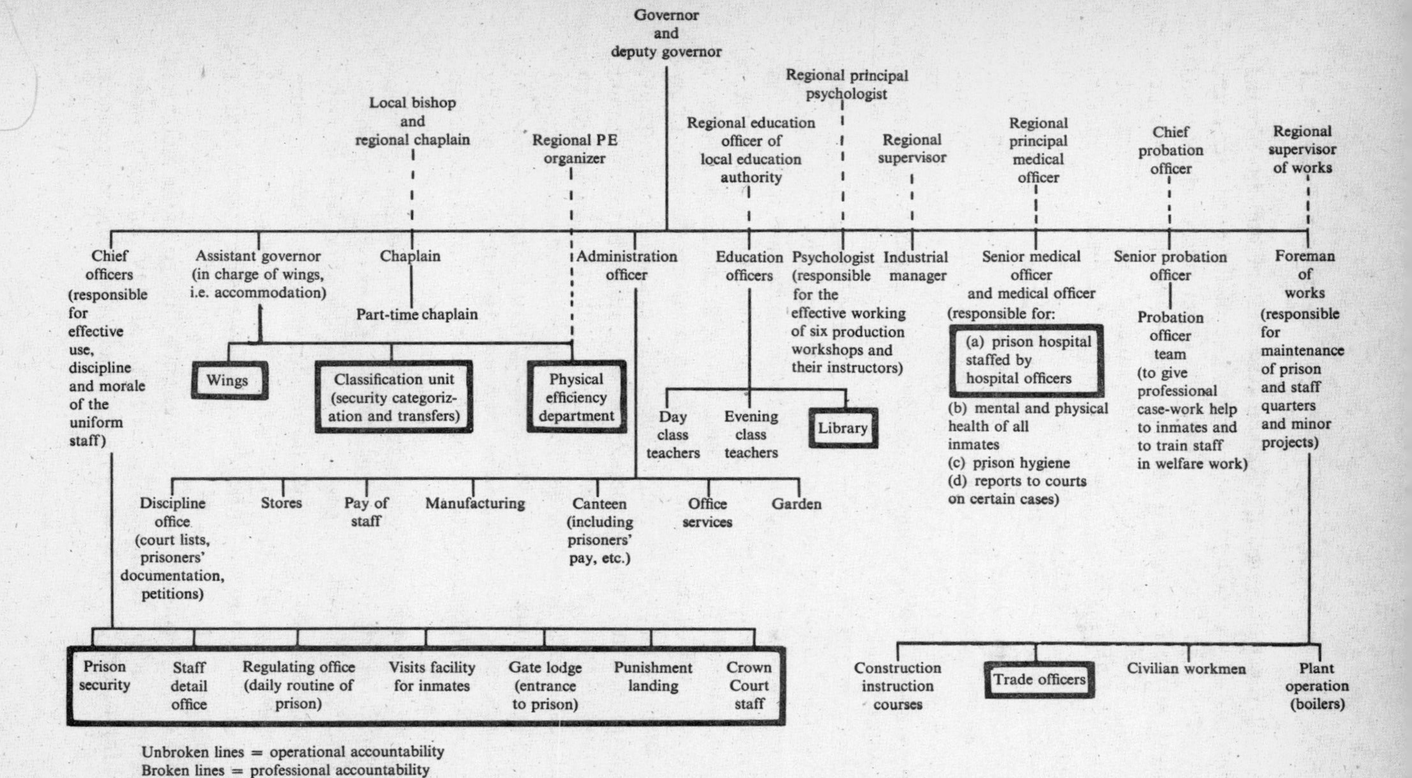

Note: This chart shows accountability; it does not show any pattern of decision making

through the uniformed staff. At one stage (1879), the clerical personnel and schoolmasters as well as taskmasters were recruited from the staff of warders. Gradually this work and additional tasks began to be performed by civilian professionals, culminating in the appointment of probation officers as prison welfare officers. Nowadays most inmate activities are supervised by civilian staff, though others are the responsibility of assistant governors accountable directly to the governor. The tasks of the prison officers are in many cases subordinate to these main tasks, which they make possible by, for example, escorting prisoners to work or to physical training. Tribute is often paid by informed opinion to the real skills of prison officers in managing difficult and aggressive prisoners, but this is often seen by the officer as lip service.

The routine of the prison still contains remnants of the old system of 'separation and silence', when the chief officer was responsible to the governor for everything in the prison except medical and spiritual care. However, there is tension between that routine and more recent additions, both because all the tasks taken away from the uniformed staff are seen by them as the more interesting ones and because the psychological roots of the old and new systems are so disparate. Evidence for this can be seen in the framed items on the management chart. These indicate the presence of uniformed staff. They show how uniformed staff have been divided into different management groups, some under a non-uniformed manager and others under the chief officer. It also illustrates the formidable extent to which non-uniformed staff are represented at management level.

The institutions

The central administration of the prison service consists of a Prison Board (and a headquarters staff) which manages four geographical regions. Within these regions are the various types of penal establishment.

Penal institutions can be conveniently divided into those for adults and those for young offenders. There are three kinds of adult establishment: local prisons, training prisons and dispersal prisons.

An institution can combine two or even three of these functions.

Most *local prisons* are the Victorian inheritance of the prison service. They sit like castles in the county towns or large centres of population. They are silent reminders to the population of the fit punishment for crime. They face outwards to keep the public out as much as the inmates in. Local prisons are all closed, i.e. with locks and bars, and bounded by a perimeter fence or wall, to prevent inmates from escaping. In modern times these institutions have two main tasks: to serve the courts (including the provision, where necessary, of reports on inmates) and to transfer sentenced prisoners to suitable training prisons.

Serving the courts involves keeping in secure conditions those persons awaiting trial or sentence who are not given bail by the courts. The philosophy governing the treatment of the first of these groups is to impose as little restriction on their liberty as is compatible with the maintenance of adequate security. They are, after all, innocent under British law until proven guilty. Serving the courts also means that the prison staff escort prisoners to magistrates' and Crown Courts, man the docks and cells at the Crown Courts and escort Crown Court prisoners back to the prison. The number of staff needed to carry out such work can vary widely from day to day. The staffing levels of a local prison therefore reflect an uneasy balance between the interests of the tax-payer in not wasting money and the interests of the prisoner in providing a reasonable regime; this problem is discussed below.

The second task of transferring men to training prisons is largely carried out as expediently as possible in view of the gross overcrowding of prisons, which is mostly concentrated in local prisons. Because of a shortage of training-prison places, most prisoners serving sentences of below eighteen months remain in local prisons. The remainder are almost always allocated to training prisons on the basis of their security category rather than training needs. The present system of security categorization was introduced by Lord Mountbatten in his report on prison security (Mountbatten Committee, 1966) and divides inmates as follows:

Category A – Prisoners whose escape would be highly dangerous to the public or the police or to the security of the state.

Category B – Prisoners for whom the very highest conditions of security are not necessary but for whom escape must be made very difficult.

Category C – Prisoners who cannot be trusted in open conditions but who do not have the ability or resources to make a determined escape attempt.

Category D – Those who can reasonably be trusted to serve their sentence in open conditions.

Prisons themselves are similarly referred to, according to the categories of prisoner for which they are considered suitable. As most inmates come into Category B or C, it is inevitable that, whilst prison overcrowding continues, training places in these categories of prison will be in short supply.

The regime for inmates in local prisons is affected by their obsolete buildings and floating populations as well as staffing problems. Prisons are staffed on the basis of managerial necessity (i.e. the need to perform the basic tasks) and not moral desirability. Management necessity in its turn is influenced by staff industrial action, in the form of restrictive practices and other pressures such as the maintenance of various forms of demarcation and excessive manning levels as in industry. But in the case of local prisons staffing levels are primarily dictated by court and escort demands and are based on average requirements. Therefore, on days of heavy court commitments, it is inevitable that some workshops are shut. As a result, the inmates who are working in these shops are locked up in their cells with breaks only for fetching their meals, having their daily exercise and, if they wish, attending evening classes.

Staffing levels in the evenings are usually such that association (when inmates are allowed out of their cells to talk to one another, to play darts, watch television, etc.) is restricted quite severely. The education and physical education departments provide opportunities, but often less than half of the prisoners will wish to take advantage of them. In fact, many inmates in local prisons appear quite content to lie on their beds all evening, or all day if there is no work for them, listening to their radios behind locked doors. After a few days of this, it is not surprising if they become irritable. Nor, of course, does their lack of reaction to being locked up mean that it is any less harmful.

It is worth remembering that the task of local prisons is, to a large extent, the mechanical one of secure containment. There is, therefore, a tendency for the management to be mechanistic in attitude. Much of the overt industrial action on the part of prison officers occurs in local prisons, particularly the larger ones, as a reaction to such attitudes. In the local prisons, management has a further problem of communication and influence: a large proportion of the staff are out at court or on escort each day and therefore out of management's direct control.

There are *training prisons* in each region; they may be either open or closed. They provide opportunities for inmates to learn trades, obtain a better education and to get and to keep fit. The general material conditions provided are better, and the degree of freedom allowed greater, than in a local prison. On the other hand, in the vast majority the general inmate culture is unhelpful to men who want to change their way of life. It is an in-group which protects the inmates against disciplinary action and is hostile to rules and rulers because these are felt to be repressive. It is a culture in which inmates exert more moral authority than the staff. All prisons have work programmes as a major element in the training of prisoners, but some training institutions have developed this further than others. The prime example of such an industrial prison is Coldingley. The whole organization of this institution is geared to efficient industrial production on a modern basis, light engineering and laundry being the two main industries. The work is financially profitable, but the regime is as much or as little reformative as any other prison. There are also management difficulties caused by the specialization. The uniform staff particularly feel deskilled, as all other departments of the prison are subordinated to industry. It could be argued, however, that the mere fact that the industrial activity saves the tax-payer money is sufficient justification for its existence.

Dispersal prisons cater for the Category A prisoners, who represent only about one per cent of sentenced adult offenders. This category contains a few spies, terrorists and a considerable number of professional criminals, many with records of violence. Others are dangerous sexual offenders. Almost all of these men are serving sentences of ten years or more and over one third have life sentences. The Mountbatten Committee's (1966) report recommended that these men be concentrated in a single prison with near-absolute security, but there was concern that such a regime might be repressive. Difficulties were also foreseen in successfully splitting up dangerous associates and keeping enemies apart. This is a necessary process to maintain effective control over dangerous prisoners. It was therefore decided, on the recommendation of a committee of the Advisory Council on the Penal System chaired by Professor Radzinowicz, Director of the Cambridge Institute of Criminology (Radzinowicz Committee, 1968), to disperse the Category A population over a small number of secure establishments. This means that so-called dispersal prisons contain a considerable number of Category B inmates in addition to those in Category A. These institutions have a very secure perimeter with reasonable freedom for inmates inside it. The regime is designed to be as humane and constructive as possible and in some prisons shows considerable tolerance for the conduct of the inmates. However, this very humanity gives opportunity for disruption to some of the prisoners, who can be highly intelligent, charismatic and sometimes intransigent in their opposition to the rule of the prison. Some are psychopaths, whom, as experience shows, neither understanding nor threats will usually restrain. Such prisoners can make use of rumours to promote confrontation, use fear to gain support and often feel that they have little to lose if they are exposed. Frequently the real leaders are neither seen nor heard in the actual trouble, whether it be a mass refusal to obey orders or an open riot. The management of these establishments is a very emotionally trying task, in that almost every day difficulties have to be met that involve anxious, sometimes angry staff and violent, often disturbed prisoners. There should be no illusions that management of a dispersal prison is anything but very difficult.

So far, no mention has been made of women in prison. The

female population is comparatively small, though there has been a considerable increase since 1973 (HMSO, 1977). Since the numbers involved are relatively low, the number of institutions is few. They therefore have to be widely spread over the country in order that the inmates, wherever possible, are not far from their homes. There is also the need for women awaiting trial or sentence to be accessible to visits from legal advisers or probation officers. The women's side of the prison staff, probably because of its small size but also because of its leadership, sets a fine example in its humanity and its desire to treat inmates as individuals.

On the young offender side there are four types of institutions, all of which are the responsibility of the prison service: detention centres (junior and senior), borstals, young prisoner establishments and remand centres.

Detention centres were first opened in 1952 as a consequence of the Criminal Justice Act 1948. They were all closed establishments. The junior centres cater for those from fourteen to sixteen years of age. Those aged from seventeen to twenty will be in senior detention centres. The two normal sentences are of three and six months, the former being the usual one. In senior detention centres, as in prisons, there is a one third remission of sentence for good conduct. In the junior centres remission of one half was brought in to alleviate a severe problem of overcrowding. One of the interesting points about detention centres is that the magistrates' courts have been asked to commit to these centres only after the warden of the centre has stated he has a vacancy, though in exceptional circumstances the court can contact the Home Office and efforts are made to find a place elsewhere in the system. (This principle does not apply to the Crown Courts.) Although it can be argued that the courts should not commit to prison without regard to the overcrowding there, it should still be possible to work out principles of sentencing that would satisfy the needs of the judiciary *and* the efficiency of the prison service. There would have to be either fewer people in custody or considerable public expenditure on a building programme. It can be argued that, at a time when the finances of the hospital service, education service and the social services are suffering severe cut-backs, such expenditure can hardly be legitimate, particularly when most authorities agree that a proportion of those in custody should not be there at all and when evidence suggests that shorter sentences would be sufficient for others (Wilkins, 1979). It is not easy to see why penal institutions should continue to be dustbins which can be filled to overflowing regardless of the consequences.

The regime in detention centres is firm but not repressive. The accent is on work, education, fitness and obedience, with a general background of personal interest in individual inmates. Recently (1979) two detention centres reverted to the original detention centre concept of a 'short sharp shock' on an experimental basis. Whilst it may be possible to justify this experiment in severity on grounds of retribution, it is difficult, from past experience, to find any hope that reconviction rates will be decreased.

The regime in junior detention centres is similar to that in senior centres except that, as many of the inmates are legally bound to attend school, education plays the most important part in the training and work takes second place. There are no detention centres for girls.

Borstals were introduced by the Prevention of Crime Act (1908), with the aim of keeping young men out of prison and providing for them a more active programme of character formation. There are both open and closed institutions, but even in the closed establishments security is much more elastic than in a prison. Borstal training came to centre on an ideal fostered by Sir Alec Patterson: young men could only be changed from inside themselves; outside pressure was not capable of bringing about any permanent change; they had therefore to be treated as self-determining individuals. It is argued in this paper that, for all practical purposes, this ideal is dead in most borstals. Most, both open and closed establishments, are merely institutions, with too many inmates and too few staff, making individual training largely impracticable. Too many managements in borstals are extensions of the bureaucracy of headquarters. Faced with a task in which they have little chance of success, they inevitably adopt new success criteria. The task is a very difficult one. The population is becoming more and more criminally sophisticated. The problem has become less one of individual psychology and more one of environment and the attitudes of society as a whole. The number sentenced by the courts means that the length of time inmates are kept is, within the legal boundaries of the sentence, largely decided by practical considerations. The staff in borstals from the governor down could benefit from more specialized training and more support from the centre. There can be few more demanding tasks than that of meeting the challenge of running a successful young-offenders institution. It was proposed – by the Younger Committee's (1974) *Report on Young Adult Offenders* – that borstals should be situated near the homes of the inmates so that, during the latter part of the sentence, training could be carried out in relation to the home environment. On grounds of finance, this recommendation was not adopted in the 1976 government green paper.

The regime in borstals is, at root, humane paternalism. Originally based on the public school system, some parts of which, such as houses and housemasters, still remain, it has since acquired some of the ethos of social work. These are combined with the requirement to maintain control of some quite difficult young men. Both open and closed borstals present inmates with educational and trade learning opportunities together with facilities for physical education. Most institutions have a programme of work by inmates in and for the local community to increase social awareness and to promote public relations. There are also normally outside sporting activities like games, canoeing, camping and hiking. However, staff influence very rarely makes an impact on the inmates except on an individual basis; even then it usually brings about conformity inside the institution rather than change on release. An exception to this is a young-adults unit at Grendon Underwood prison, which uses 'milieu therapy' to back up individual psychotherapy and counselling. Grendon has shown how to capture and mobilize the support of the inmate culture but has not succeeded in carrying such achievements forward into a decrease in reconviction rates. This may be explained by the fact that this psychiatric prison is unique within the prison service, accepting inmates from all over England and Wales (Parker, 1970). After-care is therefore very difficult to carry out effectively, particularly under the present system of imprisonment followed by complete discharge as opposed to a graduated discharge programme.

An interesting factor in the borstal sentence is that it is, apart from life imprisonment, the only sentence available to the courts that has an indeterminate element. The prison administration under the Home Secretary decides the length of sentence (between limits of six months and two years), dependent, in theory, on the progress of the inmate concerned. In practice, 'target dates' for release are set at the start of inmates' sentences and are adhered to, provided the inmates conform satisfactorily. There are two main reasons for adopting target dates. Firstly, the overcrowding of borstals caused by sentencing policies makes it convenient to use the length of the sentence as a regulator of population size. Second, there is no evidence to show that keeping borstal inmates for a longer time than the minimum produces any better result – though even before this became apparent, release was rarely based on treatment considerations, but was a way of attempting to enforce institutional conformity ('You don't get out unless you behave'). At present, many managers would prefer the judiciary to define the period of detention. They believe that the length of sentence should be determined by the seriousness of the crime and previous record rather than by hypothetical individual training needs.

Remand centres were proposed in the Criminal Justice Act 1948 but were not enacted until the Prison Act 1952. Up to that date, unconvicted young offenders who were not given bail by the courts were remanded to prison. By 1952 this was felt to be undesirable on grounds of contamination and separate remand centres were recommended. Whilst some have been built as separate establishments (Risley and Pucklechurch are recent examples), many are merely a separately designated part of a local prison. The regime of these centres aims to be occupational and humane, but there are real difficulties, with staff continuity hard to maintain in the face of the demands of the courts and demands for escorts. It is therefore difficult to keep up supportive relationships between staff and inmates. It also means that the occupations provided for the inmates can be interrupted on the days when a higher than average proportion of the staff are needed for outside duties.

In order to understand something about the dynamics of the institutions that have been described, it is necessary to attempt to interpret the group psychology that leads these establishments to function as they do. This will now be undertaken.

Aims

In a perfect society the prison system would be unnecessary. However, such a utopia is unlikely ever to exist. Faults in society are reflected in a deep-rooted organizational weakness within the prison system. This is the difficulty of finding satisfactory objectives for it – from which nearly every penal problem springs. In all organizations it is usual to find three kinds of aim: formal stated aims, pragmatic aims substituted in practice for the former, and informal aims.

The structure of any organization ought to be designed to achieve its purpose (the formal aims). But if they encounter other contradictory, irreconcilable or varying aims, this will cause organizational weaknesses and an inability to achieve any aims effectively.

These various aims will now be examined and the organization of the prison service will be measured against these with the purpose of assessing success or failure in their attainment. Penal institutions will then be analysed from what I believe to be a crucial viewpoint, their internal structure. The discussion will then be concluded by discussing the consequent effect of imprisonment on inmates.

The formal aims of the prison service, as interpreted by the writer, are, in order of priority:

(1) To protect the public from the criminal during the period of his sentence.
(2) To provide humane containment for prisoners in accordance with the current international rules on human rights.
(3) To serve the Crown Courts, i.e. escort the prisoners to and from the courts, man the docks and cells.
(4) To escort prisoners to the magistrates' courts.
(5) To provide secure conditions for certain prisoners awaiting trial in order to further an efficient and fair judicial process.

(6) To increase, in conjunction with other social-work agencies, the ability of the inmates to avoid further crime on release from prison.
(7) To manage an efficient industrial organization that will help to pay for the cost of the prison service.

The pragmatic aims are usually created to meet a long-term failure to achieve a formal aim. They are a recognition of the need of humans to have an achievable target. In 'helping' professions, they are generally a shift on pragmatic grounds, away from idealism; ironically, the substitute is often later adopted as an alternative ideal.

Substitute aims in the prison system frequently stem from what might be called the 'black bag' syndrome. Many people in social work want to be 'doctors', i.e. help to improve the physical, mental and social health of others. They feel that their success depends on their acquired professional skills. These people are usually highly motivated and failure can lead to one of two responses. The rare and difficult one is for them to reassess their skills, to find new ones and start again. The usual and easy response is to find new uses for their present skills. So, if they fail, they do not change the contents of the 'black bag' but change their objective instead. Three examples can be given. The management of the psychiatric prison at Grendon Underwood, despite that prison's many advantages, found that the reconviction rate of the prison was no different from that of any other establishment. The prison did not change its methods but altered the objective from that of reducing readmission among inmates to one of helping them to be better-adjusted human beings. On a more general level, the prison service as a whole changed its formal objective from that of affecting reconviction rates to providing humane containment. Both of these changes produced achievable aims. The third example is from a consultant psychiatrist working in a prison who, when asked about success rates, replied that he did not know them but that he could help if the medical officers referred the right type of patient to him. If he could not, it would be the responsibility of the medical officers for referring the wrong patients. The aim of the consultant, he claimed, was less one of treatment than of providing a skill. This, however, is an evasion of the success criterion, by a refusal to look critically at the methods or skills in use, the contents of the 'black bag'.

Finally there are *the informal aims*. These are the most powerful. They arise out of organizational imperatives, the cultures of staff and inmates and the pressures of public opinion – forces which tend to rule institutional life. Thus they are more deeply rooted in social realities than either of the two other kinds of aim. Furthermore, the fact that the formal aims have in any case been compromised by pragmatism makes them less defensible. Informal aims are divided for the purpose of this paper into categories according to their origins:

(1) *At headquarters*
To support the minister in his task as a member of the government accountable to parliament.

(2) *From public attitudes*
To have a regime that punishes the inmates in a covert way in response to retributive or deterrent attitudes generally held both in and outside the service. To have a quiet institution (maintenance of control) and no escapes (maintenance of security).

(3) *From institutional managers*
To run an institution that maintains a low managerial anxiety level, i.e. little staff or inmate unrest. To run a humane (and in some cases constructive) institution. To further personal career development (an aim common to most managers in all walks of life).

(4) *From prison officers*
To have a peaceful prison. To avoid the criticism of their superiors in rank. To have a status in the eyes of management, their families and outside society. Hence the lower they feel their own status to be, the greater their need to preserve the inferior status of inmates. To improve their pay and conditions of employment. (A perceptive if rather pessimistic account of the role of the prison officer is given by Thomas (1972).)

(5) *From the inmates*
To have a quiet sentence with the minimum of aggravation and the maximum of comfort. A minority will have a different aim, i.e.

to create an alternative society which is overtly against authority.

There is a thread that connects these informal aims, that of 'wanting a quiet life'. This can be described as avoiding anxiety by maintaining control over the immediate environment and in the process blunting the operation of the other informal aims. It is this shared aim and the resultant compromises that almost inevitably, and certainly understandably, dominate penal institutions. It is this shared aim that almost invariably prevents the effective implementation of three of the formal aims, i.e. rehabilitation, humane containment and efficient industry. It is this process of collusion, not only among those who work inside prisons but also between society and the prison system, which maintains a 'quiet society' by keeping trouble out of sight in a metaphorical dustbin.

It can be argued that 'the quiet life' is partly a method of living in the presence of superior power. If the power balance can be upset, there is no longer any need to lie low and other needs such as the need to rebel (particularly on the part of the inmates) can be expressed. This has happened in two areas in the last ten years within the prison service.

Firstly, the Prison Officers Association, in line with other trade unions, has shown that, in certain circumstances, it is prepared to use militant action to achieve improvements in pay and conditions. One possible cause of this is many prison officers' view of headquarters as a remote body with which they cannot communicate and an organization from which they would not, in any case, receive an understanding ear. These were seen as unacceptable attitudes on the part of those holding power. However, the use of militancy led to the balance of power shifting to the staff, so management temporarily went for the 'quiet life' while it thought about its position.

Second, the inmates have shown signs of trying to increase their power, but not so successfully as the staff. The series of prison disturbances in the summer of 1972 led to improvements in conditions, but management reasserted control shortly afterwards. In the case of the riots at Hull and Gartree dispersal prisons, the informal aims of the minority (i.e. to disrupt the prison) gave rise to a situation where other prisoners had to risk violence or intimidation from their own kind or join the uprisings. Many of them succumbed and took part in the outbreak. In dispersal prisons, where top security prisoners are held, the balance of power is bound to be uneasy because of the humane conditions that make the communication network of the inmate leaders easy to organize.

There is an important lesson to be learned by management from staff industrial action. It has been pointed out that the need to have a 'quiet life' can be affected by a change in the distribution of power. But how the newly gained power is used will depend on whether it has had to be seized or has been freely granted. Within defined boundaries, power can be given to individuals and groups at shop-floor level. This should result in increased job satisfaction. The corollary, therefore, is that if management builds in proper job satisfaction with scope for initiative, the need for the shop-floor level to use its power against management is considerably lessened. It is against the interests of anyone to destroy a building when they gain satisfaction from living in it.

As a final comment on informal aims, mention needs to be made of the aim of covertly 'punishing the inmates'. This is the punitive coercive part of prison life which links with, and in part is rationalized by, the aim of control. It is not argued that punishment is necessarily wrong, just that it is at variance with some of the formal aims. The custom of the human race is to punish the wrongdoer, but the theory of imprisonment is that incarceration is the punishment and not the *contents* of the prison sentence (Ruck, 1951, p.23). This contradiction between the form and the reality obviously leads to conflict, the severity of which is largely decided by the subcultures of the staff and inmates (see below).

Organizational problems

How far are the formal aims of the prison realized? This will be considered for each level of the organization in turn.

Headquarters

This is mostly staffed by interdepartmental grade civil servants (who move from one government department to another, unlike prison officers, for example, who are confined to a single department). Within the prison department, as elsewhere, the Civil Service operates within the boundaries of general policy decisions made by politicians, policies largely expressed in the 'formal aims' set out above. The main purpose is to carry out this political responsibility and to advise and protect the minister. This is a perfectly legitimate, efficiently executed task, on which staffing levels are based, and works satisfactorily on a routine basis. However, successful performance does depend on the 'quiet life' being maintained by the rest of the prison service. For good or ill, the 'quiet life' is no longer available, and the need of headquarters for operational efficiency can be very difficult to reconcile at times with the traditional task of the Civil Service. An example of this conflict is in the management of staff. Good and efficient management and the human touch are essential, if the large number and various grades of staff are to feel that headquarters is interested in them. Industrial unrest in recent years suggests that such management is not always available. One of the reasons for this is the structure and tradition of the Civil Service. Their preoccupations are elsewhere. Yet reconciliation is necessary. The prison service is financed by government and must therefore be financially accountable to parliament. The human-rights issues which have become central in prison administration are government's responsibility, as these transcend national frontiers. It is therefore probably impractical to resolve the conflict by divorcing the prison service to a greater extent from politics and by making it semi-autonomous, even though this would probably facilitate necessary risk-taking innovations. So the answer must lie in change within the prison department, so that management gives more of its time to the needs and problems of those actually carrying out the work in prisons.

To summarize, headquarters has difficulties in reconciling a traditional (but largely unstated) task with some of the operational needs of the service. It is designed to deal with the informal aim of preserving the 'quiet life' rather than the formal aims.

Regional offices

This intermediate administrative level is as yet undeveloped. One of the reasons for this is that power is still concentrated at headquarters. Regional offices are primarily concerned with the day-to-day operational scene, i.e. staff industrial unrest and prison security, as opposed to long-term objectives. Three items on the formal list of aims (rehabilitation, humane containment and industry) do not receive priority, as most judgements are made on, and most pressures emanate from, the operational running of the service. Further, the staff at regional level are insufficient to enable support and supervision to be provided for inmate training, except in a few specialist areas like education or physical fitness.

Regional offices end up by serving the informal aims rather than the formal, i.e. by preserving the 'quiet life'.

Institutions

Penal establishments are staffed primarily for security and control, not to enhance the training process. This is partly historical in origin as the traditional belief in imposed discipline and conformity as a training process did not demand a staffing level higher than that needed for security and control. It is also partly due to the disappointing results obtained from other methods of training or treatment in penal institutions. Whatever the reason, any assessment by headquarters of the managerial efficiency of an institution will be mostly based on security, control and the frequency of staff industrial action rather than on reconviction rates. In fact, the last has been largely abandoned as a criterion of success.

These points reinforce the pressures within the institution for a 'quiet life'. But the reasons for the success or failure of a prison organization are more complex than that. First, there is the lack of agreement over what success is, a problem shared with other institutions ranging from psychiatric hospitals to schools, which means that all involved are working at cross purposes. This is complicated by the presence of informal as well as formal organizations. When it is borne in mind that the achievement of some of the formal aims is extremely difficult, that there is conflict between the formal and informal aims and that there is unity only over the need for a 'quiet life', it will be understood why these informal organizations or subcultures have become so powerful. The function of the subcultures of the ruled (staff or prisoners) is to defend the group against threat. The more threatened the ruled feel, the more will their subculture be strengthened, the more a leader will be felt to be needed and the more power he will be given. (The parallel with Graham Sykes's (1968) 'pains of imprisonment' theory of the origins of inmate subcultures should be noted.) However, if it is accepted that the subculture is the result of the actions of the rulers, then it can be altered if the attitude of the rulers to the ruled is seen to be changed. The degree of acceptance by the prisoners of the formal aims of the prison, or, conversely, the strength of their own informal aims, will depend on the reaction of their subculture to the behaviour of the rulers. Prisoners can sometimes join together with staff against rulers who, they believe, threaten them both. For example, an inmate may warn an officer of the governor's approach. Equally, these two sides can draw together in a more positive way if management attitudes are more favourable. An example of this kind of change is at the psychiatric prison at Grendon Underwood where the treatment ethic of management was acceptable to both staff and prisoners. This was admittedly helped by the medical label attached to a psychiatric prison, which disposed inmates favourably, but was primarily due to the management being seen publicly as interested and tolerant, though firmly upholding institutional law and order. The various oppositional customs of the prisoners were considerably relaxed, primarily as a result of meetings in which free communication was encouraged. The 'no grassing' (i.e. informing on your own kind) rule was greatly loosened as staff were seen as largely non-punitive. Even the customary scapegoats, sex offenders against children, were little persecuted as the management's philosophy of 'acceptance' was seen by the inmates as genuine and in the interests of everybody. So, in many areas the formal aims of management were shared by staff and inmates.

The success of the prison service will be judged by whether it achieves its formal aims. By and large, the task of protecting the public from the criminal during sentence is successfully carried out. It is possible to argue that this is usually because the absence of a wish to escape is combined with the wish for a 'quiet life' on the part of the inmates. Prevention of escapes is largely managed by good channels of informal communication with inmates rather than by physical security measures. The exception is the dispersal prison, where perimeter boundaries are very secure.

The three aims which involve the courts are efficiently carried out. Prisoners are delivered to the courts punctually and kept securely. It is the remaining three aims (rehabilitation, humane containment and industry) that are not achieved and it is in connection with these that the informal aims of the various groups become powerful. The reformative aim has never been successfully attained, though one knows of individual cases of success – and other cases where inmates were made worse! It is of course true that some of the evaluations of the reformative achievements of prisons are so poorly carried out that their negative results count for little. Nevertheless, there is much which could be improved. For instance, after-care is often grossly inadequate and the bridge to the outside world virtually non-existent. But even if everything else were perfect, the dominant cultures of the ordinary penal institutions, if unchanged, would defeat any treatment programme.

Some staff are averse to seeing inmates as people to be helped rather than coerced. A change here means a lessening of the social distance between inmates and staff. It means assuming an authority derived from personal qualities as opposed to official status (Jones and Cornes, 1977, pp.204ff.). It means tolerating a less rigid and more elastic regime (Burns and Stalker, 1968). No group of people can be expected to change in this direction unless they feel sure that management will treat them with as great a degree of respect and tolerance as they are expected to show to the inmates. It is this, together with adequate training, that is often not sufficiently present.

In their turn, inmates understandably see themselves as self-determining individuals and not as people to be 'helped'. For them to change their social orientation or even to examine it means that a big alteration in their self-image has to take place. Gordon Hawkins (1976) refers in his book *The Prison* to remarks made by discharged prisoners. Though this example is drawn from the United States, it is of more general application:

> What seems common to all these testimonials is that officers, where these were credited as having rehabilitative influence, gave the men self-respect. This did not mean that officers were unusually lenient, lax or permissive. It meant only that they treated the men with a personal interest and without pretension or condescension. The officers were friendly in a way that inspired confidence and respect rather than contempt; they were frank, fair and considerate.

In the light of all the evidence, the prison service cannot be seen as designed to carry out rehabilitation. It is designed for control and to ensure conformity; and this produces an inmate and often a staff culture opposed to aims, about which, anyway, as we have seen, management itself is ambivalent. The formal aim of training is one that the service fails to meet because of a lack of suitable organization and because of an absence of a sufficient understanding of its deficiencies.

Humane containment is an aim that is only moderately attained. Some of the reasons for this arise from the staff attitudes described in the previous paragraph. Overcrowding and old buildings are also important influences, but perhaps the most important is the reaction of most of us to criminals, which is a wish to see them punished, or at least made to feel life is not easy for them in prison. So humane containment tends to be confined to those improvements in conditions which make control easier, i.e. further the 'quiet life'. An example is the initial resistance of many staff to prisoners being allowed radios in their cells. This was seen as making life too comfortable for them. However, when it was realized that such inmates when locked up made less disturbance and rang their cell bells less often, the staff attitude changed.

The final formal aim is that of running an effective industrial organization. There is no doubt that industry in prison could be much more efficient. The reasons for this comparative failure are interesting. They include in microcosm many of the difficulties of the prison service as a whole.

(1) If prisoners are to be motivated to work as in industrial situations outside, it is necessary to communicate with them properly and fully, to consult them and, where possible, to involve them. To treat them in the traditional way as prisoners can mean retaliatory sabotage of one kind or another. But it is difficult to treat within the same building the same inmates in two different ways, particularly when the same staff are involved. Industry, in short, is aiming more for a productive life than for a 'quiet one'. This gives rise to conflict.

(2) Industrial managers are promoted from the workshop instructor group, which are predominantly civilian grades, i.e. they do not wear uniform and have a separately negotiated system of pay and conditions from the uniformed staff. Many of the instructors are also civilians. As has been already pointed out, the uniformed staff have seen their role reduced more and more to that of turnkeys. They are caught today between a wish for status, a wish for overtime (and hence a good wage), a wish for a 'quiet life' and understandable anxieties over any change. Prison officers are in charge of discipline in workshops run by civilian instructors, who often see discipline in a different way from the uniformed staff. The officers will often be bored by the passive task, but if they ask for the post to be abolished this has implications for the overtime available to the staff group. They tend to be resentful of their status in the workshop vis-à-vis the civilian instructors, seeing the latter as having a higher professional status than themselves. In short, there is tension between the industrial situation and the traditional prison, which shows itself in a variety of resistances. It is also a tension between uniformed staff and 'intruders' who do not support the 'quiet life' on the same terms. Production is thus much reduced by the informal concerns of the uniformed staff culture, though other factors, like the difficulty of finding suitable work for inmates at a time of considerable outside unemployment, have an influence.

It has been argued in this section that the prison service succeeds in its formal aims of security and servicing the courts; that the aims of industrial efficiency and humane containment are modified by the informal aims of the prison cultures, particularly of staff; and that it fails in the aim of rehabilitation. These assertions may appear to be highly critical of the service, especially in its quest for a 'quiet life'. What else, however, can be expected? If an organization is to cope effectively with change and the resultant anxieties, it needs a positive success criterion to act as an incentive. The prison has no such standard. It has purely negative 'quiet life' criteria, such as the avoidance of disasters like riots and staff industrial action. The prison service is not alone in its search for peace above all things. In a 1979 issue of a British management magazine a contributor suggested that one of the reasons why industrial production in Britain was not rising sufficiently was that too many managers did not consider it was worth driving hard for increased production as the resultant reaction of the unions caused so much trouble. Yet these organizations have a positive production incentive, which the prison service has not, and are in a competitive market, whereas the prison service has a monopoly.

We can now summarize our conclusions up to this point:

(1) The prison service has great difficulty, as does society in general, in agreeing on the formal aims of imprisonment.

(2) There is implicit agreement about the informal aim of pursuit of a 'quiet life'.

(3) The basis on which the containment aims of the present-day service were founded was illogical, i.e. the assumption that voluntary meditation could be made compulsory without destroying its purpose.

(4) The religious basis for reformation was first replaced by a medical concept of treatment.

(5) There was then a replacement of (4) by reformative agnosticism, with the pragmatic concentration on containment.

(6) Some of the formal management aims were severely weakened by such agnosticism or scepticism as the drive that came from belief was sapped. Lack of drive to pursue the formal aims led to the

strengthening of the informal aims and hence increased their influence. It also led to the increased strength of interests such as industry, education, etc.

(7) The strongest informal aims are those of the uniformed staff, who have been, in their view, 'demoted' in the past ninety years and feel alienated.

(8) This alienation is increased as the size and influence of the civilian-run departments is increased (see (6)).

(9) The state of affairs described in (1)–(8) is against a general background of the greatly increased size of the prison department, with headquarters inevitably becoming more remote. It has not adapted sufficiently to the changed service and the increased militancy of unions in society. This failure to adapt has resulted in increased staff alienation, which has been shown by covert and overt industrial action.

The effects of imprisonment

It is important to try to assess what effect the institution has on the inmates, as they are, after all, the reason for its existence, even if not the reason for the way it operates.

There are three main schools of thought on the effects of imprisonment on inmates:

(1) That imprisonment (Clemmer, 1940) leads to a steady contamination and corruption through the effect of the inmate culture of the prison. It has been argued that that culture is partly a direct result of efforts by the inmates to mitigate the pains of imprisonment (Sykes, 1968).

(2) That the effects of the contamination are at their lowest on reception to the prison and just prior to release from it. Stanton Wheeler (1962) suggests that with each return to prison the U-curve cycle is repeated, producing, however, some overall deterioration at the end of each cycle. This U-curve pattern is in contrast to the assumption of a steady and consistent nagative pattern throughout each sentence.

(3) That inmates bring criminal attitudes to the prison with them;

this creates the inmate culture (Irwin and Cressey, 1962). They are relatively unaffected by the prison experience.

Ironically, the first theory is the most promising for those who believe rehabilitation can take place in prison. If people can be made worse by their experience of imprisonment, it could be argued that by changing the influences brought to bear on them they could be made better, presumably by reducing the 'pains of imprisonment' and thus weakening the corrupting inmate culture. This would be an argument for penal reform. The second theory has some evidence to support it apart from Stanton Wheeler's own work, but follow-up research (Atchley and McCabe, 1968) has cast a little doubt on the U-curve proposition. In considering the third, the so-called importation theory, it has been argued in this paper that management can nevertheless change the culture of the prison. However, there is a danger of confusing the process of changing institutional culture and of permanently changing behaviour. The fact that it is possible to change the general culture of the prison and therefore to reduce contamination and corruption does not mean necessarily that the initial criminality of the inmates can be lessened. At present, in the British prison and borstal service there has been only one research project (Shaw, 1974) that has shown any rehabilitation in terms of a reduction in rates of reconviction.

Not that this justifies despair. It could be contended that if better methods were used, the results could improve. Indeed, there is research evidence to this effect (Craft, 1965; Grant and Grant, 1959). Reduction in the influence of the inmate culture is probably crucial here. So the treatment issue is still a very open one. That people can influence others, given the right circumstances, is incontrovertible; that prison could do so is possible. Also, the transition between the prison and the outside community is still a problem. The working relationship between the prison establishments and the probation service is still, in the vast majority of cases, superficial. Any change of attitude in an inmate not supported or reinforced on release suffers a severe risk of reversal over a period of time, particularly, as so often happens, when the person concerned returns to the social environment he was in before he was sentenced.

It is probable, of course, that one cannot encapsulate caring in a technique, nor institutionalize love, but that says more about the professional skills needed than about the theories being discussed.

Conclusion

The prison system at present is, by reason of both its birth and its inherent contradictions, effective in its routine tasks but unsuccessful in attempts to achieve some of its formal aims. It also has to cope with the uncertainties of public opinion and the resultant political pressures, which weigh at times against managerial efficiency. There are also other problems that influence the efficiency of the prison service. The informal aim of the 'quiet life' is shared by all levels of the organization, and the organization is operated to achieve that, rather than the more recently added formal aims of rehabilitation, industrial efficiency and humane containment. The subcultures of the institution add another factor. The conclusion seems inescapable: apart from isolated ventures by charismatic governors, imprisonment can only be argued for as a period of exile. Any claims beyond these are, at present, acts of faith or prejudice, not reason.

References

Atchley, R. C., and McCabe, M. P., 1968: 'Socialisation in Correctional Communities: a Replication', *American Sociological Review*, vol. 33, pp.774–85
Burns, T., and Stalker, G. M., 1968: *The Management of Innovation*, Tavistock
Clemmer, D., 1940: *The Prison Community*, Rinehart, New York
Craft, M., 1965: *Ten Studies in Psychopathic Personality*, John Wright
Goffman, E., 1968: 'On the Characteristics of Total Institutions', in *Asylums*, Penguin
Grant D., and Grant, M. Q., 1959: 'A Group Dynamics Approach to the Treatment of Non-conformists in the Navy', *Annals of the American Academy of Political and Social Science*, vol. 322
Hawkins, G., 1976: *The Prison: Policy and Practice*, University of Chicago Press
Home Office, 1977: *Prisons and the Prisoner*
Irwin J., and Cressey, D. R., 1962: 'Thieves, Convicts and Inmate Culture', *Social Problems*, vol. 10, pp.145–55

Jones, Howard and Cornes, Paul, 1977: *Open Prisons*, Routledge & Kegan Paul
King R. D., and Elliott K, 1977: *Albany*, Routledge & Kegan Paul
Mountbatten Committee, 1966: *Report of the Enquiry into Prison Security*, under the aegis of the Advisory Council on the Penal System, HMSO
Parker, Tony, 1970: *The Frying Pan: a Prison and its Prisoners*, Hutchinson
Radzinowicz Committee, 1968: *Report on the Regime for Long-term Prisoners in Conditions of Maximum Security*, under the aegis of the Advisory Council on the Penal System, HMSO
Ruck, S. K. (ed.), 1951: *Paterson on Prisons*, Muller
Shaw, Margaret, 1974: *Social Work in Prison*, HMSO
Sykes, G., 1968: *Society of Captives*, Atheneum
Teeters, N. K., 1957: *The Prison at Philadelphia: Cherry Hill. The Separate System of Prison Discipline, 1829–1913*, Columbia
Thomas, J. E., 1972: *The English Prison Officer since 1850*, Routledge & Kegan Paul
Younger Committee, 1974: *Report on Young Adult Offenders*, under the aegis of the Advisory Council on the Penal System, HMSO
Wheeler, S., 1962: 'A Study of Prisonisation', in Johnston N. *et al.* (eds.) *The Sociology of Punishment and Correction*, John Wiley, New York, pp.152ff.
Wilkins, G., 1979: *Making Them Pay*, Barry Rose

6. Prisons in Crisis

Andrew Willis

In November 1978 the then Home Secretary, Mr Merlyn Rees, announced an urgent and independent Inquiry into the United Kingdom Prison Service, to be led by Mr Justice May. This was to investigate the size and nature of the prison population and the capacity of the prison service to accommodate it, the responsibility of the prison service for the security, control and treatment of offenders, and prison staffing levels and the efficient use of resources. In the light of these considerations, the Committee of Inquiry was asked to make recommendations about prison structure, organization, management and resources, including staffing levels, remuneration and conditions of service (*Guardian*, 18 November 1978). The establishment of this Inquiry, the largest of its kind and the most comprehensive in scope since the Gladstone Committee Report (Prisons Committee, 1895), forms the backdrop against which the contemporary problems of imprisonment are discussed.

The immediate events which led to the Committee of Inquiry involved escalating industrial action taken by prison officers in furtherance of their claims about pay and general conditions of service, accompanied by various forms of prisoner unrest and protest, ranging from passive demonstrations to violent assaults (*Guardian*, 30 and 31 October 1978 and 3, 8, 11 and 18 November 1978; *Sunday Times*, 29 October 1978 and 5 November 1978). However, rather than focusing on the proximate causes of the Inquiry, this chapter will concentrate on identifying the general features of imprisonment which, over a period of time, generated this prisoner protest and prison officer industrial action. In outlining the dimensions of what might be called the contemporary crisis of imprisonment I will be making a number of observations about the age of prisons, the extent of prison overcrowding, the general conditions of imprisonment and its gross ineffectiveness at promoting behavioural change, and the substantial costs involved. The cumulative impact of this catalogue of maladies renders the present state of the prison system critical and its future uncertain but ominous.

The age of prisons

Surprisingly, there is a certain amount of conflict and controversy about the age of British prisons. On the one hand there is the Home Office view which points to the Prison Department's large Victorian inheritance: '... the proportion of obsolete buildings is unusually high' (Home Office, 1969, p.73, para. 181); and

> The Department is handicapped by ... the failure to construct a single purpose-built closed prison or closed borstal during the forty years from 1918 to 1955. Putting it in numerical terms, of the 55 closed prisons in which male inmates were held in custody at the end of 1975, only 8 have been built as prisons since 1914 (Home Office, 1977a, p.113, para. 195.)

On the other hand, there is the claim of King and Morgan (1979, Chapter 1), in their paper arising from evidence submitted to the May Inquiry, that the prison-building programme in England and Wales has not been starved of resources, that about 61 per cent of all Prison Department establishments have been brought into use since the Second World War, and that this rate of building compares favourably with that for other buildings in the public sector (for example, schools and hospitals), so that overall 'the prison system has a remarkably high proportion of modern buildings' (King and Morgan, 1979, p.11, para. 24).

These apparently contradictory viewpoints can be resolved by taking the view that the Home Office account is substantially correct and that the assertion of King and Morgan is rather misleading, though not inaccurate. There are indeed, as King and Morgan say, 135 separate prison establishments, and it is also true that 82 (61 per cent) of these have been brought into use since 1945 (King and Morgan, 1979, p.9, paras. 21 and 22). But this general level of analysis, restricting attention to the total number of Prison Department establishments, ignores a number of important and instructive points, not least of which is the concentration of the greatest proportion of prisoners in a small number of very old prison establishments.

Using exactly the same data base as King and Morgan (Home Office, 1977a, Appendix A, pp.145–9; Home Office, 1978a, Appendix 3, pp.68–82), as well as their synopsis of the data (King and Morgan, 1979, Table 1, p.10), it is possible to analyse the age of prison establishment in relation to type of institution and category of offender, and when this is done a rather different picture emerges. For example, as the first column of Table 1 indicates, of the 135 prison establishments, just 13 are for female prisoners and, although only 69 (55 per cent) of the 125 male establishments have been built or brought into use as prisons since 1945, all the female institutions are of recent origin. Indeed 6 (46 per cent) of them have been built since 1960. Therefore half the Prison Department accommodation for male offenders pre-dates 1945, whereas all institutions for women have been built, rebuilt or refurbished since then, and nearly half since 1960. This alters the picture somewhat, especially when one takes into account the fact that in 1977 the average daily population of male prisoners was 40,212 compared to just 1,358 female prisoners – a ratio of about thirty to one (Home Office, 1978a, Table 1, p.3). Broadly speaking, small numbers of female prisoners are incarcerated in very modern accommodation, whereas large numbers of male prisoners are contained in buildings largely pre-dating 1946. A similar picture emerges with respect to young male prisoners. King and Morgan fail to stress that 42 (79 per cent) of the 53 remand centres, borstals and detention centres have been built since the end of the Second World War. Also, all nine of the open prisons post-date 1945. New prison accommodation and the post-war prison-building programme appear to be disproportionately reserved for female prisoners, young adult offenders and inmates not requiring conditions of high security. In all, 75, or well over half, of the total stock of Prison Department establishments are reserved for these categories of prisoner and as many as 64 (85 per cent) of them have been built since 1945. Yet in 1977 these institutions held an average daily population of 13,969, or 34 per cent of the total number of 41,570 prisoners. Thus, there *are* new prisons, but overall they are disproportionately reserved for minority groups of prisoners.

Table 1

Prison Department establishments in use in 1977 by age of buildings and average daily population

	Establishments		*Population*	
	No.	Per cent	No.	Per cent
Pre-1900				
Local prisons	24	18	16,567	40
Closed training prisons	17	12	5,350	13
Borstals and detention centres	5	4	1,270	3
1901–39				
Closed training prisons	1	1	487	1
Borstals and detention centres	6	4	1,189	3
1946 to date				
Closed training prisons	18	13	5,203	12
Open training prisons	9	7	3,170	8
Borstals, detention centres, remand centres	42	31	6,976	17
Women's establishments	13	10	1,358	3
Total	135	100	41,570	100

(King and Morgan, 1979, Table 1, p.10)

Conversely, the adult male prisoner held in a closed establishment is likely to find himself in very much older accommodation. Out of the 60 closed prisons for adult males only 18 (30 per cent) post-date 1945. Moreover, it is the closed prisons for men which cater for the largest single group of prisoners. From the average daily population of 40,212 male prisoners in 1977, as many as 27,607 (69 per cent) were confined in these 60 closed institutions. Clearly, over two thirds of average adult male prisoners are incarcerated in closed institutions, of which nearly three quarters pre-date 1945.

However, as King and Morgan acknowledge (1979, p.12, para. 27), the real problem of antiquated buildings is even more specific, given that all 24 of the local prisons not only pre-date 1945 but also pre-date 1900. Indeed 16 (67 per cent) of them date from before 1860 (Home Office, 1977a, Appendix A, pp.145–9; Home Office, 1978a, Appendix 3, pp.68–82). In addition, these few prisons account for a very substantial proportion of all adult male prisoners held in secure custody. In 1977, out of an average daily population of 27,607 adult males held in closed prisons, the 24 local prisons had an average daily population of 16,567, or 60 per cent of the total. Clearly, a small number of very old local prisons are coping with well over half of the adult male prisoners for whom closed conditions are necessary. To put it another way, in 1977 the 24 local prisons, which comprise just 18 per cent of the total Prison Department stock of establishments, had an average daily population of 16,567, or 40 per cent of the total average daily population of 41,570. When these predominantly mid-nineteenth-century institutions are at any one time catering for well over one third of the total number of prisoners of all types, it seems either naïve or misleading to suggest, as King and Morgan do (1979, p.11, para. 24), that the Prison Department is not working with predominantly outdated capital assets. Although it is certainly true, in numerical terms, that over half the Prison Department establishments post-date 1945, it is also true, and symptomatic of a real problem, that, in terms of the demand for accommodation, it is the small number of local prisons which figure most prominently; and all of them pre-date 1900.

Perhaps the best way to get some idea of the antiquated nature of the local prisons is to mention a few, together with the dates they were first used for the custody of offenders, the purpose for which they were first built and their average daily populations in 1977. Thus, Leeds and Liverpool prisons, built in 1860 and 1864 as city gaols, had average populations of 1,074 and 1,560 prisoners respectively; Pentonville, built as a 'model prison' in 1842, held 1,140; and Brixton and Wandsworth prisons, built in 1843 and

1849 as county gaols, had average populations of 1,025 and 1,355 respectively (Home Office, 1977a, Appendix A, pp.145–9; Home Office, 1978a, Appendix 3, pp.68–82). Taken together, these five prisons had in 1977 an average daily population of 6,154, or nearly 40 per cent of the 16,567 adult male prisoners in local prisons, despite the fact that they were all built at least 115 years ago.

The sheer age of the relatively few prisons which regularly contain the largest single group of offenders is the most obvious manifestation of the current crisis in prisons. In addition, it is clear that a disproportionate number of offenders tend to be incarcerated in these few institutions, which brings me to the second critical factor – overcrowding.

Prison overcrowding

Before I consider in some detail the evidence about the extent of prison overcrowding, a couple of preparatory points should be mentioned. First, it is again necessary to take issue with King and Morgan, who argue that the officially recorded amount of prison overcrowding may well be far in excess of the actual amount, because it is calculated in terms of the greatest amount of multiple cell occupancy, rather than the average amount in a given year, and who also suggest that prison overcrowding is almost impossible to measure because we lack an objective definition of what constitutes uncrowded normal conditions. Together, they suggest, these factors counsel caution in too readily designating prisons as overcrowded (King and Morgan, 1979, pp.15–27, paras. 31–5). Their first point may be conceded, though it is worth remembering that the method of calculation only exaggerates the extent of overcrowding by letting the unwary confuse the greatest amount with the average amount – it does not mean that none exists. Their second point must, however, be more vigorously challenged. The standard index of prison overcrowding, multiple occupancy of a single cell, seems to me a reasonable enough measure (even though, as King and Morgan point out, some prisoners prefer sharing prison accommodation to being alone, and there are no clear standards of minimum space per inmate), because nineteenth-century penal architects constructed their prisons specifically for single cell occupancy. To the extent that multiple cell occupancy now occurs, this represents overcrowding by Victorian standards of space, heat, light, ventilation and hygiene which would be regarded as inappropriate today.

Second, if prison overcrowding occurs, it would appear to be most likely within the local prison sector. Apart from the fact that it appears to be official policy to neglect local prisons – no new ones have been constructed this century (King and Morgan, 1979, pp.12–13, para. 27) – the reason for this is that the demands made of these local facilities are both varied and enormous. For example, of the 29,564 male prisoners who were received into custody under sentence of immediate imprisonment in 1977, as many as 22,678, or 77 per cent, were serving a sentence of not more than eighteen months (Home Office, 1978b, Table 4.5, p.38), often referred to as short-term imprisonment (Home Office, 1978a, Appendix 3, p.82). This sort of sentence – and even one of up to four years – would not infrequently be completely served in a local prison (Home Office, 1969, p.70, para. 170). Also, in 1977 some 12,766 adult males were received into custody in default of payment of a fine (Home Office, 1978b, Table 4.1, p.35), almost exclusively to be incarcerated in a local prison. Finally, one of the primary functions of local prisons lies in the discharge of trial and remand responsibilities to the local courts (Home Office, 1969, pp.67–8, paras. 163–5), and a very substantial proportion of their business lies in receiving and processing untried and convicted but unsentenced prisoners. In 1977, some 83,000 male prisoners were received into custody in this way (Home Office, 1978b, Table 1.1, p.5). Thus, large and increasing demands are being made of the ancient and scarce prison plant which makes up the small network of local prisons, and this could well produce overcrowding.

There is a good deal of evidence to support this view. The latest available data (see Table 2) indicates that in 1977 nearly 16,000 inmates were sleeping two or three to a cell designed for one person, 4,950 of them three to a cell and 11,040 of them two to a cell (Home Office, 1978a, Table 3, p.4). Moreover, the trend from 1969 to 1977 shows this to be a steadily worsening feature of contemporary prison life, with an increase in numbers of 5,451, or slightly over 50 per cent, during this period, and a stable rate of overcrowding of somewhere between 30 and 40 per cent for the entire prison population. With this sort of pressure of demand on accommodation, when over a third of prisoners are in conditions officially defined as overcrowded, it seems that King and Morgan are absolutely right when they say that 'the situation of the 4,950 prisoners sharing three to a cell, where they can have less than 45 square feet per person, is clearly intolerable' (King and Morgan, 1979, p.25, para. 52).

Table 2

Inmates sleeping two or three in a cell and average daily prison population, 1969–77

Year	*Total*	*Three in a cell*	*Two in a cell*	*Average daily prison population*	*Percentage of average daily prison population two or three in a cell*
1969	10,539	7,653	2,886	34,667	30
1971	14,450	8,238	6,212	39,708	36
1973	12,609	4,221	8,388	36,774	34
1975	15,640	5,298	10,342	39,820	39
1977	15,990	4,950	11,040	41,570	38

(Home Office, 1978a, Table 3, p.4; Home Office, 1978b, Table 1.4, pp.10–11)

As was suspected, it is in the local prisons that almost all the overcrowding is concentrated. As Table 3 indicates, it is only local prisons and remand centres which are subject to any degree of overcrowding whatsoever: all the other institutions were operating in 1977 at slightly under full capacity. It is also evident that the magnitude of overcrowding in these two types of institution is pretty formidable: remand centres are 23 per cent overcrowded and local prisons are 42 per cent overcrowded; or, to put it a different way, it is approximately true to say that remand centres only have accommodation for four out of every five inmates they have at any one time, whilst local prisons have facilities for only two out of every three prisoners they are required to hold in custody.

However, even this fails to reveal the true extent of prison overcrowding because it does not take into account the maximum number of inmates these local prisons were designed to accommodate when they were built over a hundred years ago. To begin with, they were built at a time when the total average prisoner population (convicts and local prisoners) was not in excess of 30,000, and in

Table 3

Prison overcrowding by type of establishment, 1977 (male establishments only)

Type of penal establishment	*Number*	*Certified accommodation*	*Average number of inmates*	*Average inmates as a percentage of certified accommodation*
Local prisons	24	11,635	16,567	142
Closed training prisons	36	11,583	11,040	95
Open training prisons	9	3,524	3,170	90
Remand centres	11	1,873	2,236	119
Borstals	24	5,752	5,412	94
Detention centres	19	1,966	1,786	91

(Home Office, 1978a, Appendix 3, pp.68–82)

decline (Prisons Committee, 1895, p.3, para. 14). Yet today much the same physical plant is being used to contain a much increased number of prisoners. For example, Walton prison in Liverpool was built in 1854 (Home Office, 1977a, Appendix A, pp.145–9) to accommodate just 800 inmates (*Guardian*, 13 February 1979), although in 1977 it had a certified population of 1,036 and an average daily population of 1,560 (Home Office, 1978a, Appendix 3, pp.68–82). Clearly, it is over 50 per cent overcrowded in terms of the number of inmates it was designed to accommodate. In addition, just 233 prisoners, or 15 per cent of the total, are in single cell accommodation.

The other local prisons present a strikingly similar picture. Here are just a few examples from 1977: Birmingham prison had certified accommodation for 603 inmates but an average daily population of 978 and was 62 per cent overcrowded: Brixton had certified accommodation for 654 inmates but an average daily population of 1,025 and was 57 per cent overcrowded; Leeds, with certified accommodation for 592 and an average daily population of 1,074, was 81 per cent overcrowded; and Manchester, with certified accommodation for 890 and an average daily population of 1,466 was 65 per cent overcrowded. Yet all of these were built between 1845 and 1869 as city or county gaols to serve the very much more limited criminal justice and penal needs of a bygone age (Home Office, 1978a, Appendix 3, pp.65–82).

Neither is there anything very new about prison overcrowding, especially in local prisons. Indeed, there is even a reference in the Gladstone Report of 1895 to the fact that unusually large drafts of prisoners into prisons have made the provision of single cell accommodation impossible, especially in London, Manchester, Birmingham and Cardiff (Prisons Committee, 1895, p.12, para. 31). In more recent years, successive Annual Reports on the Work of the Prison Department are absolutely littered with remarks about overcrowding. In 1962, for example, there is the comment that 'overcrowding has persisted in local prisons' (Home Office, 1963, p.12, para. 1).

By 1969 the position had not eased, with over 13,000 prisoners out of a population of 40,000 sleeping two or three to a cell at the highest point in June (Home Office, 1970, p.9, para. 2). By 1971, the seemingly obligatory notice on overcrowding ran: 'More than a third of those in custody sleep two or three in a cell designed for one, and most of this overcrowding is in prisons built more than a hundred years ago' (Home Office, 1972, p.3, para. 8).

The trend was maintained, and is confirmed in almost identical language at the beginning of the 1975 Report (Home Office, 1976b, p.1, para. 2). By 1976, as many as 16,435 inmates were sharing cells designed for one inmate (Home Office, 1977b, p.4, para. 12), dropping slightly to 15,990 in 1977 (Home Office, 1978a, Table 3, p.4). Indeed, the seemingly intractable nature of the problem is evidenced in the 1977 Home Office publication *Prisons and the Prisoner*, where prison overcrowding is mentioned in a glossary of difficult and technical terms (Home Office, 1977a, Chapter 3).

The whole problem is, I think, best summarized in an earlier Home Office publication on prisons which states, baldly and bluntly: 'Overcrowding is the worst feature of our prison system, worse even than the old buildings in which it takes place, and its effects are seen throughout the system' (Home Office, 1969, p.104, para. 239).

It then goes on to point out that, although some men might view 'doubling up' as an invasion of privacy whereas others would welcome the company, what is certain about prison overcrowding is that it prevents the proper use of prison workshops, strains the prison's facilities to provide food, means restrictions on opportunities for bathing, makes it difficult to provide and supervise visits, and, perhaps most important of all, makes it that much more difficult for staff to get to know prisoners.

There is little prospect of any immediate improvement in this state of affairs. Prison Department officials have estimated that on current trends the average prison population will rise from about 42,000 to nearly 50,000 by the early 1980s, with only about 4,500 new places planned, let alone under construction or actually built (*Observer*, 2 April 1978; *Sunday Times*, 5 November 1978). One estimate puts the total figure of new prison places to be available by 1982 as low as 3,200, of which only a proportion would be in the local prison sector (*Guardian*, 11 November 1978). The recent House of Commons Expenditure Committee Report comments that, although 4,760 new places are under construction, the shelving of plans for new accommodation means that the gap between daily inmate population and available places will remain substantial, the expected shortfalls for 1977–81 ranging from 1,400 to 2,600 places (House of Commons, 1978, p.xvi, para. 9). If these predictions turn out to be near the mark, it is clear that overcrowding could well increase rather than progress being made towards its elimination. And a rather fatalistic attitude towards this worsening situation seems to prevail. Thus, the Annual Report for 1977 comments: 'The essential redevelopment of the Victorian estate seemed in 1977 more remote than at any time in the past thirty years . . . The major preoccupation of the building and maintenance programme was keeping the existing deteriorating facilities in operation' (Home Office, 1978a, p.9, para. 25). Further, in a recent review of the prison system the Home Office concedes that, even though new buildings are planned:

> the plain fact is . . ., taking into account the cuts which have been necessary in public expenditure and the consequential reduction in the funds available for new prison building and improvements, that the resources to replace all the unsuitable buildings included in the present stock are not likely to be found for many years. The Service has therefore entered the last quarter of the twentieth century in the knowledge that buildings designed in the nineteenth will have to remain in use for some time. (Home Office, 1977a, p.113, para. 195.)

If there is a moratorium on prison building and improvement, it follows that there is no conceivable way, with the present levels of incarceration, that anything can be done to ameliorate, let alone abolish, prison overcrowding – indeed the situation will worsen. In addition, as a correlate of this, there will be a progressive worsening of conditions inside the various penal establishments – a situation I now want to look at in some detail.

Conditions of imprisonment

The combination of ancient prison buildings and gross overcrowding produces impoverished living conditions for many prisoners and appalling working conditions for prison officers. Although it is difficult to describe with any accuracy the way in which these conditions are routinely experienced by officers and inmates, it is possible to use their own accounts of their various prison experiences to provide an approximate portrait of some of the more disturbing features of contemporary imprisonment.

To begin with, at least in respect of the overcrowded local prisons, mention must be made of the well-known fact that there are generally no toilet facilities within the cells (sanitary recesses are provided at the ends of landings), which means that night sanitation necessarily involves the use of chamber pots inside the cells – often with two other prisoners present – and 'slopping out' every morning. Clearly, as a Home Office publication acknowledges, 'This is a disagreeable and degrading procedure; sanitary arrangements that were thought adequate in Victorian times seem quite unacceptable one hundred years later, (Home Office, 1977a, p.31, para. 37). Mr William Driscoll, the Governor of Walton Prison, Liverpool, commented with equal force, '. . . it's like living in a bathroom for seventeen hours a day with two strangers' ('A Life with Crime', BBC 2, 1 April 1979).

This is, however, more than simply an isolated example of an unpleasant and discreditable procedure, for it reflects the very precarious way in which the daily routine in prisons only just survives the enormous demands placed on outdated and inadequate resources and facilities. For example, it is not uncommon in the larger, older prisons to find as few as twenty bathing places per 1,000 inmates (and none at all for the staff), with the result that inmates do not receive their minimum statutory entitlement of one bath a week (*Guardian*, 31 October 1978). In addition, as a prison governor said in evidence to the House of Commons Expenditure Committee on prisons and the prison population, things are so bad that 'the procedure of slopping out has to be done in cyclical order, in order to provide that the drainage system is not overtaken by events. In other words, it cannot deal with the accumulated effluents collected during the night period' (House of Commons, 1978, p.xvii, para. 11).

Indeed, the capacity of the prison service to do anything more than barely meet the most minimum requirements is highly questionable. As a governor of Pentonville once summed things up, dramatically indicating how adverse conditions limit the opportunities for imprisonment to provide anything by way of training or offender rehabilitation, 'As long as we're able to bathe them, feed them and the drains can take it, we're all right' (*New Society*,

21 January 1977, p.177). The pressure is on all essential services – kitchens, laundries, bathing and visiting facilities, exercise yards and workshops – with a combined adverse effect on the health of both staff and inmates, and, perhaps more importantly, on their psychological wellbeing, both groups being regularly subjected to the intense stress of having to live or work in sub-standard establishments (House of Commons, 1978, p.xvii, paras. 11 and 12). This state of affairs caused the Institution of Professional Civil Servants to suggest in evidence to Mr Justice May's Inquiry that overcrowding combined with ancient and failing services would have resulted in the compulsory closure of some of the older gaols if they had been subject to normal public health standards (*Guardian*, 17 April 1979).

This is a problem that is well acknowledged by those who run the prison system:

> In many of the Victorian prisons, the drains, power supplies and heating systems have become inadequate for modern needs or have reached the end of their useful life. This has meant a real risk in recent years of a total breakdown of these essential services. (Home Office, 1977a, p.114, para. 198.)

But it is also a problem which will remain. Despite the specific allocation of about £1 million a year since 1969 to replace or improve these facilities (Home Office, 1977a, p.114, para. 198), it was also pointed out in the Annual Report for 1976 that the overall reduction in expenditure on new prison buildings would make it impossible to relinquish alternate Victorian cells for conversion into sanitary annexes for the remaining ones. It was then bluntly conceded: 'There is now no foreseeable prospect of progress along these lines' (Home Office, 1977b, p.10, para. 28).

It is also worth pointing out that, scarcity of resources apart, the opportunities for substantial improvements within existing prisons are very limited – literally so, by the perimeter wall. Improvements within the boundary almost invariably entail the development of one aspect of prison life at the expense of another. For example, a new prison workshop could be provided, but it is quite likely to eat into space formerly given over to exercise facilities, and so on. Furthermore, if this is the state of affairs with respect to the essential services – massive annual expenditure which scarcely maintains outdated, overloaded and deteriorating facilities – then it is quite likely that a similar situation exists for some of the other prison services, such as libraries, educational facilities, vocational training and prison welfare. Indeed, in 1977 there was either an actual cut-back or a period of non-expansion in these areas (Home Office, 1978a, Chapter V). During that year only £4.7 million was spent in all Prison Department establishments on education, training and recreation combined, whilst £5.4 million was spent on maintenance and repairs (Home Office, 1978a, Appendix 4, pp.83–5), which suggests either disproportionately high expenditure on maintenance or absurdly low expenditure on education – either way, pretty alarming.

The outdated and inadequate physical resources and the over-crowding are not without impact on both officers and inmates as the following examples of recent incidents indicate. (Accounts by both officers and inmates are included where possible.)

The first of these concerns Ashford Remand Centre, which during the Autumn of 1978 received publicity because it stood at the centre of industrial action by prison officers which involved a work to rule. Very significantly, when the ban on overtime and other sanctions started, the Home Office responded by placing a ceiling of 271 inmates on the institution, although it *normally* held about 600 (*Guardian,* 31 October 1978), which was 50 per cent in excess of its certified population of 404 (Home Office, 1978a, Appendix 3, p.75). These 'normal' conditions of overcrowding, which would presumably have continued unabated without industrial action, prompted illustrative comments about the institution from both staff and inmates. A prison officer commented, after noting an average weekly incidence of two violent assaults on prison officers, which he described as not just a push in the face but a real thumping:

> Experiments with baboons have shown that overcrowding leads to violent reactions. They turn on each other and anyone else that gets in the way – and if you keep three men in an eight by ten cell you get the same reaction. (*Guardian,* 31 October 1978.)

Then an inmate, talking about the very long periods of cellular confinement, said this:

> It's the stink – I shall never get it out of my nose. There's just one small pane that will open in the cell window and it was hotter in there than when me and my mates went on holiday to Benidorm in June. And there's just one bucket for the three of you. (*Guardian,* 31 October 1978.)

He went on to comment on the consequences of the restrictions on visits, the lack of opportunity to work, the limited periods of association and the enforced idleness in cellular confinement: 'Imagine that – in a cell for 15 days at a time. So you smash up the beds, you thump anyone in sight' (*Guardian,* 31 October 1978). In this particular case, inmates and officers are largely in agreement about the adverse consequences of prison overcrowding.

A second and more exceptional example is to be found in the case of David Evans, a seventeen-year-old boy who was remanded to Risley Remand Centre for medical reports after being found guilty of indecently assaulting a seven-year-old girl, and who was murdered by being hanged by four of his cell mates on the night of 14 April 1978. On the night in question there were some disturbing features about the remand centre. Although built in 1965 for 500 inmates, it actually accommodated 1,014 prisoners and was, therefore, in excess of 100 per cent overcrowded; it had a total of only 300 uniformed staff, which was 40 (or 12 per cent) below full strength. As many as six other inmates shared the same cell as Evans, all of them in voluntary segregation under Rule 43* because of the sexual nature of their offences or because they were informers – but segregated together. Their cell was just 23 feet long by under 8 feet wide, giving only about 25 square feet per inmate, and they were in it for up to 20 hours a day (*Sunday Times,* 5 November 1978). The question obviously arises whether, with more staff and more supervision, and less overcrowding and cellular confinement, Evans might not have been murdered.

* Rule 43 of the Prison Rules permits a prison governor to remove a prisoner from association with other prisoners in order to maintain good order or discipline or to safeguard the interests of that prisoner (Home Office, 1964, p.14). In this case it had been used to protect sexual offenders and informers against unofficial retaliation from other inmates.

Finally, the events at Walton gaol, Liverpool, during February and March 1979 are added evidence of the undesirable consequences of poor prison conditions. On 11 February 1979 the governor put the prison on full alert, following a week of unrest among over 1,100 prisoners (involving scuffles with prison officers and rooftop demonstrations). Because of a work to rule by prison officers the prisoners were being confined to their cells for up to 22 hours a day, with no opportunity for visits, work or recreation (*Guardian,* 12 February 1979). This state of affairs continued into March, with up to 1,600 prisoners mostly confined to their cells and so not getting association, exercise, baths, canteen or domestic visits (*Guardian,* 10 and 13 March 1979). Prisoner protest continued, involving barricades, hunger strikes and sit-down demonstrations (*Guardian,* 16, 17 and 20 March 1979). This red alert or crisis situation gave an opportunity for officers and inmates to comment on the usual and customary conditions in the prison. The Governor, Mr William Driscoll, said this:

> The violence was the result of frustration. The situation the prisoners are in *normally* is appalling. On average they are in their cells for sixteen hours a day. We have 285 prisoners 3 to a cell, 892 2 to a cell and 233 single cells in a prison designed for 800. The cells are thirteen feet by nine feet with three beds, three tables and three lockers. The overcrowding is very serious. (*Guardian*, 13 February 1979.)

On television the following month he repeated these remarks, again attributing prisoner unrest and prison violence to overcrowding, especially in conjunction with being locked in a cell for long periods each day. A degrading experience, he said, only likely to generate depression and tension which would eventually erupt as prison violence ('A Life with Crime', BBC 2, 1 April 1979). The inmates of this prison (built in 1854 for only 800, but holding 1,600 in early 1979) support the Governor's analysis of the situation: 'We have been locked up for about twenty hours a day. We get very bored. It affects people differently. Some can take it, some can't' (*Guardian,* 13 February 1979). To put things in perspective, a prison officer spokesman reflected on the lack of improvement since the previous crisis situation:

We had a full scale riot here only four years ago and since then the only money spent on the place was a new office block for the management. The rest of the place is still a slum. (*Guardian,* 13 February 1979.)

It seems disturbingly self-evident that essential services and facilities in the local prisons in particular are scarcely adequate for even the minimal task of providing penal conditions of reasonable decency, hygiene and safety for either officers or inmates. It is also clear that when these normal conditions of gross overcrowding in ancient and dilapidated buildings, with long periods of cellular confinement, are exacerbated by prison officer industrial action the balance of response among prisoners tends to shift away from passive acceptance of deprived circumstances and monotonous routine towards active protest. This indicates just how precarious the balance of equable social relations in British prisons today really is. Also, precisely the same inadequate conditions now no longer appear to be acceptable as satisfactory terms of employment for prison officers, whose industrial action at that time spread nationally, causing a total of seven states of 'red alert' to be declared by prison governors by April 1979 (*Guardian,* 3 April 1979). It seems, therefore, very reasonable to suppose that unless the recommendations of Mr Justice May's Inquiry dramatically improve these miserable penal circumstances (though, as already mentioned, the resources for this do not appear to have been provided) the potential for large-scale prison unrest (involving officers, inmates or both) remains undiminished.

The effectiveness of imprisonment

One of the primary goals of correction in general, and imprisonment in particular, is to promote behavioural change and to transform a predisposition towards criminal acts into a propensity for law-abiding behaviour. This was first established as a major penal task in the Gladstone Report of 1895, which laid down that the reformation of the prisoner should, along with deterrence, be the primary object of imprisonment:

... prison discipline and prison treatment should be more effectively designed to maintain, stimulate, or awaken the higher susceptibilities of prisoners, to develop their moral instincts, to train them in orderly and industrial habits, and whenever possible to turn them out of prison better men and women, both physically and morally, than when they came in. (Prisons Committee, 1895, p.8, para. 25.)

These sentiments were later encoded in Rule 1 of the Prison Rules, which states: 'The purpose of the training and treatment of convicted prisoners shall be to encourage and assist them to lead a good and useful life' (Home Office, 1964, p.4). However, the elevation of the treatment-and-training philosophy to a pre-eminent position in penal practice, so that the primary penal object is to reform offenders through discipline and training and render them useful, law-abiding members of the community (Foucault, 1977), has not been matched by evidence that training in prisons offers any degree of favourable behavioural impact. Indeed, the evidence points overwhelmingly towards the ineffectiveness of penal institutions in promoting law-abiding behaviour.

To begin with, a review of over 20,000 male prisoners discharged from Prison Department establishments in 1974 and followed up for two subsequent years (details in Table 4) indicates that, for every type of penal establishment, between five and eight out of every ten discharged inmates will be reconvicted within two years: a failure rate, by any standards, of massive proportions. Of course, the actual reoffending rate could well be substantially greater if there were a large amount of either undetected or unreported subsequent criminal behaviour, which would mean that these data represent an understated portrait of penal failure. In more detail, the proportion reconvicted within two years ranges from 50 per cent of adult male prisoners to over 80 per cent of juvenile borstal trainees. It is really a case of all groups doing badly, but some worse than others. In addition to a high probability of reconviction for all ex-prisoners, there is a substantial probability of their being given a further custodial sentence within the two-year follow-up period, which may be used as a rough indication that their reoffending is not of an extremely trivial kind. For example, 57 per cent of the reconvicted adult male prisoners were given a further custodial sentence, which means that overall, if about half of the total are reconvicted and about 60 per cent of this group reimprisoned, then about one in three of all adult male offenders who are sent to prison will find themselves subject to another custodial sentence within two years of discharge.

As a very rough picture of this state of affairs, imagine a typical prison cell, built for one but containing three prisoners. Of these three inmates, only one will remain free of reconviction for two years after discharge, the second will be reconvicted but will avoid another custodial sentence, whilst the third will be reconvicted and reimprisoned. Not, I think, a flattering portrait of prison effectiveness. Moreover, it is not possible to defend the behavioural impact of imprisonment on the grounds that at least it appears to

Table 4

Reconvictions: male offenders discharged during 1974 – two-year follow-up from date of discharge

Age of offender	*Establishment*	*Number Released*	*Percentage reconvicted*	*Percentage of those reconvicted who were given another custodial sentence within 2 years of discharge**
Juveniles (under 17 years)	Detention centre	3,564	73	31
	Borstal	1,203	81	47
Young adults (17–20 years)	Detention centre	5,326	58	35
	Borstal	4,707	63	47
	Prison	2,254	65	58
Adults (21 years and over)	Prison	20,413	50	57

* Including suspended sentences.

(Home Office, 1978b, Table 8.1, p.62, and Table 8.3, p.64)

work pretty well for the 20 to 50 per cent who avoid reconviction, because age and maturation alone (quite irrespective of any involvement in the criminal justice or penal systems) are significantly related to non-reoffending (Simpson, 1976, pp.984–1017; Walker, 1971, pp.101–9). Perhaps the best way to demonstrate the gross overall failure rate is to look at the proportion of men received into custody who have been to prison before. As Table 5 demonstrates, 70 per cent of the male adult offenders received into custody in 1977 had had previous experience of custodial confinement, 50 per cent having been inside on from one to five previous occasions, and as many as 21 per cent having received six or more previous custodial sentences. With such high rates of reconviction and reimprisonment, together with evidence of a high degree of repetitive incarceration, it is not difficult to agree with King and Morgan (1979, p.38, para. 58) that the reality of the proven ineffectiveness of imprisonment belies its philosophy of treatment and training.

Table 5

Receptions into prison under sentence by previous custodial sentences: adult male prisoners, 1977 (excluding fine defaulters)

Number of previous custodial sentences	*Receptions* Number	Percentage
0	7,816	29
1–2	7,240	27
3–5	6,099	23
6–10	3,870	14
11 and over	1,940	7
*Total**	26,965	100

* Information not available on a further 3,229 prisoners who are, therefore, excluded from this table.

(Home Office, 1978b, Table 4.3, p.37)

Neither is there any comfort to be gained from the view that penal institutions could offer improved behavioural impact if only they were to introduce more refined and sophisticated reformative strategies. To deal only with some of the English data, it is now clear that it is not a case of simply trying harder or investing more resources, because all the varieties of institutional experience investigated in a recent Home Office survey – ranging from psychotherapy in adult prisons (Newton, 1971; see also Gunn *et al.*, 1978), through an individualized approach to young adult borstal trainees (Bottoms and McClintock, 1973), to a modified therapeutic community approach for juvenile delinquents (Home Office, 1975) – suggest no greater effectiveness in terms of behavioural change than the more traditional institutional programmes (Home Office, 1976a, pp.16–27).

There is also some evidence that incarceration, certainly if it is prolonged, may well have an adverse effect upon criminal behaviour and actually promote lawlessness. The thesis that imprisonment itself is criminogenic dates back at least to the times of John Howard, who called prisons 'seats and seminaries of every idleness and vice' (Howard, 1777, p.8), and of Jeremy Bentham, who suggested that 'an ordinary prison is a school in which wickedness is taught by surer means than can ever be employed for the inculcation of virtue' (Bentham, 1864, p.351). In more recent years this view has been taken up by Clemmer (1940, pp.299–316), who suggests that, through a process he called 'prisonization', a prisoner tends to become assimilated into the culture of the penitentiary and thereby subject to influences which would deepen his criminality and progressively unfit him for re-entry into civil life. And, although the implied causal relationship between exposure to prison and increased criminality has been questioned (Hawkins, 1976, Chapter 3), there is some evidence that longer prison sentences are positively associated with an increased probability of reconviction (Eichman, 1966; Jaman and Dickover, 1969; Berecochea *et al.*, 1973). The most impressive evidence comes from Florida where, following the U S Supreme Court's decision in *Gideon* v. *Wainwright*, as many as 1,252 convicted and imprisoned offenders had to be released because it was judged they had been improperly convicted without benefit of counsel. This permitted a comparison to be made between the early releases and a matched group of prisoners released at the same time but at the end of their sentences. The early-release prisoners showed a significantly lower recidivism rate of 13.6 per cent compared with the controls' reconviction rate of 25.4 per cent (Eichman, 1966).

In addition, there is now an overwhelming research consensus that prisons, like all the other penal strategies, have negligible behavioural impact. For example, early British reviews of the effectiveness of penal treatments talked about the 'interchangeability of penal measures' (Walker, 1965, pp.257–9; 1971, pp.120–22) and consistently negative research findings (Hood and Sparks, 1970, Chapters 6 and 7). American reviews supported this analysis, with, for example, Bailey's survey of 100 separate correctional initiatives reporting that 'evidence supporting the efficacy of treatment is slight, inconsistent and of questionable value' (Bailey, 1966, p.157), and the massive review of 231 research studies by Martinson and colleagues concluding: 'this study uncovered no treatment that holds promise of easily and effectively impacting on the recidivism of all offenders' (Lipton *et al.*, 1975, p.560). As it was put in an earlier article, summarizing the survey of research findings into the effectiveness of correctional treatments, 'with few and isolated exceptions, the rehabilitative efforts that have been reported so far have had no appreciable effect on recidivism' (Martinson, 1974, p.25). This rather pessimistic research consensus has recently been confirmed both by a Home Office review of sixty-five research studies which concluded that, by and large, rehabilitative programmes have no predictable beneficial effects (Home Office, 1976a) and that research results to date 'have so far offered little hope that a reliable and simple remedy for recidivism can be easily found' (Home Office, 1976a, p.37) and by even more recent British (Brody, 1978, pp.133–48) and American (Greenberg, 1977, pp.111–48) commentaries. These conclude that correctional dispositions, achieving only a few favourable but modest results, are generally failing to reduce recidivism, and that the 'blanket assertion that "nothing works" is an exaggeration, but not by very much' (Greenberg, 1977, p.141).

The weight of evidence suggests, then, that prisons simply do not work as instruments for reforming criminal behaviour, and that the philosophy of treatment and training is bankrupt (King and Morgan, 1979, pp.27–36, paras. 56–75). This collapse of Rule 1, as it is termed, opens up a great void in penal philosophy, and in practical terms the lack of an authoritative and guiding penal purpose makes the continued use of imprisonment in its present form both problematic and anxiety-provoking. But the crisis of effectiveness is even deeper than this, for it is now acknowledged that two of the other major justifications for incarceration involve more philosophical aspiration than penal accomplishment.

On the one hand, the possible deterrent effect of imprisonment has received a considerable amount of recent attention (Zimring and Hawkins, 1973; Andenaes, 1974; Gibbs, 1975; Beyleveld, 1977, 1979) which has given little sustenance to the view that fear of incarceration acts as a psychological impediment to criminal behaviour. It is generally agreed that, for deterrence to apply, the following conditions must obtain: the potential offender must be aware of the penalty; the chances of his detection must be high; and there must be an opportunity for him to balance the likely benefits against the probable costs before offending (Brody, 1978, p.139). This clearly excludes large numbers of potential criminals – the impulsive, the irrational, the unthinking and those who are prepared to commit crime irrespective of the penalty – leaving deterrence as applicable to only a marginal group of potential offenders (Walker, 1971, Chapter 12). In addition, there is no evidence that the presumed or actual severity of punishment, usually measured by the length of imprisonment, is in any way inversely related to crime rates – that is, the notion that long prison sentences deter is false belief not penal fact (Gibbs, 1975, Chapter 5; Brody, 1978, p.140). There is an overall scepticism about these two general points which is perhaps best expressed in a recent Report from the Advisory Council on the Penal System which stated:

> Evidence about the effectiveness of general deterrence . . . is scant. Research findings are . . . inconclusive. All one can say with any degree of confidence is that nothing is likely to be lost by a general reduction in length of sentences. (Home Office, 1977c, p.3, para. 9.)

On the other hand, the notion that imprisonment affords the

public a high degree of protection against further criminal depredations is also open to question on at least three major counts. First, because there is such a large amount of unreported and undetected crime (Hood and Sparks, 1970, Chapter 1; Radzinowicz and King, 1977, pp.44–68; Sparks *et al.*, 1977; Bottomley, 1979, pp.21–32), it follows that only a very small proportion of offenders are ever actually incarcerated, the public being continually at risk from the rest. For example, one United States estimate suggests that less than 1.5 per cent of 9 million offenders a year will be incarcerated (Mitford, 1974, p.276), another, that under half of all robbery arrests ever end in a prison sentence (Petersilia and Greenwood, 1978, p.605), and a Californian study of serious, habitual offenders indicated an 80 per cent non-arrest rate for all self-reported adult felonies (Petersilia, 1977, pp. 104–23). Second, the capacity of imprisonment to offer public protection depends, according to common sense, on the length of prison sentences – longer sentences affording greater protection. But, as Table 6 indicates, of the 29,564 adult males sent to prison under immediate sentence in 1977, as many as 40 per cent were imprisoned for less than six months, with 77 per cent serving 18 months or less. Clearly, in all but a very small proportion of cases, imprisonment offers only a very temporary form of public protection – especially when remission and parole are also considered. Third, despite the growing demand for crime prevention by means of mandatory prison sentences to incapacitate recidivist offenders (Wilson, 1975, p.173), there is increasing evidence that such strategies would offer little public protection. One U.S. estimate suggests that only 8 per cent of all index crimes are prevented by present rates of incarceration, most crime being committed by new offenders and not ex-prisoners (Greenberg, 1975, pp.541–80). And, in a similar study, a hypothetical sentencing exercise which involved mandatory five-year terms for all convicted felons showed that even so severe a sentencing strategy would have reduced the crime rate by as little as 4 per cent (Van Dine *et al.*, 1977, pp.22–34). In addition, such exercises show that the marginal benefits in crime reduction would have to be balanced against massive increases in the prison population. Overall, the studies suggest that mandatory sentences entail a rise of between 3 and 10 per cent in the prison population for every one per cent reduction in the

Table 6

Reception into prison under sentence by length of sentence: adult male prisoners, 1977 (excluding fine defaulters)

	Receptions	
Sentence length	Number	Percentage
Up to 3 months	5,563	19
Over 3 months, up to 6 months	6,187	21
Over 6 months, up to 12 months	7,161	24
Over 12 months, up to 18 months	3,767	13
Over 18 months, up to 4 years	5,714	19
Over 4 years	1,172	4
Total	29,564	100

(Home Office, 1978b, Table 4.2, p.36)

crime rate (Petersilia and Greenwood, 1978, pp.604–15). In England and Wales, where the number of prisoners already exceeds available accommodation by more than 10 per cent, this penal option is plainly impracticable, because it would only place further demands on already overstretched penal resources.

It is now clear that the impact of imprisonment on behaviour is very limited, and the American Friends Service Committee wrote off treatment and training thus: 'After more than a century of persistent failure, this reformist prescription is bankrupt' (1971, p.8). There is also some evidence that incarceration may actually stimulate criminal behaviour. But, if rehabilitation as a penal aim is discredited, the alternatives of deterrence and public protection seem to offer equally little justification for imprisonment. The crisis in prisons is therefore far more than a matter of obsolete, overcrowded buildings, for it also involves the enforced recognition that there must be a fundamental reappraisal of the purposes of incarceration. A re-awakening of interest in alternatives to the defunct rehabilitative ethic has already begun, at least in academic circles, with such notions as 'facilitated change' (Morris, 1974), 'collective incapacitation' (Wilson, 1975), 'just deserts' (Von Hirsch, 1976) and 'humane containment' (King and Morgan, 1979) being bandied around. But this has not affected thinking at the level of practice: in their evidence to Mr Justice May's Inquiry, the British Association of Prison Governors and the Prison Officers Association both endorsed continued retention of the penal imperatives of treatment and training, while also aware that, as the Prison and Borstal Governors Branch of the Society of Civil and Public Servants put it, 'Nothing is more soul destroying than the present tradition of paying lip service to aims which we cannot achieve' (quoted in NACRO, 1979, p.7). To the extent that this continues, the basic contradiction of prescribing impossible penal aims will remain, and the crisis is likely to deepen, producing increasing professional disillusionment amongst prison staff and administrators.

The costs of imprisonment

Finally, it is necessary to pay some attention to the costs of imprisonment, of which there are two main types. The first, and most obvious, is the monetary cost of incarceration, though this has a number of facets. The most straightforward way to examine it is simply to total the various categories of expenditure for a given year, deduct any income received and present the remainder as the financial cost of imprisonment for that year. This information for England and Wales in 1977 is contained in Table 7, which indicates a net annual expenditure of nearly £220 million which, viewed against an average daily population of 41,548 inmates, produces an annual average cost per inmate of £4,420 (Home Office, 1978a, Appendix 4, pp.83–5). Of course, there is some variation on annual average cost depending on the type of prisoner, with, for example, adult male prisoners showing the lowest annual cost of just over £4,000 per inmate, and young adult and female prisoners costing closer to £5,000 and £6,000 a year respectively. And, as King and Morgan point out, whatever the prison system, the costs of incarcerating the serious offender in conditions of high security are likely to be much greater (1979, pp.43–4, paras. 88–90). This annual average cost, though it rises substantially year by year in monetary terms (for example, to its present level from just over £3,000 in 1975), reflects mainly pay and price increases, and in recent years the real cost has remained broadly constant and shown a similar pattern of distribution (Home Office, 1976b, p.9, paras. 24–6; Home Office, 1977d, pp.8–9, paras. 26–7; Home Office, 1978a, p.8, para. 24).

A number of points may be made with respect to this distribution of prison expenditure. First, even a rough comparison of the £135

Table 7

Expenditure on prisons, England and Wales, 1977

		£ million	*Percentage of total gross expenditure*
Current expenditure	Staff	135.5	59
	Supplies and operating expenses	25.0	11
	Prison industries	12.5	5
	Welfare and education	6.0	3
	Prison earnings	2.0	1
	Home Office administration	10.5	5
	Supply and transport	2.0	1
Maintenance, repairs, rentals	Repairs, rents	5.5	2
	Rates	3.0	1
Capital expenditure	New buildings	24.5	11
	Plant, machinery	3.0	1
Total gross expenditure		229.5	100
Current receipts and earnings		10.0	
Total net expenditure		219.5	

(Home Office, 1978a, Appendix 4, pp. 83–5)

million spent on staff and the £8 million spent on welfare and prison earnings suggests there might be an expenditure imbalance against prisoner treatment and training, notwithstanding the labour-intensive nature of custodial supervision. Second, although expenditure on welfare and education, which includes money spent on assisted visits and recreation, has increased from less than £0.5 million in 1965 (Home Office, 1977a, p.37, para. 51) to a total of £6 million in 1977, this still only represents 3 per cent of total expenditure – just over half the amount spent on administrative costs. And when this level of expenditure is considered in relation to the self-evidently huge investment in prison security (strengthening of conventional barriers, closed circuit television, personal radios, dog patrols, and so on) it prompts reflection on the priority given to these over Prison Rule No. 1. (Home Office, 1977a, pp.122–3, paras. 211–14). Similarly, the seemingly reasonable expenditure on work for prisoners conceals the fact that in local prisons, because of overcrowding and the need to use staff for court escort duties, industry assumes a very low priority (Home Office, 1977a, p.56, para. 91), and that one traditional feature of prison industry, namely sewing mailbags, will continue – albeit with a modern polypropylene dust-free product (Home Office, 1978a, p.46, paras. 152–3).

What all this suggests is that imprisonment involves high overall expenditure, with the greatest proportion of it going on custodial staff and prison security rather than prisoner welfare or training, with (as I concluded in the last section) negligible behavioural impact. To put the size of this investment into perspective, let me briefly compare the unit costs of imprisonment with those of some non-custodial dispositions. This produces some startling contrasts. A recent account of the development of community service, a disposition intended as an alternative to custody, estimated that an average order of 120 hours work completed within six months would cost just £170 (Harding, 1978, p.170). On this basis, simple arithmetic indicates a cost equivalence between an average sentence of community service and a sentence of not more than 14 days imprisonment. A similar imbalance is found when the costs of imprisonment and probation are compared. For example, at the end of 1974 there were over 140,000 people under supervision (of all types) by the probation service at a total cost for the financial year of less than £30 million (Home Office, 1976c, Table 1, p. 21, and Appendix J, p. 68). In relation to imprisonment, this represents the supervision of over three times the number of offenders at one seventh of the cost, a ratio of about twenty to one in favour of the unit cost of probation.

It seems clear, therefore, that even when due allowance is made for the fact that the comparison was not strictly between similar dispositions, there is nevertheless a massive cost advantage in non-custodial dispositions. Indeed, this advantage is actually even greater than it appears, because there are two additional fiscal costs of incarceration (which are, however, difficult to quantify). These are the hidden expenditure in social welfare payments to prisoners' dependants, and the value of prisoners' non-productivity whilst they are out of ordinary employment and being largely non-productive in prison.

Putting all this together, it really does appear that, in the words of the Advisory Council on the Penal System, 'The maintenance of the prison system is as much a direct cost to society as crime itself' (Home Office, 1977c, p.4, para. 13). However, the cost of imprisonment may also be measured in terms of its damaging social, psychological and interpersonal correlates. This human cost of imprisonment, as it is sometimes called, has been variously identified, but one of the most comprehensive and moving statements is contained in the 1971 American commentary on prisons by the American Friends Service Committee:

> We submit that the basic evils of imprisonment are that it denies autonomy, degrades dignity, impairs or destroys self-reliance, inculcates authoritarian values, minimizes the likelihood of beneficial interaction with one's peers, fractures family ties, destroys the family's economic stability, and prejudices the prisoner's future prospects for improvement in his economic and social status. (American Friends Service Committee, 1971, p.33.)

In other words, irrespective of whether imprisonment fails to reform (or even possibly fosters criminality), it can readily be viewed as a destructive, divisive and damaging instrument of social policy because of the various untoward side-effects. Although not everyone would be prepared to subscribe to the view that *all* of these are present, *all* of the time, there is now sufficient literature, including both academic commentaries (American Friends Service Committee, 1971; Cross, 1971; Mitford, 1974; Hawkins, 1976: Sommer, 1976; Fitzgerald and Sim, 1979; King and Morgan, 1979) and the often more eloquent autobiographical and literary accounts of imprisonment (Kropotkin, 1887; Serge, 1967; Cleaver, 1968; Jackson, 1970; Leary, 1970; Davis, 1971; Solzhenitszyn, 1968, 1974; Boyle, 1977), to suggest that the human cost of incarceration is far from negligible. Indeed, this feature of imprisonment is increasingly admitted as a salient factor in considerations of penal policy, not only, perhaps, because of a genuine humanitarian concern to minimize these adverse consequences for the prisoner and his family, but also because most of them – for example, destruction of marriage or inability to secure employment – carry substantial fiscal implications in terms of social welfare payments. This was recently acknowledged in a report by the Advisory Council on the Penal System, which pointed to the dangers of imprisonment and its traumatic effects, stating that it

> . . . is destructive of family relationships, and by encouraging the prisoner's identification with the attitudes of the prison community increases his alienation from normal society. In addition, long term institutionalization is all too likely to destroy a prisoner's capacity for individual responsibility and to increase the problems he must face when he returns to society. (Home Office, 1977c, pp.3–4, para. 10.)

It went on to recommend a general reduction in the length of prison sentences. Increasing awareness both of the high fiscal costs and of the severe human costs of imprisonment constitutes a real challenge to its unquestioned continuance in its present form, especially when these costs are viewed in relation to its lack of behavioural impact.

Conclusion

It is the argument of this chapter that the various features of imprisonment discussed above have given rise to a crisis: ancient and overcrowded institutions with quite appalling conditions for staff and inmates, training regimes which exert negligible behavioural impact, and all this at considerable financial and human cost – producing both disaffection in prisoners and industrial action by prison officers. In turn, as evidenced by the establishment of the May Inquiry, the crisis has prompted thought about the possibility of replacing outdated capital assets, enforced a reconsideration of the penological imperatives of imprisonment, and made a necessity of submitting any proposed changes in penal practice to a rigorous cost-benefit analysis. In Chapter 9 it is these issues, and thus the possible policy responses to the current crisis, which will be examined, with particular attention directed towards the likely future development of the prison and penal systems.

References

American Friends Service Committee, 1971: *Struggle for Justice; A Report on Crime and Justice in America*, Hill & Wang, New York

Andenaes, J., 1974: *Punishment and Deterrence*, University of Michigan Press, Ann Arbor

Bailey, W. C., 1966: 'Correctional Outcome: An Evaluation of 100 Reports', *Journal of Criminal Law, Criminology and Police Science*, vol. 57, pp.153–60

Bentham, J., 1864: *Theory of Legislation*, Trubner

Berecochea, J. E., Jarman, D., and Jones, W., 1973: *Time Served in Prison and Parole Outcome: An Experimental Study*, Research Report No. 49, California Department of Corrections, Research Division, Sacramento

Beyleveld, D., 1977: 'The Effectiveness of General Deterrents as against Crime: An Annotated Bibliography of Evaluative Research', unpublished research report prepared for the Home Office

Beyleveld, D., 1979: 'Identifying, Explaining and Predicting Deterrence', *British Journal of Criminology*, vol. 19, no. 3, pp.205–24

Bottomley, A. K., 1979: *Criminology in Focus: Past Trends and Future Prospects*, Martin Robertson

Bottoms, A. E., and McClintock, F. H., 1973: *Criminals Coming of Age*, Heinemann Educational

Boyle, J., 1977: *A Sense of Freedom*, Pan

Brody, S. R., 1978: 'Research into the Aims and Effectiveness of Sentencing', *Howard Journal of Penology and Crime Prevention*, vol. XVII, no. 3, pp.133–48

Cleaver, E., 1968: *Soul on Ice*, McGraw-Hill, New York

Clemmer, D., 1940: *The Prison Community*, Rinehart, New York

Cross, R., 1971: *Punishment, Prison and the Public*, Stevens

Davis, A., 1971: *If They Come in the Morning . . .*, Orbach and Chambers

Eichman, C., 1966: *Impact of the Gideon Decision upon Crime and Sentencing in Florida: A Study of Recidivism and Sociocultural Change*, Research Monograph No. 2, Florida Division of Corrections, Research and Statistics Section, Tallahassee

Fitzgerald, M., and Sim, J., 1979: *British Prisons*, Basil Blackwell

Foucault, M., 1977: *Discipline and Punish: The Birth of the Prison*, Allen Lane; Penguin, 1979

Gibbs, J. P., 1975: *Crime, Punishment, and Deterrence*, Elsevier, New York

Greenberg, D. F., 1975: 'The Incapacitative Effect of Imprisonment: Some Estimates', *Law and Society Review*, vol. 9, pp.541–80

Greenberg, D. F., 1977: 'The Correctional Effects of Corrections: A Survey of Evaluations', in D. F. Greenberg (ed.), *Corrections and Punishment*, Sage, Chapter 5, pp.111–48

Gunn, J., Robertson, G., Dell, S., and Way, C., 1978: *Psychiatric Aspects of Imprisonment*, Academic Press

Harding, J., 1978: 'The Development of Community Service', in N. Tutt, (ed.), *Alternative Strategies for Coping with Crime*, Basil Blackwell, Chapter 9, pp.164–85

Hawkins, G., 1976: *The Prison: Policy and Practice*, University of Chicago Press

Home Office, 1963: *Report on the Work of the Prison Department, 1962*, HMSO

Home Office, 1964: *The Prison Rules, 1964*, HMSO

Home Office, 1969: *People in Prison*, HMSO

Home Office, 1970: *Report on the Work of the Prison Department, 1969*, HMSO

Home Office, 1972: *Report on the Work of the Prison Department, 1971*, HMSO

Home Office, 1975: *Residential Treatment and Its Effects on Delinquency*, Home Office Research Study No. 32, HMSO

Home Office, 1976a: *The Effectiveness of Sentencing*, Home Office Research Study No. 35, HMSO

Home Office, 1976b: *Report on the Work of the Prison Department, 1975*, HMSO

Home Office, 1976c: *Report on the Work of the Probation and After-Care Department, 1972–1975*, HMSO

Home Office, 1977a: *Prisons and the Prisoner*, HMSO

Home Office, 1977b: *Report on the Work of the Prison Department, 1976*, HMSO

Home Office, 1977c: *The Length of Prison Sentences*, Interim Report of the Advisory Council on the Penal System, HMSO

Home Office, 1977d: *Report on the Work of the Prison Department, 1976*, HMSO

Home Office, 1978a: *Report on the Work of the Prison Department, 1977*, HMSO

Home Office, 1978b: *Prison Statistics, England and Wales, 1977*, HMSO

Hood, R., and Sparks, R. F., 1970: *Key Issues in Criminology*, Weidenfeld & Nicolson

House of Commons, 1978: *Fifteenth Report from the Expenditure Committee: The Reduction of Pressure on the Prison System*, vol. 1 (Report), HMSO

Howard, J., 1777: *The State of the Prisons*, Everyman's Library edition, J. M. Dent, 1929

Jaman, D. R., and Dickover, M., 1969: *A Study of Parole Outcome as a Function of Time Served*, Research Report No. 35, California Department of Corrections, Research Division, Sacramento

Jackson, G., 1970: *Soledad Brother: The Prison Letters of George Jackson*, Bantam Books, New York; Penguin, 1971

King, R. D., and Morgan, R., 1979: *Crisis in the Prisons: The Way Out: A Paper Based on Evidence Submitted to the Inquiry into the United Kingdom Prison Service under Mr Justice May*, University of Bath and University of Southampton

Kropotkin, P., 1887: *In Russian and French Prisons*, Ward & Downey; Schocken, New York, 1972

Leary, T., 1970, *Jail Notes*, Douglas Book Co., New York

Lipton, D., Martinson, R., and Wilks, J., 1975: *Effectiveness of Correctional Treatment: A Survey of Treatment Evaluation Studies*, Praeger, New York

Martinson, R., 1974: 'What Works? Questions and Answers about Prison Reform', *Public Interest*, vol. 10, Spring, pp.22–54

Mitford, J., 1974: *The American Prison Business*, George Allen & Unwin; Penguin, 1977

Morris, N. 1974: *The Future of Imprisonment*, University of Chicago Press

NACRO, 1979: *The May Inquiry: A Review of Submissions*, National Association for the Care and Resettlement of Offenders

Newton, M., 1971: *Reconviction After Treatment at Grendon*, Office of the Chief Psychologist, Prison Department, Home Office

Petersilia, J., 1977: 'Developing Programs for the Habitual Offender: New Directions in Research', in C. R. Huff (ed.), *Contemporary Corrections: Social Control and Conflict*, Sage, Chapter 6, pp.104–23

Petersilia, J., and Greenwood, P. W., 1978: 'Mandatory Prison Sentences: Their Projected Effects on Crime and Prison Populations', *Journal of Criminal Law and Criminology*, vol. 69, no. 4, pp.604–15

Prisons Committee, 1895: *Report from the Departmental Committee on Prisons*, HMSO

Radzinowicz, L., and King, J., 1977: *The Growth of Crime: The International Experience*, Hamish Hamilton; Penguin, 1979

Serge, V., 1967: *Men in Prison*, English translation, Gollancz, 1970; Writers' and Readers' Publishing Cooperative, 1978

Simpson, A., 1976: 'Rehabilitation as the Justification of a Separate Juvenile Justice System', *California Law Review*, vol. 64, no. 4, pp.984–1017

Solzhenitsyn, A., 1968: *One Day in the Life of Ivan Denisovitch*, Penguin

Solzhenitsyn, A., 1974: *The Gulag Archipelago*, Collins

Sommer, R., 1976: *The End of Imprisonment*, Oxford University Press, New York

Sparks, R. F., Genn, H. G., and Dodd, D. J., 1977: *Surveying Victims: A Study of the Measurement of Criminal Victimization*, John Wiley, New York

Van Dine, S., Dinitz, S., and Conrad, J., 1977: 'The Incapacitation of the Dangerous Offender: A Statistical Experiment', *Journal of Research in Crime and Delinquency*, January, pp.22–34

Von Hirsch, A., 1976: *Doing Justice: The Choice of Punishments*, Report of the Committee for the Study of Incarceration, Hill & Wang, New York
Walker, N., 1965: *Crime and Punishment in Britain*, Edinburgh University Press
Walker, N. 1971: *Crimes, Courts and Figures*, Penguin
Wilson, J. Q., 1975: *Thinking About Crime*, Basic Books, New York
Zimring, F., and Hawkins, G., 1973: *Deterrence: The Legal Threat in Crime Control*, University of Chicago Press

7. Old and New Ways in Probation

Howard Jones

Probation has been variously described as a second chance, as a lenient alternative to prison, or, most inaccurately of all, as a 'let off'. None of these descriptions does justice to its positive qualities; for many kinds of offender it is the method of choice.

Before we can speak of probation in the modern sense, all of the following conditions must be present:

(1) No punishment is imposed initially.

(2) The offender is given a fixed period to prove that he can make good.

(3) During this period he is placed under the supervision of a probation officer who will (a) keep the court informed of his progress and (b) 'advise, assist and befriend him' in his efforts to succeed.

(4) If he does complete his period of probation successfully, no further action is taken by the Court, but if he fails to cooperate with his probation officer or gets into further trouble he may be fined or may even have his probation order replaced by some other sentence for the offence for which he was originally put on probation, as well as for any further offences which he may have committed in the meantime (Jarvis, 1980).

The 'instead of prison' image has always loomed large. For over a hundred years probation has been, apart from fines, the main alternative to a custodial sentence, the main means by which offenders might be dealt with outside of prisons, borstals, approved schools, and so on. And while custodial sentences often have punishment (in the sense of retribution) and incapacitation in mind, as well as deterrence and correction, probation has from the outset been almost entirely concerned with the last two – that is, with attempting to reduce criminal tendencies. A growing awareness in recent years of the damage which incarceration does to those committed to it, plus alarm at the enormous financial and social cost of penal institutions, has produced a strong movement of informed opinion against it. If, as a result, many future offenders are kept out of custodial institutions, there will certainly be a need for new forms of sentence to be served in the open, but there will also need to be an expansion in the use of probation, the core form of non-custodial provision. The question will be raised later as to whether, as it is at present, it is even appropriate for its present role, much less a greatly expanded one.

The first use of probation is usually located in Boston in 1841, when a cobbler named John Augustus rose in court and offered to stand bail for and supervise a man charged with drunkenness. Encouraged by his success with the first case, Augustus continued with his work, and in the remaining eighteen years of his life supervised nearly 2,000 persons who had been, as he termed it, 'bailed on probation' (NPAA, 1939). This was the model for the Church of England Temperance Society, when in 1876 it set up its first Police Court Mission to try to reclaim drunkards appearing before the courts. This work was gradually extended to other types of offender. Meanwhile the magistrates cooperated by releasing offenders on bail to the missioners, even though statutory sanction for this was lacking until the passage of Acts in 1879 and 1887.

Probation still had a long way to go before achieving its present form. Supervision by the early police court missioners was dependent entirely upon the willingness of the offender to accept it. However, in the Probation of Offenders Act 1907 probation officers were mentioned for the first time, and supervision by them became enforceable on the probationer. And in 1925 the process of development was complete when the appointment of probation officers became obligatory. The expansion of the service was slow before the war of 1939–45 but accelerated rapidly in the post-war period. By 1967 there were 2,745 probation officers and over 45,000 indictable offenders on probation, 43 per cent of them juveniles. Ten years later the number of full-time probation officers had risen to 5,099 (Home Office, 1978a). But by that time the Probation

Service had taken on onerous new duties in connection with the parole and after-care of ex-prisoners, reflected in its new title, the Probation and After-care Service. Indeed, by 1977 the number of parole and after-care cases for which it was responsible exceeded the number of probationers.

The increase in involvement with ex-prisoners was paralleled by a decline in work with children. Probation was abolished for juveniles under the terms of the Children and Young Persons Act 1969, and replaced by the Supervision Order. This was more than a mere change in name: although young offenders could still be placed under the supervision of a probation officer, they could now be supervised instead by the social services department of the local authority, and many were. Under the new legislation many also received Care Orders instead of Supervision Orders, which meant that, if they were not placed in some form of residential care by the local authority social services department which was now responsible for them, they would be supervised at home by the same local authority's social workers. Add to all this the main thrust of the 1969 Act, which was to keep young delinquents entirely out of court if at all possible, treating them as 'welfare cases', and one can see that a major shift in the correction of juveniles had taken place, away from probation and towards social work. By 1977 only 14 per cent of the total caseload of the Probation and After-care Service consisted of the supervision of under-seventeens, as compared with 46 per cent of its probation caseload in 1968, the year before the passage of the Children and Young Persons Act (Home Office, 1970, p.xxviii).

The service was therefore now predominantly concerned with the supervision of adult criminals – either probationers or ex-prisoners. Meanwhile it also took on the provision of the social welfare service in prisons, previously provided by prison welfare staff, so that a number of probation officers now spend a period of years actually working amid the powerful socializing pressures of prisons. These facts may partly explain why probation officers as a group have in recent years showed signs of moving away from the main body of social work (in spite of a common training), appearing to identify more with the courts and the retributive and deterrent aspects of the penal system.

On the other hand they must also have been affected by the swing towards legalism and more severe punishment which has been such a marked feature of general opinion in recent years.

In theory, probation is a compact between the probationer and the court; a Probation Order cannot be made without his agreement. In exchange for being put on probation, the probationer undertakes certain obligations: to be of good behaviour and lead an industrious life, to notify the probation officer of any change of address, to keep in touch in accordance with such instructions as the officer may give, and to receive visits at his home from the probation officer if the latter requests this. To these standard conditions the court may occasionally also add a requirement that the probationer lives in some specified place (say, a hostel) or undergoes medical treatment. Other restrictions – for example, on who the probationer may mix with socially – may also be imposed, though this is not often done nowadays, since it is felt that such requirements are not easily enforced. They also unduly restrict the discretion of the probation officer, who is dealing with the case on a day-to-day basis and ought therefore to be free to use his own judgement in the light of his knowledge of the probationer's progress.

If the offender manages to keep the terms of this agreement for the period fixed by the court (between one and three years), the Order is discharged. It may be discharged even earlier if the court decides, on the advice of the probation officer, that the probationer has made such progress that there is no point in continuing to the bitter end. On the other hand, as already indicated, failure brings the probationer back to court. The officer may then recommend that the offender be given another chance, but often such a complaint against him will mean the end of probation and the imposition of another sentence – perhaps prison or some other custodial disposition.

How voluntary is the Probation Order as far as the probationer is concerned? Does the fact that he must accept the Order (which has first been very carefully explained to him), mean that he really is a free agent? Or is the threat of the alternative sentence, possibly imprisonment, sufficient to make him suppress any doubts he may have? This is probably an unreal distinction. In the real world people always do enter into agreements in the light of the more or less attractive (or threatening) alternatives available to them. And the requirement that the probationer accepts the Order does place some obligation of cooperation upon him which is absent from other sentences imposed more arbitrarily, giving the probation officer at least a potential area of common ground with him from which to get started. It is also more consistent with the contemporary idea that social work is only justifiable if a client and his social worker are at one about what is being attempted (Pincus and Minahan, 1973, Chapter 9).

However, the Probation Order itself is no more than a piece of paper. It is the probation officer who makes a reality of it, and research has shown that differences in probation practice are very considerable. An unpublished Home Office study of how one group of officers used their time showed wide variations. Some met their clients frequently, others less so; some preferred long interviews, others short. Some carried large caseloads, while others had smaller ones. Yet all wrote of their work in similar terms, related to a conventional or 'textbook' view of how it should be conducted. What this very brief investigation made quite clear was the importance of the personal element, overriding to a large extent the legal or professional definitions of the task. This has been confirmed by other researches in respect of both custodial institutions and probation (Brody, 1976, p.63). As long ago as 1959, in a study of correctional effectiveness in a U S naval detention barracks, the Grants were able to distinguish between the results achieved by the 'best', 'next best' and 'worst' supervisors. Johnson in 1962 found that more 'adequate' probation officers also secured better results. In a study of probation hostels in 1971, Sinclair concluded that success or failure depended partly on the personal characteristics of the wardens. In the most sophisticated of these studies, Palmer (1968) found that appropriate matching of types of 'treatment' with types of young offender in the California Community Treatment Project halved the failure rate.

These results are probably not very surprising, bearing in mind the fact that the correction of offenders, like all forms of interpersonal influence, is brought about through a personal relationship between the worker and his client. And although the fact that the penal experience (the 'suffering'?) can vary according to the kind of probation officer or custodial staff to whom you are assigned does detract somewhat from the even-handedness of justice, it also offers special opportunities for correction by providing an almost infinite variety of approaches, to complement the variety of types of offender. More will be said about this at a later stage.

The potential range of approaches is not limited, but rather underpinned, by the way in which the role of the probation officer is defined in the law. He is adjured first of all to 'advise, assist and befriend' his probationer. Over the years this everyday language has been reinterpreted to mean the use of the social casework method, in which subtle interpersonal skills are used to help the probationer examine his present mode of adjustment to society and work out a better one. Intensive casework is not often practicable in the busy life of the probation officer, but it has become the ideal, and under the influence of psycho-analytic theory probation has emphasized patience and tolerance, and allowing the probationer to discover himself, rather than trying to impose on him ideas from other people which, it is claimed, he would not assimilate with any real conviction.

At the same time, however, the officer has the responsibility of 'policing' the Probation Order on behalf of the court which imposed it. Only if he reports the probationer as in breach of the Order will the court consider setting it aside in favour of some other (possibly more onerous) imposition.

The probation officer, then, who in one of these characterizations is to be seen as a 'friend', albeit a somewhat manipulative one, is in the other expected to become an instrument of the deterrent threat implicit in probation. There are two ways of looking at this. It could be (and has been) argued that suspicion or fear of the officer in his 'watchdog' capacity may prevent probationers from being honest and frank with him in his casework role. Since he needs their confidence if he is going to be able to understand and help them, this could constitute a serious handicap to effective correctional work (Jones, 1971, pp.258–9; Hauge, 1968). The alternative view is that this apparent contradiction merely increases the repertoire of approaches available to the officer, who can be gentle or tough as the case demands. The power to 'breach' a probationer means that both he and the officer know that if the officer does adopt a 'tough' stance, there is muscle behind it (Foren and Bailey, 1969).

In practice the deterrent element usually looms very much less large than that derived from casework, mainly because probation officers have been trained on social work courses in company with those who intend to work in the social services, helping the unhappy and underprivileged members of society. Probation officers in general still show great tolerance, admitting that they 'breach' only reluctantly and as a last resort. Yet this mode of working rests on nothing more concrete than the current attitudes of probation officers, and with the present shift in public opinion away from correction and towards a more punitive approach it could all be changing. There is nothing in the law or even the philosophy of probation to prevent this. Indeed Chief Probation Officers (CCPO, 1978) and the authors of a recent critique of probation (Bottoms and McWilliams, 1979) would restrict casework to those probationers who opted for it, the Order imposing solely an obligation to report. The length of the Order and the frequency of reporting would be laid down by the court, presumably on the basis of some assumptions about deterrence or a retributive tariff.

An important part of the work of the Probation Service has always been the preparation of reports for the guidance of the courts, mainly magistrates' courts, and especially in the case of children. But in 1962 the Interdepartmental Committee on the Business of the Criminal Courts (the Streatfeild Committee), in considering how to make sentences more correctionally relevant, recommended that both judges and magistrates should be trained in sentencing, and also that the role of probation officers in supplying information to the courts at all levels should be extended (Streatfeild Committee, 1962). By 1977 over 223,000 'social inquiry reports', as they are called, were being submitted to courts, as compared with under 100,000 in 1960 (Home Office, 1978a) and it has been estimated that officers spend 22 per cent of their working week preparing them (Davies and Knopf, 1973, Table 3, p.12). This is clearly a substantial time commitment, and it is worthwhile asking: to what end?

Although the British court of law has an unequalled reputation for incorruptibility, legal erudition and the protection of individual rights, its performance as a sentencing body has often been challenged. This is partly because of the conflicting aims which it tries to achieve; correctional motives are rarely uncontaminated by retributive or deterrent considerations. But the courts have also been criticized because, though correctional sentencing calls for social and penological knowledge, the training of judges has been exclusively in the law, and that of magistrates has hardly existed. The traditions of the courts and the social background of sentencers have also been said to be such as to make them backward-looking and uncomprehending of the life and social circumstances of the mass of working-class people. Criticisms such as these led some states of the USA to transfer part of the sentencing function to Youth Correctional Authorities consisting of social and medical experts. In more traditional Britain it was hoped that social inquiry reports supplemented by reports from the police would make it possible for the courts as at present constituted to function more effectively.

The police can of course supply information about the offender's previous criminal record and his personal reputation and criminal connections, as well as anything they happen to know about his family and social background, education, employment, and so on. The probation officer supplements all this with a report based on an interview (and sometimes a home visit), in an attempt to broaden and deepen the amount of personal information provided for the court. Much of this information is subtle and concerned with personal relationships, and therefore difficult to obtain and to be sure about. Nevertheless it is this kind of intangible information which social workers believe to be of most importance in understanding people's motives and behaviour. Doubt has been cast on this by statistical researchers who argue that the best predictors of future criminality are previous criminal record, age, previous work record and type of home area – relatively objective facts (Simon, 1971, p.145). Nevertheless, to argue that family and personal relationships, which mean so much to us all, have no influence on our behaviour is to strain credibility beyond what is reasonable. And that these factors play some part is shown by the evidence for what is called 'clinical prediction' – that is, judgements about the future prospects of criminals based on qualitative assessments rather than so-called 'hard data' (Simon, 1971, pp.143–4).

There is a danger that we may be 'blinded by science' into overlooking simple truths which even statistically minded criminologists accept as self-evident in their everyday lives. It has been suggested, for instance, that to adopt, as the statisticians do, the level of reconviction as the ultimate test of correctional success or failure may be too simple to fit the facts. Many desirable changes in the offender's life and social adjustment may have been brought about even though he has got into further trouble. In its simplest form the reconviction criterion does not even have the justification that it satisfies society's demand for a pay-off in the form of a reduction in the crime problem. This is partly because it does not usually concern itself with any qualitative changes in crime patterns (for instance, in the seriousness or frequency of crimes committed) which may be brought about by measures which have a correctional bearing (such as the use of social inquiry reports). But there is an even more fundamental point: because of the existence of a 'dark' figure of crime, the crimes we get to know about are a highly selected minority of the total. For example, police investigation procedures being what they are, a man with a long previous record of criminality is much more likely to be picked up than a beginner in crime. This must cast considerable doubt on the reconviction criterion.

However, facts of any kind, whether objective or not, mean very little until they are arranged to form some meaningful pattern. Probation officers set out to make sense of the material included in their reports by selecting what they feel to be most relevant to an understanding of the particular case and then arranging it in such a way that it throws light upon the offender's criminality and how he should be dealt with. Therefore, even if the officer does not make a recommendation to the court, he often cannot avoid implying one.

There is little doubt that this highly subjective process of structuring the report is influenced by the officer's own personal beliefs, or what is often the same thing – his theoretical views about the nature of criminality. It is argued that this is an unsafe basis on which to provide information for the courts, and certainly it is likely to be affected by differences in personality and personal values, as well as variations in insight and sensitivity. It is important, therefore, that social inquiry reports should contain a certain common framework of significant facts out of which the officer must deduce his interpretation. Courts can then evaluate those interpretations for themselves.

Probation officers, however, do not always confine themselves to innuendoes about the most appropriate disposition. The Streatfeild Committee said that they should express an opinion on the best sentence, and many probation officers are prepared to make recommendations about this, though some do so only in relation to probation. It is not easy to decide how much influence such recommendations have on the sentences ultimately passed. Where recommendation and sentence coincides, it may be because the court had independently come to the same conclusion as the officer. Or it may be, as is often suggested, because the probation officer has successfully managed to 'second-guess' the court's ultimate decision. Officers will often express their concern about the dangers of being 'way out' in their recommendations and thus damaging the credibility of their reports.

In a study of the socal inquiry reports presented to a juvenile court between 1965 and 1967, an attempt was made by Mott (1977–8) to get round these ambiguities. The magistrates concerned made sentencing judgements at three stages: before hearing the report, after hearing it but before discussing it between them, and, finally, after discussing it. Any changes made at the second or third stages which were in the direction of the probation officer's recommendation were seen as evidence of 'deference' by the court towards the recommendation. She found a high overall correlation between the probation officer's recommendations and the decision ultimately made by the magistrates. Most of these were 'obvious' decisions, in the sense that both parties agreed from the outset about what ought to be done. In a substantial group of cases, however, magistrates actually changed their minds after reading the reports. Only 10 per cent of their decisions actually differed from the advice given by the officers. Significantly enough, in the light of the points made earlier, the factors on which magistrates laid most stress were home background and the seriousness of the offence.

This, however, was a juvenile court. One might expect that the probation officer would be more influential in cases involving children, where correctional rather than punitive motives should prevail, at any rate more than in the adult courts. Probation officers have also traditionally had a close relationship with magistrates, especially with those in juvenile courts, whereas their contacts with judges were slight before the Streatfeild Report. How much influence then are they able to exercise in cases involving adults, especially those heard in the higher courts?

Perry (1974) found that in 60 per cent of the reports on adults which he studied the probation officer made definite recommendations. Understandably, the higher the court the less frequently did the officer presume to advise it on sentence, though, paradoxically, the higher the court the more likely it was to agree with the officer's recommendations. It is not possible to say whether this was simply agreement on obvious sentences, 'second-guessing' by the officer, or genuine 'deference' to his recommendations by the court. However, in only 58 per cent of cases where the reports did contain recommendations were these reflected in the sentences actually passed. Thus only 35 per cent of all reports were followed by sentences which coincided with explicit advice given in them – and even this may have been the result of 'obvious' sentences or 'second-guessing'. There might also, of course, have been some cases in which the advice remained implicit but the 'message' got over nevertheless.

In a more recent study by Thorpe (1979), it was found that in areas producing many reports there tended to be a smaller proportion making specific recommendations. Where such recommendations were made, however, they had more influence on the sentence passed than any amount of detail in the reports themselves. So neither the number nor the length of reports seems to be a criterion for this influence.

Such research on social inquiry reports certainly does not justify any fear that courts are in danger of having their sentencing function usurped by probation officers. On the contrary, the amount of influence officers exercise outside the juvenile courts is not nearly enough to put court decisions on a sound correctional footing. Current attacks on the correctional approach are often justified by its lack of success, but improvement cannot be expected until sentencing itself improves. No matter how good a correctional method may be, it will not succeed if it is applied at the wrong time or to the wrong people.

Not that existing correctional methods are as good as all that, and that includes probation. For a long time there has been an untested assumption that, while prison, say, was self-evidently damaging, probation was self-evidently helpful, so that all we had to do was impose fewer custodial sentences and use more probation instead. Research, on the other hand, has shown little or no difference in their success rates. Bearing in mind, however, the much greater cost of custodial sentences, both in financial terms and in social and personal deprivation to the offender, it is arguable that there is a case for more probation even if results are not better than for prison and other institutional forms of correction. Both Wilkins in Britain and Davies in America showed that probation could replace prison more often than at present without serious adverse consequences (Brody, 1976, p.28), and trends in the use of probation will be examined later in this chapter. But these results will, as already stated, have been partly an artefact of sentencing practice. And this almost random choice among different motives in the course of sentencing could only have been exacerbated by the particular way in which the researchers in these studies compared like with like in the prison and probation cases whose success or failure was being compared. To match cases in a general way is to ignore (that is, to randomize) the special appropriateness of cases to one form of correction or another. Much interest has therefore focused on the attempt made in experiments by the Youth Authority of California to work out ways of matching types of offenders more precisely to type of 'treatment' (Brody, 1976, p.59).

In what was called the Community Treatment Project (CTP) a

group of young offenders were allocated at random, either to a period in custody followed by parole, or to casework in the community (Brody, 1976, p.31). In the latter cases the personality classification system known as 'I-levels' (interpersonal maturity levels) was used as a basis for matching caseworker to offender and for determining the approach to be adopted. In spite of the initial random allocation between custody and community-based correction, the latter achieved the better results, supporting the general assumption in favour of probation, but this depended on the probationer being allocated to an officer whose personal qualities closely matched the offender's needs. This limitation might have been expected, in view of what has been said about the role of personality (as against technique) in determining how the face-to-face work of correction is actually conducted.

Although all I-level types did better in the community than in custody, some did less well than others, suggesting that there might be a case for institutional correction of a less traditional kind. This proved to be the case. Four samples were allocated to either custody or CTP, one of each being considered suitable on I-level grounds for the form of disposition chosen, and one of each unsuitable. The offenders allocated to the institution were subjected to a more intensive programme than that of the traditional regime. The 'suitable' cases were all more successful than the unsuitable ones, including those placed in the institution, who actually did better than 'unsuitable' cases allocated to the CTP.

The basic process involved here is the development of a typology of correctional approach (community treatment versus custody) and a parallel typology of offenders (I-levels), and then the marrying of the two for maximum effectiveness. Such single-minded correctionalism seems to leave little scope for the operation of other sentencing aims such as retribution, deterrence or incapacitation. Nevertheless it could provide an empirical yardstick against which to estimate the cost, in loss of correctional effectiveness, of any departures from rehabilitation, whether proposed by traditional jurists or contemporary deviance theorists.

Not all recent studies of the 'matching' hypothesis have taken enough account of the personal element in a probation officer's style of work. A case in point is the 'Impact' experiment conducted in Britain by the Home Office Research Unit (Home Office, 1976). In this study no difference was found between a group of probationers given more intensive and 'situationally orientated' correction, and a control group dealt with mainly by the traditional brief 'office interview'. More significant for present purposes appears to be the fact that matching officer to probationer showed only very limited benefits. But although the personality features of probationers were taken into account, officers were classified only according to whether they (a) operated in a supportive *or* a controlling fashion, and (b) paid most attention to factors affecting the probationer as an individual *or* to the situation in which he found himself. Although theoretical or ideological beliefs are often presented in support of one or other of these choices, they almost certainly also depend to some extent on the personalities of the officers concerned. What is equally true is that these choices do not exhaust, or even do justice to, the personality element. One could, for example, imagine officers who all used a controlling and individualistic approach, but because of differences in personality used more or less direct methods of control and also utilized either cold and punitive or warm and paternal relationships to achieve such control. Such differences are well-known to anyone with experience of correctional work. There is no easy behavioural basis for developing typologies of either offenders or probation officers; more general features of personality are involved.

'Matching' is, however, no more than a refinement of the conventional 'advise, assist and befriend' or casework function of the probation officer. It represents no challenge to the individualist model of criminality on which conventional probation practice rests. Yet that model cannot be convincingly supported nowadays. Criminality is not solely a characteristic of the individual, to be modified simply by exercising personal influence upon him without any regard for his relationships with other people and with other aspects of his environment. To argue that it is, is almost like postulating a kind of medieval doctrine of 'possession'. The individual is possessed by the evil spirit of criminality, which must be cast out by the application of the appropriate casework (or psychiatric) ritual. To put it in less theological terms: 'Thus for Aristotelian physics, a stone fell because it had the property of heaviness; modern physics explains its fall by showing it to be the resultant forces of gravity and air resistance acting upon it in accordance with certain general laws' (Frank, 1942). The human being is, of course, not as passive and helpless as this in the face of the forces impinging upon him. As a self-conscious creature with his own goals and his own creative potentiality he can react powerfully to his environment. But it will nevertheless have its effects, of which, indeed, this need to counter-attack is itself one. As the psychoanalysts have shown, many of our own behaviour patterns are just such attempts to defend our satisfactions and our identities from what seem to us to be threats from the outside.

Criminal behaviour is, then, a byproduct of the criminal's relationships with his environment. A person may commit crimes because of the effect upon him of stress or deprivation within his home, of deviant subcultural norms in the neighbourhood in which he lives, of his sense of being underprivileged either materially or in social status. More recently, emphasis has been placed upon the amplification of criminality which results from the stigmatization and segregation of 'primary deviants' by the operation of the criminal justice machinery itself (Lemert, 1971, Chapter 3). Also present will usually be an individual selective factor which originally caused one person in such situations to fall foul of the law, and allowed another to escape scot-free, but that factor is meaningless unless seen in its specific environmental context. It is that environmental pressure or temptation which draws out and gives form to personal traits which are otherwise criminologically neutral.

If all this is true it is only to be expected that our correctional efforts, concentrated as they are on the individual, will be of limited effectiveness. And it is very surprising, considering the widespread acceptance of the importance of the social factor, that the probation service itself should continue to be so committed to the traditional approach. The only new idea to emerge within the service, apart from the sterile 'reporting' proposal already referred to, is the plan for prefabricated 'probation packages' to be made available to the court, consisting of 'a combination of workshop, work experience, day centres, accommodation, special education, training in social skills etc.' (CCPO, 1978). This is an imaginative proposal, but it does not sufficiently engage the wider social setting of the probationer.

A custodial sentence tears the individual physically out of context, but so does probation. In particular, and especially when it consists mainly of office interviews, it facilitates the compartmentalization of behaviour – or what Merton (1961, p.374) calls, believe it or not, 'insulating role-activities from observability by members of the role-set'. Like the working-class child who suppresses his natural accent in the classroom, the offender on probation can present an image in the probation office, in response to the demands of his officer, which bears little resemblance to his self-image or to his behaviour at home. To see this as deception is to fail to recognize the extent to which we are all, in the course of our social interactions, engaged in 'presentations of self' (Goffman, 1969).

Group interviews make compartmentalization more difficult. Thus a home visit, when a probationer is interviewed in the presence of some other member of his family, forces him to assimilate his probation office 'presentation' to that which he uses at home. Interviewing probationers as a group, if they share a common subcultural affiliation, has a similar effect in producing more authentic behaviour from them all. Probation officers who have used the group method in this way sometimes complain at first that the response of their probationers has deteriorated – has become less compliant and submissive, perhaps even more overtly delinquent. Only later do they come to realize that this is not deterioration, that they are now obtaining a more accurate picture of what their probationers are really like. This must be a gain; social work based on a false (and usually over-optimistic) perception of the client cannot be expected to succeed. Equally important, any readjustment which group members make is also going to be more realistic, since it will be based on their continuing awareness, through the presence of their peers in the group, of the subcultural norms and life-style to which they will have to go on accommodating in the future.

Group work has another very important advantage. Casework for many probation officers is more of an aspiration than a feature of daily practice. This is because it calls for fairly long interviews repeated frequently. With average caseloads of 35 to 40 (Home Office, 1978a) this is not possible except for one or two special cases. Many probation officers will rationalize this by saying that these 'special cases' are the only ones who need intensive casework – but it is astonishing how often they turn out to exist in just those numbers which the officer finds the pressure of work allows him to cope with. For the rest it is the very brief, rather didactic and infrequent office reporting session.

If, however, these short individual interviews are replaced by a group session, the situation is transformed. If, say, fifteen minutes is available for office interviews with each of nine probationers, this permits, if they are seen as a group, a session of an hour and a half plus a little slack. Nor does this mean any dilution in the impact of the correctional process. Group work method, which involves each member of the group as a correctional influence on the other members, actually increases the pressure for change on the probationers present. Requests by members of a probation group to go back to individual interviews because what they want to discuss is 'personal' or 'confidential' only bears witness to this pressure, which escape from the group would enable them to avoid.

There are difficulties in the way of expanding the use of group work in this field because of the traditional assumption that probation is essentially, and should remain, a means by which personal counsel can be provided for individuals. This is the heritage of John Augustus and is reflected in what might be called the 'advise, assist and befriend' philosophy. Courts see it in this light and allocate cases accordingly, so that it is sometimes difficult for officers to construct viable groups from within their own caseloads. This is a particular problem in rural areas where cases are thinly scattered over a wide area anyway. Judges and magistrates also expect the officer to have the kind of intimate and detailed knowledge of a probationer's affairs which might be acquired by a friend and counsellor. And of course there is the constant preoccupation of the courts and the penal system with the dangers of contamination if groups of malefactors are brought together (Barr, 1966; Jones, 1962, 1965). The Chief Probation Officers' proposal for probation packages includes a number of valuable pointers to ways of extending the use of the group method (CCPO, 1978).

Group work goes part, but only part, of the way towards taking account of the essentially social origins of crime. It gives some expression to the subcultural factor. It also provides exercise in the handling of multilateral personal relationships for those who lack confidence or are inept at relating to other people, in a way that a one-to-one contact between probationer and officer could never achieve. And it enables the officer to maximize the value of his time. But it does not deal with such conditions as employment, material deprivation, life chances, housing, recreation and friendship, all of which may play a part in determining whether a person becomes delinquent or not.

It is often argued that some of these factors are political in origin and can only be solved by means of political action (Pritchard and Taylor, 1978, Chapter 5). Thus it is political decisions which determine the level of social welfare support for the underprivileged, and also the level of public intervention in the economy which ultimately decides whether an area or an industry shall be allowed to decline, with catastrophic consequences for those living in the area or employed in the industry. Some say that these same problems are inseparable from the present crisis of the capitalist system, so that only the root-and-branch transformation of society will remedy them – and therefore the crime problem to which they give rise. Many social workers and some probation officers have therefore become 'politicized', with varying degrees of radicalism, in recent years, seeing rehabilitative activity as doomed to failure until some more basic reconstruction of the social order has taken place.

There are many difficulties of principle and practice confronting those who take such a view. For probation officers, with their unambiguous obligation to readjust the offender to society, any attempt to adjust society to the offender instead is bound to lead to conflict with representatives of the established order. This does not mean that the officer cannot be a reformer or even a revolutionary if he wishes, but that, in the industrial cliché, he will be expected to do so 'in his own time', and not to introduce more conflict into the role of the probation officer than already exists. Much alarm has already been expressed by, for example, traditionally minded magistrates about the political positions taken up by some probation officers. To put this matter into perspective, however, it must be made clear that political radicalism is a minority tendency in the service.

Whatever one's sympathies it is difficult to see how probation officers can expect to be allowed to subvert the social fabric which they are appointed and paid to preserve. They can work within that fabric, certainly, so as to help probationers to secure all their benefits, to get a job or to join a union to improve their bargaining power. But beyond this it becomes a breach of the officers' implicit contract with society, and it may also be a form of tyranny, for it may involve using their special position in society to propagate their own views and foist them on their probationers and on society at large. That others do such things is no excuse for their doing violence both to the individual's right to choose for himself and to the democratic machinery of society.

Is there then no way out? Must probation officers go on carrying out functions which some of them believe are quite futile for the purpose of reducing criminality? Classical social work theory would answer no, arguing that the solution is to be found in strengthening and equipping probationers to take political action for themselves, as they see fit. For many of them this appears unrealistic. Heavily stigmatized or in other ways socially alienated, their underprivileged socio-economic position allowing them no influence on the course of events and leaving them with little confidence and determination, they are not going to represent much of a force for change. Unless, that is, they can also be helped to a better adjustment to and a more influential role in society. This is not merely an aim which is compatible with the formal responsibilities of the probation officer, but one which will put the probationer in a better bargaining position for improving the situation in life of people like himself.

The adjustment aim in probation (and in social work generally) is often seen as opposed to desirable social reform, and some will go so far as to say, 'Don't relieve people's sufferings, because if you do you make present-day society, with all its contradictions and injustices, more tolerable, and therefore help to perpetuate it.' Leaving aside the callousness of such a view, it seems that it may actually be wrong in principle. Maybe it is not abject misery which makes revolutions (in the sense of radical change) but confidence bred of education, a full belly and the possession of political muscle. Incidentally, such a programme would also be aimed against those factors in the wider environment which we have seen to be connected more immediately with criminality. But it is a programme which cannot be achieved solely through individual casework or even group work. These techniques have to be utilized within a broader strategy of what is called community work.

By this time we may seem to have wandered so far from the traditional individuation of the probation service as not to be discussing probation at all, but something entirely new. On the contrary. The probation idea is being set in a broader and more realistic social context without changing any of its basic features as enumerated at the beginning of this chapter. It must be remembered that it is not probation as an approach to the individual offender which matters, but probation as a complex amalgam of support and deterrence which has always provided the main correctional alternative to custody. The signs are that as such an alternative it will be called upon more and more in the future.

Community work was originally defined by Clifford Shaw, in the crime prevention work of his Chicago Area Projects, as 'changing the street' – that is, changing social attitudes in high-crime-rate areas. This has proved an impossible task, and, even if it were not, many would see it as a form of cultural imperialism. Bottoms and McWilliams suggest (1979) that probation officers should do community work, in the sense of trying to improve social conditions in such areas. Important though this is in its own right, it is very remote from the acts of criminality against which it would be directed. It could be expected to work, if at all, only in the long term. As to its long-term value, this seems a common-sense expectation, though research evidence for this is weak. A community approach of this kind also ignores the personal and immediate dangerousness and distress of the individual offender, which calls for more direct action.

What can be aimed at instead is helping probationers to reattach themselves to existing social networks in a more successful and less offending way than they were able to achieve in the past. The Dutch probation service provides a clue as to how this might be approached by the more extensive use of voluntary helpers (Wilson *et al.*, 1975). The important thing is that such volunteers should be 'matched' culturally, economically and even personally with the probationers they are seeking to help, which will mean calling on the assistance of a much wider selection of the population than gives most of our voluntary social service at the present time. The Dutch can call on the church as an avenue of recruitment because of the central position which denominational religion plays in Dutch society. We still have to find social levers strong enough to achieve such a purpose for us.

Once an appropriate voluntary supervisor has been identified, however, it will be found that much more than an individual 'befriender' has become available to the probationer. The whole social network of the volunteer opens up to him, including friends, leisure activities, contacts with employers. An important art of the probation officer then becomes that of enabling the probationer to exploit these opportunities in order to increase his understanding of himself and his social situation and to find a stable niche for himself in society. It will be clear that the value of the volunteer consists in his continuing to be himself, rather than becoming an unqualified social worker. This means that many people can be enrolled as volunteers whose personal qualities might unfit them for social work. All that is required is that they are appropriately matched to their probationers: that each is the kind of person who can help such a person as the probationer is. Therefore a second important skill for the probation officer of the future will be matching people up like this.

There will be plenty of scope meanwhile for him to exercise his other skills – as caseworker, group worker, marshaller of welfare and other resources for the benefit of the offenders in his charge. It is merely the theatre within which all these activities take place which has changed – from the office to the community.

It has already been pointed out that probation has been losing ground over the years. The trend over a period of ten years depicted in the following table shows a decline in the use of probation for all age-groups and both sexes. Another feature of this table is the much decreased use of probation with older age-groups. This is probably partly because many of the older offenders will have had their chance on probation earlier in their criminal careers. Another reason, however, must be the assumption that younger offenders are more malleable and therefore better prospects for a predominantly correctional approach like that of probation. Any move away from custody in the future is going to bring about a dramatic increase in the proportions placed on probation. It is perhaps also worth noting that the decline in the use of probation is steepest not among the oldest people but among those between 17 and 21. This may be a punitive reaction to the prominence of this group in the crime picture in recent years, especially in connection with the more newsworthy offences such as vandalism and acts of personal violence.

Table 1

Probation/supervision as a percentage of total sentences

	Age-groups					
	10–16		17–21		Over 21	
	M	F	M	F	M	F
1968	26	33	14	34	7	16
1969	25	32	14	32	7	16
1970	24	30	13	29	6	15
1971	22	28	13	28	7	15
1972	20	29	13	26	7	15
1973	20	28	11	24	7	15
1974	19	28	10	23	6	14
1975	18	27	9	22	6	13
1976	17	24	8	20	5	12
1977	17	24	7	19	5	12

(Home Office, 1978b, Table 6.1, p.87)

What has been happening to that increasing number who are no longer being placed on probation? As far as the two older age-groups (17 to 20 and 21 and over) are concerned, over the last three years of the decade 1968–77 it has been the popularity of the Community Service Order (see Chapter 8) which has made the difference. In the previous seven years the slack from the 17–20s group was taken up by an increase in the use of fines. Only in the youngest group has probation been partly replaced by an increase in custody. Detention centre and borstal sentences doubled for boys under 17 over the ten years concerned. This is very surprising in view of the frequent complaints of magistrates and others that the Children and Young Persons Act 1969 has resulted in too few children being sent away from home.

With this one exception, then, there is no reason to believe that probation is losing ground to institutional sentences. It is being replaced by other non-custodial sentences, and especially by the pioneering new sentence of Community Service. Such innovations are needed if we are to try to improve the correctional effectiveness of our penal system, and they can also help to reduce the populations of prisons, borstals, and so on. It should be remembered that, although the number of prison sentences is not increasing, the lengths of sentences are (Home Office, 1977, Appendix C, pp.156–60), and this alone must mean that the proportion of our convicted offenders in prison is still increasing. But the financial and social costs of imprisonment argue strongly for an actual decline in this proportion, and it would be profligate not to continue using probation as the main alternative. We have seen that even as it stands it could be expanded without any risk of increasing recidivism. Given a probation system which took more account of the social nature of crime, we might expect it to produce results in preventing reconviction which even the most sceptical researcher would find it difficult to gainsay.

References

Barr, Hugh, 1966: *A Survey of Groupwork in the Probation Service*, HMSO

Bottoms, A. E., and McWilliams, W., 1979: 'A Non-Treatment Paradigm for Probation Practice', *British Journal of Social Work*, vol. 9, no. 2, pp.159ff.

Brody, S. R., 1976: *The Effectiveness of Sentencing*, Home Office Research Study No. 35, HMSO
CCPO, 1978: *Residential Conference Papers*, Conference of Chief Probation Officers
Davies, M., and Knopf, A., 1973: *Social Enquiry Reports and the Probation Service*, HMSO
Foren, R., and Bailey, R., 1969: *Authority in Social Casework*, Pergamon
Frank, J. D., 1942: 'The Contribution of Topological and Vector Psychology to Psychiatry', *Psychiatry*, vol. v, no. 1
Goffman, E., 1969: *The Presentation of Self in Everyday Life*, Allen Lane; Penguin, 1971
Hauge, R., 1968: 'Institutional Dilemmas in Probation and Parole', in N. Christie (ed.), *Aspects of Social Control in Welfare States*, Scandinavian Studies in Criminology, vol. 2., Tavistock; especially pp.49–50
Home Office, 1970: *Criminal Statistics, England and Wales, 1969*, HMSO
Home Office, 1976: *Intensive Matched Probation and After-Care Treatment*, vol. 2, HMSO
Home Office, 1977: *Prisons and the Prisoner*, HMSO
Home Office, 1978a: *Probation and After-Care Statistics, England and Wales, 1977*, HMSO
Home Office, 1978b: *Criminal Statistics, England and Wales, 1977*, HMSO
Jarvis, F. V., 1980: *Probation Officers' Manual*, Butterworth
Jones, Howard, 1962: 'The Group Approach to Treatment', *Howard Journal*, vol. xi, no. 1, pp.58–63
Jones, Howard, 1965: 'Group Work: Some General Considerations', *Probation*, vol. xi, no. 3, pp.91–4
Jones, Howard, 1971: *Crime and the Penal System*, University Tutorial Press
Lemert, E. M., 1971: 'Deviance and Social Control', in L. Radzinowicz and M. E. Wolfgang (eds.), *The Criminal in Society*, Basic Books, New York
Merton, R. K., 1961: *Social Theory and Social Structure*, Free Press, New York
Mott, Joy W., 1977–8: 'Decision Making and Social Enquiry Reports in one Juvenile Court', *British Journal of Social Work*, vol. 7, no. 4, pp.421–32
NPAA, 1939: *John Augustus, First Probation Officer*, National Probation Association of America
Palmer, Ted, 1968: *Community Treatment Project: Report*, vol. 9, no. 2, Youth Society, State of California, pp.44ff.
Perry, F. G., 1974: *Information for the Court*, Cambridge Institute of Criminology
Pincus, A., and Minahan, A., 1973: *Social Work Practice: Model and Method*, F. E. Peacock, Itasca, Illinois
Pritchard, C., and Taylor, R., 1978: *Social Work: Reform or Revolution?*, Routledge & Kegan Paul
Simon, Frances H., 1971: *Prediction Methods in Criminology*, HMSO

Streatfeild Committee, 1962: *Report of the Interdepartmental Committee on the Business of the Criminal Courts*, HMSO
Thorpe, Jennifer, 1979: *Social Enquiry Reports: A Survey*, HMSO
Wilson, Thelma, Harper, J., and Willis, P., 1975: *Probation Service in England and the Netherlands*, North East London Polytechnic

8. Other Non-Custodial Measures

Andrew Willis

As Cohen argues (1979), the last ten years or so have witnessed a new romantic movement in corrections, one with an Arcadian vision of deviancy control which rejects the use of penal institutions as places of first resort and stresses the need for offenders to be more appropriately dealt with through community control and supervision. This has had some effect on official attitudes:

> With varying degrees of enthusiasm and actual measurable consequences, officials in Britain, the United States and some Western European countries, became committed to the policy labelled 'de-carceration', the state-sponsored closing down of asylums, prisons and reformatories. (Cohen, 1979, p.609.)

The purpose of this chapter is both to document the apparent strength of the movement and to investigate the extent to which the rhetoric of community corrections finds true expression in penal practice.

Towards community corrections

There appears to be a consensus amongst academics, government advisory bodies and legislators that high levels of incarceration are ineffective and inhumane, and disenchantment with institutional penal programmes generates enthusiasm for community care. On the academic side, a recent American volume on alternatives to imprisonment expresses this view with a pleasant mixture of romantic vision and hard-headed pragmatism: 'By bringing them back into the community, by enlisting the good will and the desire to serve . . . we shall meet the challenge . . . and at the same time ease the financial burden of . . . confinement in institutions' (Alper, 1973, pp.vii–viii).

Also, the 1976 edition of a prestigious American anthology on contemporary practice in probation and parole finds it necessary to add a completely new section on community corrections. (See Carter and Wilkins, 1976.) Indeed, what appears to be happening, as Scull observes (1977, pp.41–3), is that academic commentators are ushering in a new Golden Age of corrections, a therapeutic millennium in which the adverse consequences of imprisonment are avoided to the mutual benefit of offender and community. Moreover, this tendency is evident in England. A recent volume on non-custodial penal strategies is introduced as containing recommendations which offer justice to both offender and community:

> Justice to the offender is attempting to offer him an opportunity to change his life style while avoiding double-think and brutalization. But equally important is justice to the community in offering it protection, freedom from exaggerated claims and value for money. (Tutt, 1978, p.20.)

In addition, government agencies now endorse the value of community corrections. The influential American National Advisory Council on Criminal Justice Standards and Goals bluntly concludes that it 'considers community based corrections as the most promising means of accomplishing the changes in offender behaviour that the public expects' (Carter and Wilkins, 1976, p.486). This is because they offer the humanitarian advantage of eliminating the unfavourable consequences of incarceration, a reformative impact no less than incarceration, and large fiscal savings. Similarly, an American Public Health Service publication argues that 'a large number of offenders who are candidates for incarceration may instead be retained in the community as safely, as effectively and at much less expense' (Carter and Wilkins, 1976, p.530). This view is echoed on the other side of the Atlantic. A report of the Advisory Council on the Penal system in 1970 suggested that 'there is room for further development of alternatives to deprivation of liberty. Imprisonment is not only inappropriate and harmful . . . it is also a wasteful use of limited resources' (Home Office, 1970, p. 3, para. 9). And in 1978 the Fifteenth Report from the House of Commons Expenditure Committee proposed that, although imprisonment must remain the penalty of last resort, increased use must be made of existing non-custodial sanctions and new ones deployed, if only for financial reasons. (See House of Commons, 1978, pp. lxviii–lxxxi, paras. 182–230.) The report concluded:

> . . . such a community based approach will provide a surer foundation for developments in the field, make better use of resources, both human and financial, and would in the long run lead to a reduction of the pressure on the prison system. (House of Commons, 1978, p.lxxxii, para. 239.)

This groundswell of informed opinion is reflected in recent legislation which seeks to expand non-custodial penalties at the expense of incarceration. For example, California during the 1960s witnessed the quiet revolution of Probation Subsidy (R. Smith, 1971, pp.136–43). The profile of the entire correctional system was modified by offering the incentive of state financial aid to those counties which reduced commitments to prison below a calculated level and used probation instead. This form of subsidy produced astounding results and the proportionate use of probation for adult offenders rose from under 45 per cent to over 65 per cent in the period 1960 to 1969 (Scull, 1977, Table 3.5, p.55). As R. Smith points out (1971, pp.49–50), fiscal bribes on a sliding scale resulted in a 25 per cent reduction in state-wide commitment rates within two years of introducing the programme, though there have been less enthusiastic interpretations (Lerman, 1975, Chapter 7).

In England and Wales, the Criminal Justice Act 1967 introduced the suspended prison sentence and parole, whilst the Criminal Justice Act 1972 brought about community service, compensation and restitution, and day training centres (Home Office, 1978a, Part One). This proliferation of new non-custodial measures came about, according to Hawkins (1975, pp.68–77), for reasons of expediency and economy; ever-increasing inmate populations at ever-increasing costs and little positive behavioural impact made imprisonment progressively less attractive. As Table 1 indicates, these new custodial measures do appear to have been well received by sentencers and used as alternatives to imprisonment. With respect to young adults, the slight proportionate increase in the use of immediate imprisonment seems more than compensated for by a substantial decrease in the use of borstal training and detention centre orders.

Table 1

Young adult and adult male offenders sentenced for indictable offences by type of sentence or order, 1967–77

Age	*Year*	*Total number sentenced*	*Dispositions by percentage*							
			Absolute or conditional discharge	Probation Order	Fine	Community Service Order	Detention centre or borstal	Imprisonment		Other
								Sus-pended	Imme-diate	
17–20 years	1967	58,147	8	15	54	—	17	—	4	3
	1977	95,107	8	7	57	5	12	4	5	2
21 years and over	1967	117,208	8	9	57	—	—	—	24	1
	1977	180,923	9	5	53	2	—	12	17	1

(Home Office, 1978b, Table 6.2, p.90, and Table 6.3, p.93)

And community service now seems well established as a major penal sanction. A similar picture emerges with respect to adults: the use of immediate imprisonment decreased sharply, and there was an impressive use of new non-custodial dispositions, so that community service and suspended prison sentences accounted for one in seven of all sentences. In addition, for both groups financial penalties remained the dominant sanction. Clearly, there appears to be good *prima facie* evidence for the dawning of the new age of community corrections. However, the purpose of this chapter is to question the extent to which these purported alternatives to imprisonment really operate as substitutes for custodial sentences, and the extent to which they could do so. I suggest that, in all cases, their roles as alternatives to imprisonment are fiercely circumscribed. In making this argument, rather than cataloguing and commenting on all custodial dispositions, I shall pay attention to three separate types of sentence. First, individual deterrent penalties (fines and suspended prison sentences); second, a sentence which promises to be both punitive and reformative (community service); and, third, measures intended predominantly to offer social welfare benefits (day training and detoxification). If restricted potential for decarceration is shown in all three areas, irrespective of the distinct penal philosophies involved, the general conclusion that there are limits beyond which non-custodial measures are unlikely to expand is greatly reinforced.

Deterrent penalties

Deterrent penalties are intended to reduce an offender's disposition either to repeat his offence or to break the law in any other way through the application of an unpleasant measure (Walker, 1972, p.72). Where pro-social conduct is achieved through psychological coercion deriving from the unpleasantness of actual punishment, this is called 'specific' or 'individual' deterrence (Andenaes, 1971, pp.17–18; Gibbs, 1975, pp.34–5). Very clearly, the unpleasantness of a financial penalty actually imposed and the threat of a suspended sentence of imprisonment being activated represent individual deterrent penal sanctions.

Table 2

Defendants found guilty and fined by type of court and type of offence, 1977

		*Number found guilty**	*Number fined*	*Percentage fined*
Magistrates' Courts	Indictable offences	371,510	205,877	55
	Non-indictable offences (excluding motoring)	426,193	286,298	67
	Motoring offences	1,147,154	1,121,687	98
	Sub-total	1,944,857	1,613,862	83
Crown Courts	Indictable offences	68,795	10,228	15
	Non-indictable offences (excluding motoring)	906	114	13
	Motoring offences	3,251	1,220	38
	Sub-total	72,952	11,562	16
Grand total		2,017,809	1,625,424	81

*The figures in this column with respect to the Crown Courts refer to offenders found guilty and offenders sent for sentence following conviction at magistrates' courts.

(Home Office, 1978b, Table 1a, pp.146–65, and Table 5a, pp.272–81)

To begin with fines, it is clear, as Table 1 demonstrates, that they account for over half of all penal dispositions. And, as Table 2 indicates, although the greatest number of financial penalties are awarded for motoring offences and non-indictable offences (about 1.5 million), it is also the case that as many as 216,105, or 49 per cent, of the 440,305 persons found guilty of indictable offences received monetary penalties. But, despite the evident popularity of fines, four factors collectively inhibit the extent to which they might be used as alternatives to incarceration.

First, they are of questionable penal effectiveness. Early Home Office research into the comparative efficacy of fines involved calculating the expected rates of reconviction for offenders with respect to factors in their criminal biographies and comparing these to actual reconviction rates for a group of offenders subject to a variety of penal dispositions (Home Office, 1964, Part VI, pp.40–51). As Table 3 indicates, fined offenders were actually being reconvicted at much less than the expected level, imprisoned or discharged offenders about the expected level, and offenders placed

Table 3

Indices showing results of sentence compared with expectation for adult male first offenders

Disposition	*Offenders aged 17 years and over*		
	England and Wales 1932	Scotland 1947	Metropolitan Police District 1957
Discharges	90	103	102
Fines	86	96	75
Probation	120	108	124
Imprisonment	100	104	116

(100 = expected rate of reconviction within five years)

(Home Office, 1964, Table 4, p.48)

on probation at a higher than expected level. This held true for all three areas studied, and prompted the conclusion that 'Fines ... appear to be among the most "successful" penalties for almost all types of offender' (Home Office, 1964, p.51, para. 163), a view endorsed in the most recent edition of a Home Office advisory booklet to sentencers (Home Office, 1978a, p.85, para. 289). This view is supported by Walker who argues that to reject the 'face-value' interpretation would entail the implausible belief that sentencers regularly put highest-risk offenders on probation rather than unsophisticated or non-hardened criminals whose circumstances offer hope of reform (Walker, 1968, pp.251–4; 1971, pp.113–16; 1972, pp.118–22). Against this view, however, Bottoms (1973, pp.543–52) argues the case for 'agnosticism', suggesting that magistrates do tend to reserve probation for poor risks, that is, offenders with domestic, employment, financial and other problems, and impose fines on the better risks, that is, offenders with steady employment and regular incomes. Indeed, a Home Office

Table 4

Amount of time taken to complete payment of fines and compensation, Home Office survey, 1974

Payment of total sum completed	*Offenders*	*Percentage*
Within 1 month of sentence	911	35
Within 3 months of sentence	1,279	49
Within 6 months of sentence	1,593	61
Within 12 months of sentence	1,873	72
Within 18 months of sentence	1,999	77
Payment not completed within 18 months of sentence	597	23
Total	2,596	100

(Home Office, 1978c, Table 10, p.15)

survey found that whereas over three quarters of the offenders who were employed were fined, only half of those unemployed received financial penalties (Home Office, 1978c, Table 4, p.5). To the extent that Bottoms is correct, fines are clearly limited as alternatives to custody in two ways. On the one hand, because they offer nothing special in the way of effect on recidivism, imprisonment may well be preferred on other grounds – for example, public protection or greater retributive impact. And, on the other hand, fines look suspiciously as if they are being reserved for offenders with a low probability of reconviction – the sort who would anyway be unlikely to be imprisoned.

There is also the problem of enforcing the payment of fines, which may involve the sanction of imprisonment. A recent Home Office survey of fining practices in magistrates' courts, which involved 3,240 adult offenders in England and Wales convicted of common indictable offences (burglary, theft, fraud, criminal damage, malicious wounding), confirmed the popularity of fines, with 2,596 or 80 per cent of the sample adjudged to pay fines, compensation or other sums, totalling £125,000 (Home Office, 1978c, p.14). However, although three quarters should have paid their fines within three months, there was a problem of non-payment. As Table 4 indicates, only 1,279 (49 per cent) had paid within three months and as many as 597 (23 per cent) had failed to complete payment within 18 months. Indeed, at this point, 222, or 9 per cent, had paid nothing at all and only three quarters of the monies due to the courts had been received (Home Office, 1978c, pp.14 and 15). These data support the findings of an earlier survey, in which 25 per cent of fined offenders had outstanding balances to pay after nine months and one in ten had something still to pay after twelve months (Home Office, 1973, Appendix G).

Moreover, action taken to remedy non-payment was not particularly successful. Reminder letters, means summonses, the issue of warrants of commitment to prison and other actions only yielded payment in from half to two thirds of the cases. In fact, of the 194 offenders against whom warrants of commitment were issued, as many as 119 (61 per cent) failed to pay in full and were presumably received into prison in default of payment (Home Office, 1978c,

Chapter 5). On a national scale, in 1977 as many as 16,040 people were received into custody for non-payment of fines. Although this is only a tiny proportion of about 1.75 million offenders fined, it still represents a quarter of all receptions under sentence for the year (Home Office, 1978d, p.51, para. 1). More important than the numbers, though, is the impact of imprisonment on defaulters. As Table 5 shows, despite the fact that over half were committed for under one month, about one in five of all receptions paid their fines within three days, thereby securing their release (Home Office, 1978d, p.53, para. 8). Similarly, a study of fine enforcement in Manchester confirmed that a strict policy of imprisonment for default (following letters and visits by enforcement officers) was productive of almost immediate payment (Latham, 1973, pp.552–9).

This strongly suggests that imprisonment is a necessary measure of last resort for enforcing the payment of fines, especially in view of the fact that the rate of default is proportionately greater for the more serious offences of robbery, burglary and violence against the person than it is for motoring or drunkenness offences (Home Office, 1978d, Table 7(a), p.51). But this creates a dilemma: the

Table 5

Fine defaulters by length of sentence and release within three days of reception, England and Wales, 8 September–31 December 1977, taking into account changes in the law introduced by the Criminal Law Act 1977

Sentence length	*Percentage by sentence length*	*Percentage released within 3 days of reception*
Up to 1 month	54	24
Over 1 month, up to 3 months	41	22
Over 3 months	5	19

(Home Office, 1978d, Table 7(c), p.52, and Table 7(d), p.53)

Table 6

Percentage of offenders fined by number of previous convictions, Home Office survey, 1974

Number of previous convictions	*Percentage fined*
Nil	75.2
1 or 2	73.0
3 or more	47.5
Total	66.0

(Home Office, 1978c, p.3, Table 2)

greater the use of financial penalties, the more the prison population is likely to be swollen as commitment rates for non-payment increase, especially if fines tend to be reserved for the less serious offenders who would be unlikely to go to prison.

In addition, it does appear that fines are largely used for the less serious offenders and offences. On the one hand, as Table 6 demonstrates, offenders with no previous convictions are most likely to be fined, the proportion decreasing as criminal record increases. This suggests that fines are used as a penalty of first resort, a common disposition for new offenders, but one which has an attenuated importance for recidivist offenders. On the other hand, the data also suggest that fines are largely reserved for trivial offences, a view derived from the fact that the vast majority of fines are for relatively small amounts. Thus, in 1977 as many as 35 per cent of adult male offenders fined in magistrates' courts for indictable offences were fined not more than £20, with 60 per cent fined not more than £30 (Home Office, 1978b, Table 6.13, p.104), which merely confirms the Home Office survey data of 1974 (Home Office, 1978c, Table 7, p.10).

Finally, if fines were to be used as a substitute sentence for imprisonment, the amount of the penalty would have to be substantially increased in proportion to the increased gravity of the offence. However, the ability of offenders to pay these inflated fines has to be taken into account. The Home Office survey points to the fact that as many as 38 per cent of the sample were unemployed offenders (Home Office, 1978c, p.6), and three quarters of those fined reckoned they made payment wholly or partly out of current income, which in some cases necessitated reduced spending on clothing, food and housekeeping (Home Office, 1978c, Chapter 6). It would appear, then, that any increase in the level of financial penalties would only give rise to greater levels of imprisonment for default in payment.

Despite the fact that fines are already widely used, they therefore appear to offer little opportunity to expand community corrections at the expense of imprisonment: they are no more effective than other penalties, and were they to expand they would be productive of increased levels of imprisonment as the absolute numbers of defaulters increased, as well as a proportionate increase due to inability to pay. The only solution to these difficulties, apart from overcoming the tendency to reserve fines for new, non-serious offenders, would be to relate the amount of the fine to an offender's ability to pay (Home Office, 1970, Chapter 2, pp. 5–11; Appendix B, pp.74–7).

Similar difficulties also exist with the implementation of suspended sentences of imprisonment. This innovation was introduced as 'a focused deterrent – a threat addressed to an identified offender' (Walker, 1972, p.109) under the Criminal Justice Act 1967 as amended by the Criminal Justice Act 1977 and the Power of the Criminal Courts Act 1973. These provide that a court which passes a sentence of immediate imprisonment for a term of not more than two years may order that the sentence shall not take effect unless, during a specified period of up to two years, the offender commits another offence punishable with imprisonment (Home Office, 1978a, pp.41–2, paras. 137–43). In effect, the court first awards a custodial sentence but then immediately puts it into abeyance for a specified period, subject to no further offence being committed. The purpose of the sentence is to 'give an offender an incentive to avoid trouble by making a set period of imprisonment contingent on his committing a further imprisonable offence' (Home Office, 1978a, p.42, para. 141).

The value of the sentence is reckoned to lie in the fact that the courts can distinguish between the seriousness of the offence, which they mark by the length of the sentence, and the needs of the offender, which may be better served by release into the community. But, should the offender be reconvicted of an imprisonable offence within the specified period, the court is required to activate the suspended sentence unless in view of all the circumstances it would be unjust to do so (Home Office, 1978a, p.42, para. 142).

More recently, additional legislation under the Criminal Law Act 1977 has conferred power on courts to partially suspend prison sentences of between six months and two years, the period of suspension to be not less than a quarter and not more than three quarters of the sentence (Home Office, 1978e, pp.118–23, paras. 268–82). The rationale for this is that it improves on the ordinary suspended sentence by offering double deterrence – a deterrent element in actual custody and postponed deterrence during the suspended period (Home Office, 1978e, pp.118–19, para. 268).

The appeal of the suspended sentence, in either of its forms, is immediate: it minimizes or removes the actual term of imprisonment with all its attendant deformative influences, and yet maximizes the deterrent impact by insisting on a short period of incarceration or by holding the threat of imprisonment over the offender. Not surprisingly, the penal intent in the suspended and partially suspended prison sentence has received recent endorsement from both the Advisory Council on the Penal System (Home Office, 1978e, Chapter 13) and the House of Commons Expenditure Committee investigating ways to reduce the pressure on the prison system (House of Commons, 1978, pp.xxxiii–v, paras. 57–64). But good penal intentions are not always realized in penal practice, and it is now apparent that in four interrelated ways the implementation of the suspended sentence has actually had the opposite effect to the one intended and has ended up increasing the amount of incarceration.

As is evident from Table 1, despite an apparent decline in the use of custody during the period 1967 to 1977 inferred from the proportionate decrease in the use of immediate imprisonment, this is

Table 7

Suspended sentences awarded, breached and activated, 1977

	Number	*Percentage*
Sentences awarded	35,068	
Sentences breached	10,205	29
Sentences breached	10,205	
Sentences activated	7,289	71

(Home Office, 1978b, Table 6.20, p.113, and Table 6.21, p.114)

more than compensated for by the utilization of the suspended sentence. If suspended sentences are aggregated with sentences of immediate imprisonment, the proportionate use of all forms of imprisonment is much higher in 1977 than in 1967. With respect to young adult males it nearly doubles from 4 to 9 per cent, and for adult males it rises from 24 to 29 per cent. Thus the proportion of offenders actually awarded prison sentences, as opposed to having to serve them, is on the increase. This means that some of the 35,000 offenders who receive suspended prison terms each year (Home Office, 1978b, Table 6.5, p.97) would not have been subject either to the sentence of imprisonment or to the risk of actually having to serve it prior to the introduction of the suspended sentence. This surreptitious increase in social control under the guise of de-carceration is a phenomenon Cohen refers to as *widening*, pointing to the irony

> . . . that the major results of the new network of social control have been to increase, rather than decrease, the amount of intervention directed at many groups of offenders; and, to increase, rather than decrease, the total number of offenders who get into the system in the first place. (Cohen, 1979, p.610.)

In response to the possible objection that the suspended sentence has only resulted in an increase in the threatened as opposed to the actual amount of incarceration, it is necessary to consider breaches of suspended sentences and subsequent activation of terms of imprisonment. One measure of the breach rate is to compare the number of suspended sentences awarded with the numbers breached and activated in a given year. Table 7 presents this information for 1977, showing that nearly one in three of the sentences were breached – a breach rate half as large again as the breach of probation rate calculated in the same way (Home Office, 1978b, p.113, para. 6.20 and Table 6.20). In addition, a very high proportion of those dealt with by the courts for non-compliance with the terms of the suspended sentence – nearly three quarters – were awarded sentences of immediate imprisonment (Home Office, 1978b, p.114, para. 6.21 and Table 6.21). In effect, of the 35,068 suspended sentences awarded, as many as 7,289 (21 per cent) were to result in an actual sentence of imprisonment which had to be served. Indeed, even when breach rates are calculated in years subsequent to the award of the suspended sentence, the result is the same – a breach rate in excess of 20 per cent, and which appears to be increasing (Home Office, 1978e, pp.226–7, para. 4 and Table 2). Clearly, the practice of suspending prison sentences is actually generating imprisonment.

This effect is even greater if the suspended sentence is awarded not as an alternative to immediate imprisonment but as a substitute for another non-custodial measure. The evidence for this is overwhelming, and illustrates the 'widening' referred to above. If levels of immediate imprisonment and suspended prison sentences combined are greater than the level that immediate imprisonment alone might have been expected to reach, the suspended sentence must have displaced some non-custodial penalties as well as immediate imprisonment (Home Office, 1978e, p.226, para. 1). According to Hawkins (1975, p.76), Home Office estimates suggest that only 40 to 60 per cent of those given suspended sentences would have received sentences of immediate imprisonment before 1968, and that what has happened is that courts have extended 'the potential application of imprisonment to a wider range of offenders, thus ensuring that what had been meant to be used as an alternative to imprisonment was in some cases being used as an alternative to other non-custodial measures'. Similarly, an analysis by Sparks (1971, p.387) suggests that about a quarter of those awarded a suspended sentence in 1969 would have received financial penalties before its introduction. As an example, compare the levels of imprisonment for the indictable offences of theft and handling stolen goods in 1977 with those for similar offences of larceny in 1967, for adult offenders convicted in magistrates' courts. In 1977, of the 117,204 offenders found guilty, 6,414 (6 per cent) were sentenced to immediate imprisonment and 8,243 (7 per cent) received suspended sentences (Home Office, 1978b, Table 1(e), pp.232–51). And in 1967, of the 86,743 offenders found guilty, 9,497 (11 per cent) were sent to prison (Home Office, 1968, Table 1(b), pp.42–61). There is clearly a drop in the use of immediate imprisonment but an overall proportionate increase in the use of immediate imprisonment plus suspended sentences from 11 to 13 per cent. And, other things being equal, the additional 2 per cent are offenders now receiving a suspended prison sentence who would probably have received a genuine non-custodial sentence prior to the Criminal Justice Act 1967.

Finally, there is the probability that sentence length has increased as a function of introducing suspended sentences, having been adjusted upwards by sentencers so as to maximize the deterrent effect and compensate, so to speak, for the conditional liberty. The early review by Sparks (1971, p.393) was emphatic on this point, suggesting that implemented suspended sentences were doubling effective terms of imprisonment, resulting in substantial increases in the prison population. Support for this view can be derived from Home Office data presented in Table 8, which indicates a reduction over the period 1967–76 in the total numbers sent to prison, together with a substantial fall in the use of short sentences. Clearly some offenders have been kept out of prison by the use of suspended sentences. Equally clearly, however, the post-1967 period has seen a large rise in the number given medium-term sentences. This is probably attributable to the use of longer prison terms in suspended sentences and the subsequent activation of some of these. Whatever the explanation, a larger proportion of receptions into custody involve longer sentences now than was the case before the introduction of the suspended sentence.

Table 8

Receptions into prison under sentence of persons aged 17 and over (excluding fine defaulters) by length of sentence, 1967–76

	1967	*1970*	*1973*	*1976*
Sentence length				
Up to 6 months	21,625	12,935	9,493	13,136
Over 6 months, up to 4 years	12,820	20,811	16,517	19,873
Over 4 years	772	1,161	1,149	1,462
Total	35,217	34,907	27,159	34,4711

(Home Office, 1978e, Table 3, p.227)

A consequence of the failure of individual deterrent penalties to decrease levels of imprisonment is that it becomes necessary to examine other non-custodial dispositions informed by alternative penal philosophies which might operate to displace custodial sentences.

Social control and the reintegration of offenders

The Criminal Justice Act 1972, now superseded by the Power of Criminal Courts Act 1973, introduced Community Service Orders, under which an offender surrenders his leisure time to perform unpaid service within a community organization (Harding, 1978, p.164). A court may make a Community Service Order for a period of between 40 and 240 hours of work, provided the offender is aged 17 years or more, the offence is one punishable with imprisonment, the offender consents to the Order after having its nature explained to him in ordinary language, and the court is satisfied, after considering a probation officer's report, that the offender is a suitable person (Home Office, 1978a, pp.20–21, para. 65). This work is to be completed within twelve months of the imposition of the Order, and so far as is practicable the offender will be given a task which will not conflict with his work or religious beliefs (Home Office, 1978a, p.21, para. 68). The sentence was first proposed in a 1970 report of the Advisory Council on the Penal System (Home Office, 1970, Chapter 3), introduced experimentally in 1973 in six petty sessional areas (Durham, West London, Kent, Shropshire, Nottingham and South-west Lancashire) and gradually extended so that by the spring of 1977 it covered, in whole or in part, 53 of the 56 probation areas (Wootton, 1978, p.127).

The penal intent in community service may be looked at in two ways. On the one hand, as suggested by Hawkins (1975, pp. 67–87), recent new non-custodial sentences may be regarded as little more than expedient responses to relieve serious levels of prison overcrowding, a view supported by a statement from the then Home Secretary (quoted in Hawkins, 1975, p.77) that offenders 'should be punished in other ways in the interests of relieving the strain on the prison service'. In other words, as J. Smith argues (1974, p.245), community service owes its origins largely to gross prison overcrowding and, in the long term, will be judged by its ability to reduce the numbers of men in prison; what it really represents is an offender suffering 'a substantial invasion of his liberty without the community providing him with free lodgings'.

More positively, the Advisory Council on the Penal System put forward the view that community service fulfilled a range of quite distinct, though not incompatible, penal objectives:

> To some, it would simply be a more constructive and cheaper alternative to short sentences of imprisonment; by others it would be seen as introducing into the penal system a new dimension with an emphasis on reparation to the community; others again would regard it as a means of giving effect to the old adage that punishment should fit the crime; while still others would stress the value of bringing offenders into close touch with those members of the community who are most in need of help and support. (Home Office, 1970, pp.12–13, para. 33.)

Under community service, then, the traditional aims of punishment and reformation are not seen as mutually exclusive but as both applying: deprivation of leisure and the requirement to work is clearly punitive, but the work element is also regarded as a constructive activity generating the probability of a changed outlook on the part of the offender (Home Office, 1970, p.13, para. 34). Indeed, the early commentators all stressed the multi-dimensional penal philosophy embedded in community service (Harding, 1978, p.169; J. Smith, 1974, pp.245 and 264), perhaps no one more succinctly than West (1976, p.69), who viewed it as 'designed to punish, treat, exact vengeance or reparation, control, cure, or provide help to, and save expense for, the community'.

This lack of specificity in the penal objectives of community service can, however, be criticized as a weakness or applauded as a virtue (Wootton, 1978, p.128). It has been criticized as a 'vaguely determined project' (Home Office, 1975, p.6), while others view its penal character as its strength: 'It is this very versatility that provides the community service order with its greatest potential, (Home Office, 1975, p.6). Indeed, Baroness Wootton, the Chairman of the Advisory Council sub-committee which proposed community service, conceded that the paragraph referring to the multiplicity of penal aims was nothing more than 'an undisguised attempt to curry favour with everybody' (Wootton, 1978, p.178).

This philosophical uncertainty is not, however, without practical consequences. In particular, no one is exactly certain of the extent to which community service should be used as an alternative to imprisonment. As I have suggested elsewhere (Willis, 1977, pp.120–25), the Advisory Council report is fatally ambiguous. On the one hand it asserts that community service is 'inappropriate for trivial offences' (Home Office, 1970, p.13, para. 37) and proposes that it should 'constitute an adequate alternative to a short custodial sentence' (Home Office, 1970, p.14, para. 37). Yet on the other hand it goes on to imply the opposite by proposing community service as suitable for not-so-serious offences: for 'some cases of theft, for unauthorized taking of vehicles, for some of the more serious of traffic offences, some cases of malicious damage and minor assaults' (Home Office, 1970, p.13, para. 37). As any quick inspection of the criminal statistics will show, these offences very rarely result in imprisonment. For example, in 1978, of the 17,403 males found guilty in magistrates' courts of all indictable offences of criminal damage (including arson and criminal damage endangering life), only 861 (5 per cent) were sent to prison (Home Office, 1979a,

Table 1(e), pp.276–95). And the report heaps uncertainty on confusion by then proposing that community service should not be precluded from use in certain cases where there is no liability to imprisonment, as well as suggesting that it should be regarded as an alternative to a fine (Home Office, 1970, pp.13–14, para. 37). Indeed, this uncertainty finds expression even in a Home Office handbook for sentencers which holds that, although community service may be used for any offence punishable with imprisonment, and 'could thus be regarded as a viable alternative to a custodial sentence', it is not a requirement of the law 'that the court would have imposed a prison sentence on that particular offender had it not given him a community service order' (Home Office, 1978a, p.21, para. 67). This point is more than academic for, as J. Smith (1974, p.254) points out, if community service is interpreted only as another alternative to existing non-custodial penalties, the crisis in the prisons will deepen, and a new future for penology and community correction is passed by.

First impressions suggest that community service might well be being used as an alternative to imprisonment. Declining rates of imprisonment (see Table 1) and spectacular increases in the use of community service look promising. For example, in 1976, the first year in which the sentence was available in most probation areas, some 9,133 orders were made (Home Office, 1977a, Table 5.11, p.58), increasing to 11,768 in 1977 (Home Office, 1978b, Table 6.9, p.100, and Table 6.10, p.101) and up to 14,155 in 1978 (Home Office, 1979a, Table 6.1, p.120). Indeed, the very swift transition from an Advisory Council on the Penal System report to legislation (Harding, 1978, p.165), the availability of community service on a national basis within three years (Home Office, 1977b, p.58, para. 5.25), and its increasing use, all suggest, as Pease noted (1978, p.269) that it represents a real growth area in penal policy. Indeed, according to the recent House of Commons Expenditure Committee report on ways to reduce the pressure on the penal system, community service is regarded as: 'one of the most notable recent developments of alternatives to imprisonment' (House of Commons, 1978, p.lxxiii, para. 201). The report also recommends that its use should be further extended.

However, evidence from three principal sources suggests that community service largely operates as an alternative to existing non-custodial measures, rather than to imprisonment. First, following an early review of the operational viability of the experimental scheme (Home Office, 1975), a later investigation paid attention to the extent to which Community Service Orders displaced sentences of imprisonment (Home Office, 1977b, Chapter 2). It assessed the level of sentence substitution by examining circumstantial evidence in a number of areas. To begin with, a sample of probation officers was asked to speculate on the likely sentences for a group of offenders awarded community service if this measure had not in fact been used. As Table 9 indicates, nearly half thought imprisonment very probable, and only one in five discounted it altogether. Then 111 breach cases under Section 16 of the Power of the Criminal

Table 9

Judgements by probation officers of likely sentences in the event of community service not being awarded

	Number	*Percentage*
Imprisonment probable	19	49
Imprisonment possible	13	33
Imprisonment unlikely	7	18
Total	39	100

(Home Office, 1977b, p.4)

Courts Act 1973 were studied to see which sentence was imposed in breached cases, which might count as evidence for the sort of sentence offenders might have got originally instead of community service. As Table 10 shows, under half the breach cases were awarded immediate imprisonment, with slightly more getting a non-custodial disposition, and nearly two thirds if suspended sentences are counted as non-custodial. Another approach involved monitoring 102 cases in which the court had, at the social inquiry stage, specifically requested the probation service to consider community service, but this had not finally been awarded. As Table 11 indicates, in less than one in five of these cases was immediate imprisonment the eventual sentence. Finally, nearly 1,200 cases were examined in which community service had been recommended in

Table 10

Disposal in community service breach cases

	Number	*Percentage*
Immediate imprisonment	49	44
Suspended sentence	17	15
Non-custodial sentence	45	41
Total	111	100

(Home Office, 1977b, Table 1, p.5)

Table 11

Disposal in cases where courts asked for community service to be considered but where it was not awarded

	Number	*Percentage*
Immediate imprisonment	18	17
Suspended sentence	16	16
Non-custodial sentence	68	67
Total	102	100

(Home Office, 1977b, pp.6–7)

social inquiry reports but the courts had refused to accept the recommendations. As Table 12 demonstrates, under half of the sample received immediate imprisonment.

Overall, this review suggested that under half of those awarded community service were actually being displaced from custody, and even this was regarded as a probable exaggeration of the displacement rate (Home Office, 1977b, pp.9–10). And recent data on breach action confirms this picture. In 1978, as Table 13 shows, 14,155 offenders were sentenced to community service and, in the same year, 1,742 offenders were breached for failure to comply with the terms of the Order – an approximate breach rate of 12 per Cent. Of these, just over one third received sentences which immediately deprived them of their liberty, the rest getting non-custodial dispositions. Bearing in mind that the breach sentencing will involve reconsideration of the initial offence as well as taking into account the subsequent misbehaviour, the low rate of incarceration seems very difficult to reconcile with community service being used as an alternative to custody. With these sort of data the conclusion of the Home Office Survey that community service, though viable, 'has not as yet made much impact on the prison population' (Home Office, 1977b, p.70) seems a fair assessment.

Table 12

Disposal in cases where probation officer recommended community service but courts rejected this advice

	Number	*Percentage*
Immediate imprisonment	561	47
Suspended sentence	245	21
Non-custodial sentence	388	32
Total	1,194	100

(Home Office, 1977b, pp.8–9)

Table 13

Disposal in cases where community service awarded and breached, 1978

	Number	*Percentage*
Persons awarded community service	14,155	100
Persons breaching community service	1,742	12
Sentence in breach cases		
Immediate incarceration (detention centre, borstal, imprisonment)	668	39
Suspended sentence	179	10
Non-custodial sentence	895	51
Total	1,742	100

(Home Office, 1979a, Table 6.28, p.148, and Table 6.30, p.149)

Table 14

Community service offenders by instant offence and most common type of previous offence

	Instant offence		*Most common type of previous offence*	
	Number	Percentage	Number	Percentage
Offences				
Offences against the person	89	12	58	8
Property offences	380	50	485	71
Motoring offences	182	24	97	14
Miscellaneous	106	14	47	7
Total	757	100	687*	100

*70 offenders had not previously committed offences.

(Home Office, 1975, pp.40–43)

The second area of supportive evidence derives from studies of the criminal records of offenders made subject to Community Service Orders. As Table 14 clearly shows, the early Home Office study of 757 offenders on community service found that only 89 (12 per cent) were placed on community service for offences against the person, whereas 182 (24 per cent) were awarded it for motoring offences. With respect to prior involvement in criminal activities, only 58 offenders (8 per cent) were persistently involved in crimes of violence, as against 97 offenders (14 per cent) in motoring offences. In addition, as many as 435 (57 per cent) had no previous experience of custodial institutions, and no less than 594 (78 per cent) had no more than one previous experience of incarceration (Home Office, 1975, pp.40–43). In addition, a Kent survey found

Table 15

Community service dispositions by type of offence, 1978

	Number	*Percentage*
Indictable offences		
Violence against the person	842	6
Sexual offences	53	0.5
Burglary	3,153	22
Robbery	66	0.5
Theft and handling	6,256	44
Fraud and forgery	552	4
Criminal damage	706	5
Other	153	1
Total	11,781	83
Non-indictable offences		
Motoring offences	961	7
Other	1,413	10
Total	2,374	17
Grand Total	14,155	100

(Home Office, 1979a, Table 6.3, p.122)

that 70 per cent of Community Service Orders were made for thefts and motoring offences and just 11 per cent for assaults and sexual offences, though even these were by no means serious enough to warrant imprisonment, since they involved affrays and unlawful sexual intercourse (Sussex, 1974).

More recent data supports the view that community service is being reserved for the relatively trivial offender with little prior experience of the criminal justice system and, by implication, little prospect of being imprisoned. For example, as Table 15 indicates, a large minority of the offenders who received community service in 1978 (some 2,374, or 17 per cent) were being sentenced for non-indictable offences – the sort of offences, generally speaking, for which imprisonment is unlikely. Moreover, this is a stable proportion over time, being 16 per cent (or one in six) in both 1976 and 1977 (Home Office, 1977a, Table 5.11, p.58; Home Office, 1978b, Table 6.9, p.100, and Table 6.10, p.101). Also, the small proportion of violent or sexual offences is clear enough.

What seems to be happening is that community service is being used for offences which are amongst the most common and are the least serious – that is, offences which would be unlikely to be dealt with by prison terms, were community service not available. Indeed, in the early Home Office survey, it was discovered that although probation officers failed to agree on the factors pertaining to offenders' biographies or circumstances which would incline them to recommend community service, this would definitely be precluded if the offence was of a violent or sexual nature (Home Office, 1975, pp.16–19).

In addition, it is possible to study community service dispositions in relation to alternative non-custodial penal options within given offence categories. For example, in 1978 31,919 offenders were found guilty of all types of violent indictable crime in magistrates' courts. Of these, just 554 (under 2 per cent) received community service, whereas 18,624 (59 per cent) were fined. Similarly, of the 216,294 persons found guilty of indictable thefts, just 4,958 (slightly over 2 per cent) were given community service, whereas 128,469 (59 per cent) were fined. (See Home Office, 1979a, Table 1(a), pp.192–211.) As already established in Table 1, the vast majority of offenders, of all ages and for all but the most serious categories of offence, receive non-custodial sentences, especially financial penalties, so any new non-custodial sentence is as likely to replace an existing one as it is to serve as a substitute for a term of imprisonment. Indeed, since the proportionate use of imprisonment for young adult offenders has increased in recent years, it is possible to surmise that in their case community service is definitely not acting as a substitute for imprisonment (Home Office, 1979a, Table 6.15, p.134). Similarly, the proportionate use of custodial sentences for adults has increased slightly since the availability of community service (Home Office, 1979a, Table 6.17, p.136). Assuming constancy of offence–offender characteristics, the new non-custodial sentence is having a negligible impact on the rates of imprisonment.

Community service may be expanding, but taken together these three points all suggest that it is not yet flourishing at the expense of imprisonment. Whatever the good intentions behind community service – to keep offenders out of prison (Home Office, 1970, p.v) and to operate as an exciting innovation in penal treatment (Home Office, 1975, p.70) – the reality of community service is that it competes with existing non-custodial penalties rather than displacing offenders from prison. The problem, as both Pease and West have suggested, is that the uncertain position of community service on the tariff enables probation officers to restrict its use to those offenders whose offences and criminal records are insufficiently serious to warrant imprisonment (Pease and West, 1977, pp.16–20; Pease, 1978, pp.269–75). And, as West puts it (1976, p.71), once its position slides, 'the downgrading is inexorable and irreversible'. All the evidence suggests that this is precisely what has happened, and that community service does not substitute for imprisonment. In effect, as McEwan asserts (1978, p. 773), 'no claim more extravagant than that of sheer novelty can be made'.

Social welfare strategies

Finally, there remains the residual category of non-custodial dispositions which place almost exclusive emphasis upon the social welfare of the subject, and on improving either the offender or his circumstances as well as keeping him out of prison. Intervention could take place either at arrest or at the court sentencing stage (Marshall and Fairhead, 1979, p.616). An example of the former, a sort of pre-emptive penal strike, would be the introduction of detoxification centres for habitual drunken offenders, and an example of the latter would be the setting up of day training centres for inadequate repetitive offenders.

In response to a Home Office report on habitual drunken offenders (Home Office, 1971a), a number of pilot and experimental refuges were established for homeless, vagrant alcoholics. Hospital-based centres opened in Edinburgh in 1973 and in Manchester in 1977, whilst a community-based centre opened in Leeds in 1976 (Melville, 1979, p.400). With respect to the Leeds centre, Department of Health and Social Security funding was guaranteed for three years, its future thereafter depending on an assessment of its operational viability and effectiveness, as well as the willingness of the local authority to assume financial responsibility for the venture (*Observer Magazine*, 16 September 1979, pp.124–7).

The aim of the Leeds centre, which is staffed by social workers, nurses and assistants on a twenty-four-hour basis, is 'to provide an alternative to the penal system; and to give homeless alcoholics the opportunity to get the medical, social work and other care they need' (Melville, 1979, p.400). The centre caters for habitual drunkards who can only be referred by the police following an arrest for being drunk and incapable or disorderly. Section 34 of the Criminal Justice Act 1972 as amended by the Criminal Law Act 1977 permits the police to take habitual drunken offenders to treatment centres instead of charging them with public drunkenness. In addition, referrals must have had previous convictions for drunkenness, be without accommodation and not be wanted for any other offence. Upon reception there is an initial phase, lasting up to twelve hours, during which subjects are dried out and allowed simply to work through their withdrawal symptoms. The new arrival then transfers to the main part of the centre for a ten-day period which sees the introduction of individual counselling and group discussions about drink problems and controlling drinking behaviour. In addition there are medical and psychiatric facilities (Melville, 1979, pp.400–401; *Police*, July 1979, pp.32–3). The only rule is that absolutely no drink is allowed, and referrals are allowed to leave at any time.

However, despite the clear intention of these centres to cater for men who would otherwise be processed through the criminal justice system and might well end up in prison, either directly or through default in payment of fine, their future is in jeopardy. With an annual average conviction rate for drunkenness of 20 per 1,000 population (*New Society*, 5 April 1979) – over 100,000 convictions in magistrates' courts in 1978 for simple drunkenness or drunkenness with aggravation (Home Office, 1979a, Table 1(a), pp.192–211) – it seems clear that the demand for the centres is strong enough. Yet only two centres were ever established in England and Wales, and those with no great haste, following the 1971 report. Furthermore, the Leeds centre looks like losing its £165,000 a year DHSS grant (*Observer*, 18 March 1979) and the funding for a proposed centre in London at St Thomas' Hospital has been withdrawn (*Social Work*, 1979, no. 294, p.1).

The extraordinary aspect of this likely termination of experimental programmes and the withdrawal of finance is that it comes in spite of favourable accounts of the operation of the centres, rather than because of proven ineffectiveness. For example, since opening, the Leeds centre has catered for over 3,000 offenders diverted from the criminal justice system (Melville, 1979, p.400). To be fair, in the first two years of operation the Leeds centre had 1,892 cases but only 571 separate offenders (*Police*, July 1979, p.33), which indicates a small number of repetitive offenders making use of the centre on numerous occasions. Also, it could be the case that the police are now picking up cases they would have ignored before the centre opened. However, taken at face value, the throughput represents substantial savings when the £167 admission cost is compared to the conventional costs of arrest, charge, court appearance and disposition (*Police*, July 1979, p.33). Indeed, given that an average arrest of this kind involved about twelve hours of police work and every prosecution cost about £30 in court expenses (*Observer Magazine*, 16 September 1979, p.124), as well as the £100-a-week cost of imprisonment (Home Office, 1979b, Appendix 4, pp.76–8), it is difficult not to agree with this. In addition, when over 2,000 offenders a year are received into custody in default of payment of fines for drunkenness offences (House of Commons, 1978, p.xli, para. 78), the potential saving in the time and trouble of prison staff is considerable, apart from the benefit of avoiding unnecessary periods of incarceration for persistent drink offenders.

Morever, there is some evidence that the effect of detoxification centres is positive. The Edinburgh centre reported that over half the people treated described some improvement in the quality of their life, and that one third of the patients move out of night shelters and common lodging houses into flats or after-care houses, which suggests a steadier pattern of life (*New Society*, 5 April 1979, p.22). However, it was also the case that there was no difference between attenders at the centre and a control group of non-attenders with respect to drinking behaviour. But, as Don Steele of the Federation of Alcoholic Rehabilitation Establishments points out, this is a misleading criterion for success, because when the centres do dry offenders out, provide access to medical care and social work support, as well as keeping people out of the courts, in a sense they *cannot* fail (*New Society*, 19 April 1979, p.159). This more optimistic view is taken by Ronald Gregory, the Chief Constable of West Yorkshire, who said that detoxification was

> . . . one of the most humane experiments for social welfare with which I have had the privilege to be associated. These men have been rescued from incarceration and the humiliating process of the penal system. On the credit side, many of them have been rehabilitated and much police time has been saved. (*Observer*, 18 March 1979.)

Like detoxification, day training is a penal experiment with an uncertain future. Under Section 20 of the Criminal Justice Act 1972, now Section 4 of the Power of Criminal Courts Act 1973, provision was made for the establishment of day training centres, of which four were brought into operation on an experimental basis in West London, Liverpool, Sheffield and Pontypridd during 1973 (Home Office, 1978a, pp.18–19, para. 58).

Attendance at a day training centre can be made a requirement written into a conventional probation order. This obliges an offender to present himself at a centre for a period of not more than 60 days, and whilst attending to comply with the instructions of the person in charge of that centre (Savage, 1977, p.3). Before any such order is made, however, the sentencing court must be notified of the availability of such a centre in the offender's locality and must obtain his consent to the condition written into the order (Adams, 1976, p.48).

Right from the earliest days when NACRO mooted the idea (Priestley, 1970), the express intent has been to provide a service for the more inadequate offender, the sort who might well otherwise go to prison. As the latest edition of a Home Office Advisory booklet to sentencers puts it, the centres should offer 'intensive full time training for socially inadequate offenders ... directed particularly to the needs of offenders whose criminal convictions seem to stem from an inability to cope with the demands of modern life' (Home Office, 1978a, pp.18–19, para. 58). This view was confirmed by the House of Commons Expenditure Committee report which stated that the four centres try to take offenders who 'already have a number of convictions and a record which included imprisonment' (House of Commons, 1978, p.lxx, para. 189), as well as the inadequate and the withdrawn, in order to 'provide in some cases a breathing space in what has been a steady criminal career' (House of Commons, 1978, p.lxxi, para. 191). The consensus view, as expressed by the then Home Secretary, Mr Robert Carr, is that day training offers an opportunity to cater 'for the inadequate, the type who repeatedly runs into trouble because he cannot cope adequately with the behaviour of modern life' (quoted in Adams, 1976, p.48).

Just as it is very clear who the prospective trainee is, it is also evident that there is a high level of agreement on the nature of the training programme. The centres adopt what might broadly be termed a helping approach (Bottoms and McWilliams, 1979, pp.159–202), one which stresses the opportunities for trainees to acquire practical, social, work and interpersonal skills which will enable them to survive without recourse to crime or long-term reliance on social welfare agencies. The agreed emphasis is upon a 'broad-based social education' (Home Office, 1978a, p.19, para. 58), which involves basic training in work routines and practical exercises to acquire social skills, as well as group discussions to try and control feelings which give rise to law-breaking (Adams, 1976, pp.51–3; House of Commons, 1978, p.lxx, para. 189). As a director of one of the centres put it, the idea is

> . . . to help people develop effective ways of solving problems in areas like money, work, relationships, drink and welfare rights. This involves the learning of social and life skills and the increasing of confidence in the management of day-to-day living. (Vanstone, 1979, p.1.)

In theory, then, day training offers realistic and practical help for repetitive and inadequate offenders who might well otherwise go to prison.

In practice, the data is supportive of this view, pointing towards the viability of the schemes and their value as alternatives to imprisonment on two separate counts. First, there is every reason to believe that many day trainees would go to prison if day training were not available. Predominantly the trainees are young men in the early twenties (Savage, 1977, Table 1, pp.8–10; Vanstone, 1979, Table 1, p.14), with three quarters having six or more previous convictions (Willis, 1979, Table 2, p.17) and 55 per cent having over ten previous convictions (Savage, 1977, Table 1, pp.8–10). In addition, a survey in Pontypridd found that only a quarter of day trainees had no previous experience of imprisonment, borstal training or detention centre, and over 15 per cent had served six or more custodial sentences prior to day training (Willis, 1979, Table 4, p.18). This incarceration rate is confirmed by the Sheffield study (Savage, 1977, Table 1, pp.8–10). Overall in Pontypridd, the trainees showed a mean number of three prior prison sentences, each with an average length of twelve months (Willis, 1979, Table 4, p.18). Collectively, these data suggest that day trainees are repetitive, non-trivial offenders with a long history of involvement with the crininal justice system, so much so that day training 'is mainly catering for people who have either completely or partially exhausted the disposal facilities of the court and failed to respond' (Vanstone, 1979, p.15).

This impression is confirmed by a content analysis of 42 social inquiry reports accompanying the 1977 Pontypridd day training intake, of which 33 (79 per cent) make explicit reference to possible incarceration should day training be unacceptable to the sentencing court. The sorts of remarks which predominate in the social inquiry reports (see Willis, 1979, p.19) are:

The court may feel that day training would be a viable alternative to custody

Day training is an alternative to what would otherwise be an inevitable custodial sentence

The court may feel that a period of day training would be a suitable alternative to a custodial sentence.

In addition, day training offers reasonable impact on criminal behaviour, which is an imperfect though not entirely useless way of measuring penal effectiveness (Walker, 1971, p.105). Although 60 per cent of a Pontypridd sample were reconvicted within twelve months of completing the day-training order component of probation (Willis, 1979, Table 5, p.24), this seemingly high failure rate is somewhat tempered by the high expectation that young men like this with substantial criminal records would offend again at this sort of level (Home Office, 1964, Part VI; Home Office, 1971b), and by the comparable failure rate of discharged prisoners (Home Office, 1979c, Chapter 8).

Alternatively, penal effectiveness could be assessed by analysing the impact of day training on the employment of offenders. It is possible to compare the complete lack of employment at the beginning of day training (Savage, 1977, Table 1, pp.8–10; Vanstone, 1979, Table 6, p.16) with trainees who find employment as a consequence of day training. In the Sheffield survey, 45 per cent of the trainees found employment within twelve months (Savage, 1977, Table 4, pp.15–16), and in Pontypridd 30 per cent had jobs to go to on completion of training (Vanstone, 1979, Table 6, p.16). This compares very favourably with the 15 per cent of discharged prisoners who are employed on release from prison after being unemployed at reception into custody (Corden *et al.*, 1978, Chapter 4).

Clearly, both day training and detoxification offer genuine displacement from custody and positive behavioural impact. Yet, although these social welfare strategies stand out as dispositions which live up to the name of community corrections, their success is not without qualification. In particular, they are prominent in having only experimental or temporary status and singularly failing to receive government endorsement by being made available nationally. True, they work, but only at the margin of the criminal justice system.

Conclusion

This overview of the deployment of some non-custodial dispositions prompts two important observations. First, it is far from being the case that the Golden Age of decarceration has arrived: the rhetoric of community corrections proves empty and is largely unaccompanied by substantial diminution in the use of imprisonment. On the contrary, the individual deterrent penalties may inadvertently add to the prison population, whilst community service is arguably doing little to reduce levels of incarceration. Together, community service and suspended sentences account for about 50,000 penal dispositions each year (Home Office, 1979a, Table 6.1, p.120), dispositions which singularly fail to achieve the intended displacement from custody and reduction of pressure on the ever-swelling prison population (Home Office, 1979b, p.3, para. 7).

Secondly, however, the failure of community corrections is very much more complex than these apparent failures to substitute for imprisonment. The social welfare strategies alone appear to offer both genuine displacement and positive impact. Yet these penal options, in stark contrast to suspended sentences and community service orders, have existed at the margin of the criminal justice system on an experimental basis for an extended period of time. In consequence a strange state of affairs prevails in which there is an inverse relationship between the courts' use of non-custodial measures and their displacement potential: sanctions which divert substantially are little used and retain an extended provisional status, whilst those which divert not at all are increasingly used and prove very acceptable, even when they add to the prison population.

One possible reason for the non-implementation of the genuine displacement strategies is a deep-seated conviction on the part of sentencers and their advisers of the penological inappropriateness of further reducing incarceration. Perhaps, once a certain very marginal level of displacement has been achieved, a more uncompromising retributivist view prevails which limits further decarceration, especially with respect to the more serious offender. This would explain the selective use of, say, community service, but not the non-proliferation of detoxification units. An alternative reason may turn out to be fiscal and not philosophical. It is interesting to note that considerations of financial expediency accompanied the community corrections movement, and that in practice the sanctions involving least cost, for instance, suspended sentences, are those used most. Conversely, those of greatest cost, such as day training, are more sparingly deployed. Perhaps the relationship is not coincidental and reflects fiscal limits beyond which even well-intentioned penal aspirations founder. No doubt both penological and financial considerations apply, and it is to these questions that I direct my attention in the following chapter.

References

Adams, J., 1976: 'Day Training Centres', J. King (ed.), *Control Without Custody*, Cambridge Institute of Criminology, pp.48–65

Alper, B., 1973: Foreword to Y. Bakal (ed.), *Closing Correctional Institutions*, D. C. Heath, Lexington, Massachusetts, pp.vii–x

Andenaes, J., 1971: 'The Moral or Educative Influence of Criminal Law', *Journal of Social Issues*, vol. 27, no. 2, pp.17–31

Bottoms, A., 1973: 'The Efficacy of the Fine: The Case for Agnosticism', *Criminal Law Review*, pp.543–52

Bottoms, A., and McWilliams, W., 1979: 'A Non-Treatment Paradigm for Probation Practice', *British Journal of Social Work*, vol. 9, no. 2, pp.159–202

Carter, R., and Wilkins, L. (eds.), 1976: *Probation, Parole and Community Corrections*, John Wiley, New York

Cohen, S., 1979: 'Community Control: A New Utopia', *New Society*, 15 March, pp.609–11

Corden, J., Kuipers, J., and Wilson, K., 1978: *After Prison: A Study of Post-Release*

Experiences of Discharged Prisoners, Papers in Community Studies No. 21, University of York

Gibbs, J., 1975: *Crime, Punishment and Deterrence*, Elsevier, New York

Hawkins, K., 1975: 'Alternatives to Imprisonment', in S. McConville (ed.), *The Use of Imprisonment*, Routledge & Kegan Paul, Chapter 6, pp.67–87

Harding, J., 1978: 'The Development of Community Service', in N. Tutt (ed.), *Alternative Strategies for Coping with Crime*, Basil Blackwell, Chapter 9, pp.164–85

Home Office, 1964: *The Sentence of the Court: A Handbook for Courts on the Treatment of Offenders*, HMSO

Home Office, 1968: *Criminal Statistics, England and Wales, 1967*, HMSO

Home Office: 1970: *Non-Custodial and Semi-Custodial Penalties*, Report of the Advisory Council on the Penal System, HMSO

Home Office: 1971a: *Habitual Drunken Offenders*, Report of the Working Party on Habitual Drunken Offenders, HMSO

Home Office, 1971b: *Prediction Methods in Criminology*, Home Office Research Study No. 7, HMSO

Home Office, 1973: *A Survey of Fine Enforcement*, Home Office Research Study No. 16, HMSO

Home Office, 1975: *Community Service Orders*, Home Office Research Study No. 29, HMSO

Home Office, 1977a: *Criminal Statistics, England and Wales, 1976*, HMSO

Home Office, 1977b: *Community Service Assessed in 1976*, Home Office Research Study No. 39, HMSO

Home Office, 1978a: *The Sentence of the Court: A Handbook for Courts on the Treatment of Offenders*, HMSO

Home Office, 1978b: *Criminal Statistics, England and Wales, 1977*, HMSO

Home Office, 1978c: *Fines in Magistrates' Courts*, Home Office Research Study No. 46, HMSO

Home Office, 1978d: *Prison Statistics, 1977*, HMSO

Home Office, 1978e: *Sentences of Imprisonment: A Review of Maximum Penalties*, Report of the Advisory Council on the Penal System, HMSO

Home Office, 1979a: *Criminal Statistics, England and Wales, 1978*, HMSO

Home Office, 1979b: *Report on the Work of the Prison Department, 1978*, HMSO

Home Office, 1979c: *Prison Statistics, 1978*, HMSO

House of Commons, 1978: *Fifteenth Report from the Expenditure Committee: The Reduction of Pressure on the Prison System*, vol. 1 (Report), HMSO

Latham, C., 1973: 'Enforcement of Fines', *Criminal Law Review*, pp.552–9

Lerman, P., 1975: *Community Treatment and Social Control*, University of Chicago Press

Marshall, T., and Fairhead, S., 1979: 'How to Keep Homeless Offenders out of Prison', *New Society*, 20 September, pp.616–17

McEwan, J., 1978: 'Assessing the Value of Community Service', *New Law Journal*, vol. 128, no. 5865, pp.772–3

Melville, J., 1979; 'You'll Find Leeds Billy down at the Detox', *New Society,* 23 August, pp.400–401

Pease, K., 1978: 'Community Service and the Tariff', *Criminal Law Review,* pp.269–75

Pease, K., and West, J., 1977: 'Community Service Orders: The Way Ahead', in *Home Office Research Bulletin No. 4,* Home Office Research Unit, pp.16–20

Priestley, P., 1970: *The Problem of the Short Term Prisoner,* National Association for the Care and Resettlement of Offenders

Savage, A., 1977: *The Sheffield Day Training Centre,* unpublished report from the Day Training Centre, Sheffield

Scull, A., 1977: *Decarceration: Community Treatment and the Deviant –A Radical View,* Prentice Hall, Englewood Cliffs, New Jersey

Smith, J., 1974: 'The Community Service Order', in L. Blom-Cooper (ed.), *Progress in Penal Reform,* Clarendon Press, Chapter 19, pp.245–53

Smith, R., 1971: *A Quiet Revolution – Probation Subsidy,* U.S. Department of Health, Education and Welfare, Washington, D.C.

Sparks, R., 1971: 'The Use of Suspended Sentences', *Criminal Law Review,* pp.384–401

Sussex, J., 1974: *Community Service by Offenders: Year One in Kent,* Barry Rose

Tutt, N. (ed.), 1978: *Alternative Strategies for Coping with Crime,* Basil Blackwell

Vanstone, M., 1979: *Pontypridd Day Training Centre: An Alternative to Prison,* Mid Glamorgan Probation and After-Care Service

Walker, N., 1968: *Crime and Punishment in Britain,* University of Edinburgh Press

Walker, N., 1971: *Crimes, Courts and Figures,* Penguin

Walker, N., 1972: *Sentencing in a Rational Society,* Penguin

West, J., 1976: 'Community Service Order', in Joan King (ed.), *Control Without Custody,* Cambridge Institute of Criminology, pp.68–90

Willis, A., 1977: 'Community Service as an Alternative to Imprisonment: A Cautionary View', *Probation Journal,* vol. 24, no. 4, pp.120–25

Willis, A., 1979: 'Displacement from Custody: A Review of the Day Training Experiment', unpublished paper, University College, Cardiff

Wootton, B., 1978: *Crime and Penal Policy: Reflections on Fifty Years' Experience,* George Allen and Unwin

9. The Future of Corrections

Andrew Willis

In Chapter 6 I detailed the dimensions of the contemporary crisis in the prison system of England and Wales, suggesting a number of factors in combination as the primary cause: ancient and overcrowded buildings give rise to appalling living conditions for inmates and inadequate working conditions for prison officers, little or nothing is achieved by way of behavioural reform or societal protection – and all this costs very much more than non-custodial alternatives. This state of affairs prompted prisoner protest and industrial action by prison officers, and caused the Home Secretary to establish in November 1978 an independent Inquiry into the United Kingdom Prison Service under the chairmanship of Mr Justice May. It seems appropriate, therefore, to discuss the future of corrections in general against the topical backcloth of crisis in prisons and possible government response. Having established the dimensions of the present crisis, I will proceed to show that there is nothing very new about it, which in turn raises the interesting question of why it is that so very little has been done to remedy or ameliorate what has long since been widely and openly regarded as an urgent and pressing problem. In discussing this inertia in penal reform I will elaborate on the two principal variables – cost unattractiveness and political disadvantage – which seem to me to explain the lack of substantial penal reform. Then, using these two variables, I intend to predict the way in which I believe penal policy will tend to develop in forthcoming years. This predicted development turns out to be rather complex: penal policy appears to be moving in quite different directions for three separate categories of offender.

Inertia in penal reform

The argument in this section involves three stages: first, that the crisis in prisons and corrections has remained acknowledged but unattended for a considerable period of time – that is, that the response of successive Home Secretaries has been that of inertia; second, that the opportunity for fundamental prison and penal reform is at best limited and at worst non-existent, irrespective of the personal wishes of any particular Home Secretary; and, third, that the reasons for this inertia constitute the critical variables for comprehending the likely development of penal policy.

With respect to the first part of the argument, it is clear that, although there have been recent developments in penal policy, each has tended to focus on just one aspect, namely sentencing – for instance, non-custodial dispositions (Home Office, 1970), young adult offenders (Home Office, 1974), maximum prison sentences (Home Office, 1978a) – to the exclusion of attending to and making proposals about the old and decaying physical fabric of British prisons. Yet, despite this neglect of prison conditions, it has been evident for a considerable period of time that the situation is both poor and deteriorating. For example, in the 1969 descriptive pamphlet on the English prison system, *People in Prison*, the Home Office authors identify 'the rise in numbers and the consequent overcrowding' as the principal factors dominating the development of the prison system since 1945 (Home Office, 1969, p.104, para. 237). Yet this was a period when, by contemporary standards, overcrowding was of minor proportions, there being in 1968 an average daily prison population of just 32,500 inmates (Home Office, 1969, p.104, para. 238). But even this was regarded as intolerable:

> There are today about 9,000 prisoners sleeping two or three to a cell. Overcrowding is the worst feature of our prison system, worse even than the old buildings in which it takes place, and its effects are seen throughout the system. (Home Office, 1969, p.104, para. 239.)

Comments of this kind were not confined to the occasional glossy Home Office publication, but appeared with monotonous and predictable regularity in prominent positions at the beginning of

Annual Reports on the Work of the Prison Department. Thus, the very first paragraph of the 1975 Report states that 'the main problem with which the prison service has had to grapple in 1975 has been the steady upward rise of the prison population' (Home Office, 1976a, p.1, para. 1). And in 1976 the point is reiterated:

> The three factors to which the opening chapter of the 1975 Report drew particular attention – the rising prison population, the cutback in the prison building programme and reductions in staffing resources – continued to dominate the prison system. (Home Office, 1977a, p.1, para. 1.)

Similarly, the 1977 Report begins with a statement that these problems continued to figure prominently (Home Office, 1978b, p.1, para. 2), and the Prison Statistics for the same year note prison overcrowding as again a problem, with the records showing the highest average daily prison population this century (Home Office, 1978c, p.3, para. 1). It is probably not unfair to suggest, in the light of these observations, that the rhetoric of ancient, overcrowded and poorly provided-for prisons is a constant feature of these Annual Reports, the only element of change being the number of prisoners spiralling ever upwards. Yet despite these clear official acknowledgements of this problem of imprisonment, there were no reform initiatives.

The media (not well known for an abiding interest in penal reform) have also been articulately conscious of the appalling prison conditions and deteriorating facilities. Indeed, the *Sunday Times* ran an article headed 'Why the Prisons Could Explode' nearly two years before the crisis of late 1978, describing in some detail the extent of prison overcrowding, the miserable conditions and the likely consequences in terms of unrest and industrial action (*Sunday Times*, 23 January 1977). Prophetically, Walton Gaol was specifically mentioned as a possible source of future trouble. But this and other press reports did not serve to stimulate penal reform.

In addition, recent government publications on prisons and related matters have also shown awareness of the defects in current prison arrangements, and in particular the over-use of prisons. In 1977 the Advisory Council on the Penal System bluntly concluded in an Interim Report that prisons were overfull mainly because of over-use, stating 'that a large number of sentences of imprisonment, especially in the short and medium term band of sentences, are longer than they need be, in the interests either of society or of the offender' (Home Office, 1977b, p.1, para. 3). The Report went on to assert in forthright terms the view that prisons now offered very little by way of reformation; that they were positively damaging in that they destroyed family ties and increased alienation from conventional society whilst fostering pro-criminal identifications; and that they were extremely costly (Home Office, 1977b, pp.3 and 4, paras. 8, 10 and 13). Hard on the heels of this came the substantial 1978 Report of the Expenditure Committee of the House of Commons, which made fifty-two specific recommendations for reform, among them that alternatives to custody should be increased, that conditions for staff and inmates should be improved, and that prisoners' rights should have greater protection (House of Commons, 1978). This report, as a *New Society* editorial said on 9 November 1978,

> ... was a timely initiative which could have provided a platform for immediate intervention. It won approval from most of the interested parties, an unusual enough achievement to suggest that, here at last, was the chance the government needed.

But whether the advice and proposals came from its closest penal policy advisers or even from within the ranks of an all-party committee of the House of Commons, the government took no action, and the crisis deepened as overcrowding continued to increase within deteriorating physical conditions.

Finally the prison governors made a direct approach through their union, the Society of Civil and Public Servants, to the then Secretary of State, Mr Merlyn Rees, complaining vehemently of the conditions of service for prison staff, of what they termed the deplorable lack of leadership from the Home Office, and of the critical state of prisons. They commented:

> If the present trend continues, there will be a serious loss of control which would have to be quelled by an armed intervention by another service. The Home Office has produced no initiative. Governors see no sign of firm leadership in this crisis. The service is drifting towards a major catastrophe. (*Sunday Times*, 29 October 1978.)

There was no immediate response, and it was another three weeks – weeks punctuated by prison officers' industrial action, prisoners' unrest and prison governors declaring 'states of emergency' in their prisons – before the May Inquiry was established.

All this indicates that the crisis could not have been more clearly signposted – by government, media and independent bodies – over a considerable period of time, and also highlights the official response of total inaction and inertia. This lack of response requires explanation. It might be possible to explain it principally in terms of the personal characteristics of the then Home Secretary, Mr Merlyn Rees. It could be suggested that procrastination and avoidance of decision-making were primary features of his period of tenure at the Home Office – not just on prisons but also on police pay, child pornography and official secrets (*Sunday Times*, 5 November 1978). Such an explanation would not, however, account for the fact that inattention to prison conditions and overcrowding goes back more than ten years and, therefore, spans the stewardship of a number of very different Home Secretaries. A more reasonable approach might seek to explain the prolonged evasion of the prison problem in terms of the political and economic realities within which *any* Home Secretary operates. What I want to suggest is that the inactivity of successive Secretaries of State with respect to the problems of imprisonment was equivalent to the behaviour of a frightened ostrich burying its head in sand when it feels threatened. In particular it reflects their complete inability to implement either of the two possible remedies which would have resolved the prison crisis: a massive prison-building programme or, alternatively, large-scale decarceration – giving people who might be sentenced to imprisonment a non-custodial sentence instead. These two courses of action seem to offer possible solutions to the present crisis; but, as I will show, for different reasons neither is a realistic option.

First, Government could embark on a large-scale prison-building programme designed to eliminate overcrowding and enforced cell-sharing as quickly as possible. This would provide prisoners with tolerable living conditions, including reasonable facilities for education, work and leisure, prison officers with improved working conditions, and all the other interested parties – visitors, probation officers, solicitors – with appropriate facilities. However, for a number of reasons, all related to cost, this option must be viewed as unrealistic and, practically speaking, out of the question.

There are some very unambiguous statements to this effect in the same Home Office publications which detail the dimensions of the problem. Thus, in *Prisons and the Prisoner*, despite observations about antiquated, overcrowded and underfinanced prisons, there are also comments on the practical feasibility of injecting substantial resources in order to ameliorate this critical situation. The publication notes that it would cost 'scores of millions of pounds' (Home Office, 1977c, p. 113, para. 195) and that finance of this sort is unlikely to be forthcoming:

> ... it will be some considerable time before the service can be within sight even of the limited goals of eliminating overcrowding; of providing acceptable living conditions for all those in custody; and thus of relieving the feelings of very real and immediate pressures under which members of the service are undoubtedly operating. (Home Office, 1977c, p.115, para. 200.)

Even more explicitly, the recent Green Paper, *Youth Custody and Supervision*, in discussing the possibility of a new generic custodial sentence for young adult offenders, first concedes that there is at present a critical shortfall of available institutional places (Home Office, 1979a, p.18, paras. 45–7), and then promptly admits: 'There is no prospect of a prison building programme on a sufficient scale to meet this surplus [of inmates over accommodation] with new buildings, (Home Office, 1979a, p.20, para. 51).

Indeed, even a brief look at the probable costs of a large-scale prison-building programme serves to substantiate this sombre prognosis. Consider the £14 million expenditure on the recently completed prison for 800 Category C prisoners at Wymott in Lancashire (*Guardian*, 29 January 1979 and 12 February 1979), which works out at about £18,000 per new inmate place. At these prices, the likely cost of providing new prison accommodation for those offenders presently incarcerated in local prisons is something of the order of £300 million; and for replacing all but the very newest prisons the figure would be well in excess of £700 million. Another estimate, found in a letter to *The Times* from P. Davis, suggests that a complete prison rebuilding programme spread over a fifty-year period would cost £70 million a year for the first twenty-five years and then £55 million a year for the second twenty-five years – at current prices, a grand total of £3,175 million, or well over £50,000 for each inmate's cell and other facilities. Clearly, whatever the assumptions upon which the calculations are based, the gross capital expenditure seemingly required for prison rebuilding is, putting it bluntly, absolutely enormous. In addition, it should be borne in mind that any prison-building programme would almost certainly be accompanied by a substantial rise in both numbers of prison staff and their salaries: new institutions alone would be of limited value without a commensurate investment in staff numbers, staff training and staff facilities. And when current staff costs are about £135 million a year, or 60 per cent of the total prison expenditure (Home Office, 1978b, Appendix 4, pp. 83–5), it is self-evident that any additional expenditure represents a far from marginal extra burden to the public purse, and a recurring one.

The point I want to make is rather simple. The prison crisis of 1978 coincided with the last few months of a government which not only presided over some fierce public expenditure economies, but, according to an Opposition spokesman of the time, Mark Carlisle, also cut a prison expansion programme by two thirds, from 10,000 new places to just over 3,000 (*The Times,* 11 November 1978). According to a Home Office spokesman, this would leave a shortfall of nearly 4,000 places by 1981, with no improvement in existing facilities (*Sunday Times,* 5 November 1978). Since this Government was superseded by one even more committed to restriction in public expenditure, it seems quite unrealistic and absurd for the penal reformer, any more than the prison administrator, to conjure up images of a splendid range of purpose-built, brand new penitentiaries constructed in order to eliminate prison overcrowding. I strongly suspect that at the present time the country cannot afford the luxury of new prisons, quite irrespective of whether it desires them: economic recession and limits on public expenditure (with all that this implies about increased competition for priority allocation of scarce resources) mean that a large-scale prison rebuilding programme is a penological pipe-dream.

Second, and in complete contrast, it might be possible to find a solution by dramatically reducing the present levels of imprisonment. A number of strategies, alone or in conjunction, would work towards this end. These could include extending remission or loosening the criteria for awarding parole – measures designed to shorten the period of incarceration. Alternatively, steps might be taken to limit the power of the courts to imprison certain types of offender, or some offences could be decriminalized and community-based corrections could be expanded – all measures designed to avoid imprisonment in the first place. However, irrespective of the strategy employed, at least two apparently intractable problems emerge which, taken together, put stringent limits on any such restrictions of the use of imprisonment.

To begin with there are, at least in the short term, fiscal disadvantages, in that community alternatives to incarceration (of whatever type and however deployed) would require considerable financial support for a period of time before they began to divert offenders away from prison. So decarceration initially involves double costs – those of both community corrections and imprisonment. Putting it a slightly different way, the marginal costs of imprisonment – the extra cost involved in sending just one more offender to prison when no new staff or facilities are required – is very low, perhaps a matter of just a few pounds a week. Thus, the diversion of small numbers of offenders away from custodial sentences would only involve marginal savings, and when these were set against the extra costs of expanding non-custodial measures there would probably be an overall increase in expenditure. In addition, there is some evidence that even in the long term the supposed fiscal benefits of community correction prove illusory, and that intensive community supervision costs more than the incarcerative disposition it is replacing (Lerman, 1975).

There are also, however, what might be termed general political considerations which serve to limit the potential for expanding non-custodial dispositions. When law and order is something of a national preoccupation, as evidenced in the campaign preceding the 1979 General Election, the politician who advocates massive reductions in the prison population is probably committing political *hara-kiri.* Indeed, the major political parties and pressure groups were all trying to curry political favour by advocating sterner and more repressive penal sanctions. For example, in September 1978 the Conservative Party ran an advertisement which offered tougher penal measures as the solution to increased lawlessness and the breakdown of order, appealing to the electorate as follows: 'Mugging up 205 per cent, criminal damage up 135 per cent . . . is it safe to vote for another Labour government?' (Quoted in Wright, 1978, p.80.) Similarly, the Labour Party passed a resolution at its October 1978 Party Conference calling for bold and resolute action against crime. It was proposed by Mr A. Williams of Liverpool West Derby, whose speech referred to 'murder and assassination in our streets, vicious attacks on our police officers, and doorstep crimes of mugging and vandalism' (*Guardian,* 6 October 1978). And a national advertisement placed by Mr J. Jardine on behalf of the Police Federation in April 1979 discussed the intolerable growth in serious crime, citing as evidence the 2.5 million indictable crimes recorded in 1978 and the 6 per cent rise in mugging, armed robbery and wounding over the previous year, and then asserted that 'crimes of violence must be met with the severest penalities' (*Guardian,* 20 April 1979).

When there is this measure of party political and pressure group consensus on both the extent of the crime problem and the punitive measures required to control lawlessness, it is reasonable to suppose that the scope for decarceration must be fiercely circumscribed. Evidence for this was provided in Chapter 8 where I argued that new non-custodial alternatives to imprisonment (whatever their original penal intent) often turn out to be nothing more than replacements for existing non-custodial measures.

That political considerations are always important in penal reform is shown by the fact that very few MPs are known for their interest in prisons or penal reform. As a *New Society* editorial pointed out (9 November 1978), 'the tragic fact seems to be that although there are no votes in prisons, there are votes to be won by advocating measures that will lead to more people being sent there'.

Conversely, votes or public support may very well be lost to the politician who advocates measures which would result in prisoners either being released from prison or not being sent there at all. To the extent that this is true (or felt to be true by Front Bench politicians), there can be no substantial reduction in the prison population. It is perhaps worth stressing that this argument applies to all politicians, irrespective of their party affiliations. It could well be the case, for example, that personally and privately both the Home Secretary and the Opposition home affairs spokesman would favour a substantial reduction in the prison population. But I am quite certain that, if this were so, each would prefer the other to be in office and responsible for it!

Together, then, these two variables of cost unattractiveness and political disadvantage operate to inhibit easy resolution of the crisis in prisons. Rebuilding prisons, especially in times of public expenditure restraint, looks more like a fiscal impossibility than merely being cost unattractive; and massive decarceration is politically unacceptable to any Home Secretary, who knows that if he endorses such a policy he will only generate parliamentary brickbats and media disapproval, not to mention electoral disfavour. The impracticability of these two courses of action explains, to a large extent, why inertia has been the constant companion of penal crisis.

The future of corrections

It is possible to use the two variables identified above, not just to account for the present state of affairs, but also to predict the likely development of prison and penal policy. Although there is an undoubted overall tendency towards inaction and inertia, there have been some changes and there will be more, and these can best be understood by using the two variables to show that for three quite separate groups of offenders penal policy is moving in different directions, and for different reasons. In order to examine this further it is necessary to divide the present prison population somewhat artificially and very crudely into three analytically distinct categories: at one extreme, non-persistent minor offenders convicted of relatively trivial offences; at the other, major offenders convicted of very serious offences; and in the middle an intermediate group of persistent, though not necessarily very serious offenders. This tripartite distinction has a certain common-sense validity and superficial plausibility, and will serve for present purposes even if (as is undoubtedly the case) the behavioural criteria for including a particular offender in a given category are incomplete or vague. Using this rather basic typology of the incarcerated offender and the variables discussed above, I shall now examine the likely development of penal policy for each group in turn.

Minor offenders

Where minor offenders are concerned, I want to suggest that there has already been a certain amount of decarceration – that is, movement away from institutional dispositions towards community corrections – and I anticipate this trend to be maintained and perhaps to increase slightly. As described in Chapter 8, recent years have witnessed the introduction of new non-custodial measures specifically designed as alternatives to incarceration. In particular, I noted that suspended prison sentences accounted for some 35,000 dispositions each year (Home Office, 1978d, Table 6.5, p.97) and that Community Service Orders were made in nearly 12,000 cases in 1977 (Home Office, 1978d, Table 6.6, p.98, and Table 6.7, p.98). But, in addition to these and other new non-custodial measures already discussed, there is some evidence of increasing pre-trial diversion of offenders away from the formal court system through the use of police cautions, which, as Table 1 shows, rose for juveniles from about 34,000 a year during the 1960s to well over 100,000 a year by 1974 (Home Office, 1976b, Chapter 2). Finally, some decarceration has been achieved by limiting the amount of time spent in custody through executive release in the form of parole. In 1978, 4,815 (44 per cent) of all parole-eligible prisoners were released before their expected date of remission (Home Office, 1979b, Appendix 3, Table 1, pp.20–21). This reflects a gradual upward trend in the use of parole (Home Office, 1976c, Appendix 3, Table 1, pp. 24–5).

Taken together, these data are strongly supportive of the view

Table 1

Juveniles cautioned for indictable and non-indictable offences in England and Wales, 1960–74

	Percentage of known offenders cautioned				
Age group	*1960*	*1968*	*1970*	*1972*	*1974*
10–13 years	33.0	39.1	51.7	65.7	66.2
14–16 years	21.1	18.6	25.5	34.1	36.1
Total number cautioned	34,977	33,703	53,478	82,099	101,235

(Home Office, 1976b, Table 1, p.6, and Table 2(b), p.7)

that there has been real growth in diverse penal strategies designed to prevent offenders appearing before the courts or intended to avoid or restrict the use of imprisonment. Indeed, at a general level, despite the overall increase in the numbers sent to prison each year in England and Wales, the proportionate use of imprisonment for adult male offenders is actually decreasing. For example, the proportion of offenders in this category sentenced to immediate imprisonment by all courts fell from 24 per cent in 1967 to 17 per cent in 1977 (Home Office, 1978d, Table 6.3, p.93, and Figure 6.5, p.94). Moreover, this substantial trend away from incarceration is to be found in other countries. In the United States, for example, as Table 2 indicates, both the absolute and proportionate use of imprisonment contracted during the 1960s. Despite a massive increase of 176 per cent in the number of reported index crimes and a 30 per cent increase in arrests during this period, the rate of imprisonment fell from 118.6 to 96.7 per 100,000 population between 1960 and 1970 – a decrease of nearly 20 per cent (Scull, 1977, pp.46–7). So, despite the reservations detailed in the previous chapter concerning the extent to which community dispositions were being used as alternatives to incarceration, especially for the more serious offender, there is substantial evidence that a certain amount of this is taking place. However, it also appears that the burgeoning use of non-custodial penalties is largely reserved for the relatively minor offender who might not otherwise be sent to prison.

Table 2
United States prison population and prisoner rate per 100,000 population, 1960–70

Year	Prison population	Prisoner rate per 100,000 population
1960	212,953	118.6
1965	210,895	109.5
1970	196,007	96.7

(Scull, 1977, Table 3–1, p.46)

The reasons for these trends are twofold. On the one hand, both sentencers and penal policy-makers are now to some extent sensitized to the fact (discussed in detail in Chapter 6) that imprisonment shows a lack of positive and reformative impact (Home Office, 1976d; Brody, 1978; Greenberg, 1977) and in other respects can be regarded as positively damaging (American Friends Service Committee, 1971; Hawkins, 1976; Home Office 1977b; Mitford, 1974). Increased awareness of these factors has probably resulted in imprisonment being less frequently the first-choice penal sanction. But on the other hand, as Scull argues (1977, Chapters 3 and 8), the likely major cause of the increased use of non-custodial dispositions is not humanitarian concern about the ill-effects of incarceration but, rather, the pressure of financial necessity. The provision of institutional resources can no longer keep pace with the ever-increasing demand for places. Scull suggests that in Western developed countries in the period since the Second World War a rapidly increasing pool of economically redundant, unskilled workers has come to form a large and permanent welfare class at the margin of the economy, necessitating ever-increasing social welfare provision. So when, for example, about 25 per cent of the GNP of the United Kingdom is already spent on welfare programmes of one sort or another, there is nothing left for the high-cost provision of institutional care – whether for delinquent youth, adult criminals or the mentally disordered (Scull, 1977, pp.134–51). Hence the tendency is towards non-institutional treatment. As evidence for this, Scull traces the development and rapid expansion of new non-custodial penal measures in the United States from a time of acute financial crisis in the 1960s. The 1967 President's Crime Commission found that an examination of current trends in the demand for institutional places for juvenile offenders projected a 70 per cent increase by the mid 1970s – with no resources available to fund this expansion (Scull, 1977, p.48). Similarly, official forecasts of the rise in the state correctional population of California in the mid 1960s indicated that it would double within a decade, the only solution (other than inventing decarceration) being a $90 million prison construction programme for a period of ten years, even without allowing for inflation (Scull, 1977, p.54). In short, Scull argues that expanding state welfare measures generate a monetary crisis as expenditure threatens to outrun resources; economies must be made, and costly institutional care is sacrificed on the altar of fiscal expediency.

In all probability the two factors outlined operate in conjunction to stimulate non-custodial measures. So far as the future is concerned, Scull's analysis would suggest an ever-increasing role for such measures, and in times of economic recession and public expenditure restrictions this seems plausible enough. To be balanced against this, however, is the 1979 Conservative Government's apparent commitment to an increased role for custodial sentences, especially for juvenile and young adult offenders (*Guardian*, 17 May 1979), and the problem of what I called in Chapter 8 the 'empty rhetoric' of non-custodial sentences, which means that, contrary to the initial penal intent, the deployment of non-custodial measures tends to be largely reserved for offenders who would otherwise have received some other non-custodial disposition rather than imprisonment. My own feeling is that cost considerations alone will be sufficient to ensure the future of community corrections, but that they will tend to be reserved for the not-too-serious occasional criminal offender.

Major offenders

At the opposite end of the penal spectrum, however, a very different development appears to be taking place. This is not a cost-saving exercise designed to keep minor offenders out of prison: on the contrary, it is a potentially very expensive penal exercise designed to keep serious offenders in prison for a very long time indeed. It is almost as though some sort of penal equilibrium is being maintained, whereby, for it to be acceptable on humanitarian and cost grounds to decarcerate a proportion of imprisoned offenders, it is necessary to pay a political price for this exercise in penal clemency – namely, longer sentences and/or more repressive penal conditions for the small minority of very serious offenders. In other words, the tendency towards more lenient treatment for occasional and minor offenders is compensated for by a more vigorous penal approach towards the more serious offenders. As Bottoms puts it (1977, p.88), what we now see emerging is a bifurcation in sentencing policy with 'on the one hand, the so-called "really serious offender" for whom very tough measures are typically advocated; and, on the other hand, the "ordinary" offender for whom, it is felt, we can afford to take a much more lenient line'. Two related pieces of evidence spring to mind as confirmation of this trend.

To begin with, in the last thirty years the average length of prison sentences has increased, despite an overall decrease in sentencing severity. For example, in the period 1948–74 the proportion of adults tried, found guilty and sentenced to immediate imprisonment fell from 71 per cent to 41 per cent in the higher courts, and from 22 per cent to 14 per cent in magistrates' courts (Bottoms, 1977, p. 88). However, this was accompanied by a substantial rise in the average length of prison sentences. As Sparks noted (1971, pp.56–9), this was particularly true during the mid 1960s, when there was a 150-per-cent increase in the prison population of long-sentence prisoners (those serving sentences of over five years) during a period when the total prison population increased by less than 60 per cent. Table 3 dramatically illustrates this trend over a very much longer time scale. What is perfectly clear is that there is a very well-established trend towards longer sentences, particularly since the Second World War and especially in the 1960–75 period, which shows a 50-per-cent increase in average sentence length. Part of this might be explicable in terms of the increase in the number of life-sentence prisoners since the abolition of the death penalty – up to 600 by

Table 3
Index of the average length of prison sentences for all offenders, 1913–74

Year	*Index of average length of sentence**
1913	17.0
1938	38.9
1948	82.9
1958	98.8
1961	100.0
1968	119.3
1975	150.9

* Indices relative to a 1961 baseline of 100

(Home Office, 1977c, Appendix C, Table 5, p.157)

1968 (Sparks, 1971, p.59) and over 1,300 by 1977 (Home Office, 1978b, p.20, para. 72) – and part might be nothing more than an inevitable by-product of decarceration, which, to the extent that it occurs, diverts less serious offenders away from custody, leaving the more serious offenders who are serving longer sentences, and thus increasing average sentence length. Nevertheless, the increase probably does reflect a genuine tendency towards severer penalties.

In addition, trends in sentencing practice suggest that this represents more than merely the lengthening of the average prison sentence: it also seems to involve attempts to create a special innovative type of penal sanction to cater exclusively for the more serious offender. Specifically, in the last five years, three prestigious bodies have produced influential reports incorporating special sentencing provisions for this type of offender – the so-called dangerous offender.

In 1975 the Scottish Council on Crime proposed the introduction of a new court disposition called a 'Public Protection Order', which would secure the indefinite detention of violence-prone adult offenders until such time as it was safe for them to be released – all this being done in order to protect the public (Scottish Council, 1975, p.39, para. 74). This sentence was seen as warranted if there was evidence concerning the likelihood of future serious personal violence, and a record of past acts suggesting a persistent tendency towards violence (Scottish Council, 1975, p.62, para. 130). Additionally, there was explicit recognition that such a sentence made protection of the public (by the indeterminate incarceration of violence-prone offenders) of greater importance than the right of the individual offender only to be punished for what he has already done rather than what he might do (Scottish Council, 1975, pp.60–61, paras. 125–6).

Similar reasoning is to be found in the 1975 Report of the Interdepartmental Committee on Mentally Abnormal Offenders (the Butler Committee), which proposed an indeterminate period of incarceration, called the 'reviewable sentence', for adult offenders showing signs of mental disorder who were also deemed to be dangerous – that is, having a propensity to cause serious physical injury or lasting psychological harm (Butler Committee, 1975, p.59, para. 4.10, and p.71, paras. 4.39 and 4.40). Again, the balance between the right of the public to protection and the right of the offender to be incarcerated only for what he has done, and not what he might do, is tilted in favour of the former (Butler Committee, 1975, p.62, para. 4.16, and p.71, para. 4.39).

Finally, the 1978 Report of the Advisory Council on the Penal System develops the same theme of using special penal sanctions against a minority of serious or dangerous offenders. In proposing an overall reduction in maximum penalties (Home Office, 1978a, Chapters 3–9), the Advisory Council finds it necessary to suggest the introduction of a determinate prison sentence which may be of any length, to be called the 'exceptional sentence', as a safeguard to ensure the public protection against the approximately 10 per cent of the offending population who are likely to persist in committing seriously harmful offences (Home Office, 1978a, Chapter 10: especially p.89, paras. 195–6; p.90, para. 202; and p.91, para. 205).

What all these proposals have in common is that a minority of offenders (the dangerous, the violent, the harmful) should be treated disproportionately severely; as the Advisory Council puts it, 'anyone seeking the protection of the public must be prepared to contemplate really long sentences, and not merely a slight stretching of the normal range of sentences' (Home Office, 1978a, p.90, para. 201). This view is restated later when the Report urges: 'The possibility that a court might impose a sentence of quite inordinate length has to be faced' (Home Office, 1978a, p.94, para. 214). But the innovatory character of these proposals involves far more than their obvious severity. First, because they are specifically intended to provide protection for the public rather than to punish or rehabilitate the offender, they have what might be called a future orientation, in which pre-emptive penal action prevents further harm by prophylactic detention, rather than punishments being imposed for harms already done. This, quite clearly, represents a substantial shift from traditional sentencing practice, according to which, following Hart's (1968, Chapter 1) restrictive principle of retribution, punishment is normally and properly applied 'only to an offender *for* an offence' (my italics) (Hart, 1968, p.9). This restriction eliminating vicarious punishment is, according to Hart, important as the cornerstone of justice, which thereby offers fair terms within which any more general aim of punishment – for instance, reformation – may be pursued. Under these new proposals, however, offenders would be subject to incarceration not so much for what they had done, but more because they were likely to offend in future (Scottish Council, 1975, p.61, para. 128; Butler Committee, 1975, p.73, para. 4.42; Home Office, 1978a, p.90, para. 198).

Second, even if the principle of preventive sentencing proves acceptable, there are difficulties with predicting accurately just which offenders are likely to be repetitively harmful. It is now generally conceded that actuarial or clinical predictions of dangerous behaviour are highly inefficient (Kozol *et al.*, 1972, pp. 371–92; Wenk *et al.*, 1972, pp.393–402; Morris, 1974, pp.63–72; Steadman and Cocozza, 1974; Butler Committee, 1975, pp.39–62, paras. 4.11–4.16; Greenberg, 1975, pp.541–80). But this certainty of mis-classification, false diagnosis and, therefore, improper detention in no way inhibits the proposed use of these preventive measures. Indeed, in discussing this issue, the Advisory Council actually suggests that unnecessary detentions are preferable to mistaken releases (Home Office 1978a, p.90, para. 200). Again, this seems an inversion of the traditional practice of the criminal justice system, which places a premium on avoiding erroneous conviction and imprisonment.

Finally, whereas there are normally explicit and easily identifiable biographical and behavioural criteria which have to be met before any prison sentence is awarded (for example, those of age, current offence, criminal history and prison record) this is not so in the case of the new proposals for preventive sentences. It seems to me very much open to question precisely what criminal behaviour is likely to cause, and what constitutes, 'serious, irremediable, personal injury' (Scottish Council, 1975, p.60, para. 122) or 'serious, physical injury or lasting psychological harm' (Butler Committee, 1975, p.59, para. 4.10) or 'serious physical injury; serious psychological effects . . . exceptional personal hardship . . . and damage to the security of the state . . . or to the general fabric of society' (Home Office, 1978a, p.89, para. 196). It is not just that 'serious' is nowhere defined, nor that I have no idea what is meant by 'psychological harm' or 'psychological effects', but that I have no idea of exactly what behaviour would be *excluded* from falling under one or more of these criteria, especially 'damage . . . to the general fabric of society'.

Taken together, these features of the new sentencing proposals for serious offenders add up to a radical shift in sentencing policy. According to vague criteria which exclude no criminal acts, offenders may be incarcerated for prolonged periods largely because of what they might otherwise do rather than what they have done, even though it is acknowledged that many of them will be misdiagnosed as dangerous and erroneously imprisoned. The explanation for this development, as well as the trend towards longer prison sentences, is to be found in the political advantage to be gained either by proposing or endorsing such policies. As was evident in the 1978–9 General Election campaign and the pre-election hysteria concerning law and order, votes are certainly not going to be lost (and are probably there to be won) by exploiting to the hilt existing or imagined public fears about serious, dangerous offenders and the threat they pose to public safety. Equally important, however, is the fact that by concentrating public attention on a small minority of serious offenders, public interest and (possibly critical) attention is diverted away from the trend towards greater use of non-custodial measures at the other end of the penal spectrum. And this development could well reflect, as Bottoms, following Durkheim, suggests, an attempt to 'reassert an agreed *conscience collective,* or other kind of consensus, in a time of great social and moral doubt and confusion (Bottoms, 1977, p.90). In other words, in an increasingly secular and differentiated society, an attempt to identify and dispose of a common enemy (the dangerous offender) may help to bind together fragmented social elements.

Whatever the exact relationship between these variables, they all seem to offer a measure of political advantage to those who foster the trend in favour of preventive sentencing. Such moves reassure the community of government determination to fight lawlessness, thereby perhaps binding society more closely together; they earn for the government the electoral gratitude of the society which feels thus protected; and, they help divert attention from what, out of financial necessity, is happening at the other end of the penal spectrum.

Intermediate offenders

There remains a substantial residue of currently incarcerated offenders who are neither obvious candidates for decarceration nor serious enough offenders to warrant preventive detention. For this class of offenders I suggest that the paradigmatic response of penal inertia will prevail; but first it is necessary to provide a brief descriptive overview of this residual type.

A Home Office survey of the prison population in the south-east of England in 1972 provides some startling data on the type of prisoner generally in custody in English prisons (Home Office, 1978e, pp.12–24). A 10-per-cent sample drawn at random from all adult male prisoners under sentence of immediate imprisonment (excluding life sentence prisoners) provided a total of 771 prisoners about whom data was gathered from their prison records. These data fall into three major categories.

First, their criminality was examined and it was found that minor offenders predominated. For example, as many as 299 (39 per cent) were serving short sentences of up to 18 months; a further

328 (42 per cent) had received medium sentences of between 18 months and 4 years; whilst only 144 (19 per cent) were serving long sentences of over 4 years. This corresponds pretty closely with national data on adult prisoner receptions for 1977 (Home Office, 1978c, Chapter 4). In addition, police antecedents and criminal records were examined in order to assess the criminal history of these prisoners, and an approximation was made of the seriousness of the men's total criminal careers on the basis of information about such things as the degree of planning, the value of property and the degree of injury or distress to victims involved, as well as such factors as persistence and frequency of offending. All this information was combined to produce a table containing six composite categories of offending seriousness (Table 4).

This indicated that a large proportion of prisoners had throughout their criminal careers displayed only a very unsophsticated level of criminal behaviour, as many as 227 (30 per cent) being categorized as either petty or minor offenders. The group of petty offenders (13 per cent of the total) consisted of those who tended only to commit trivial offences. The property offenders amongst them derived no substantial gains and included no housebreakers, and the

Table 4

Categories of criminality: south-east prison population, 1972

Category	*Number*	*Percentage of sample*
Petty offenders	100	13
Minor offenders	127	17
Average offenders	272	35
Serious offenders against property	109	14
Serious offenders against persons	131	17
Serious offenders against property and persons	32	4
Total	771	100

(Home Office, 1978e, Table 3, p.15)

offenders against the person tended to cause only minor injuries or a minimum of distress. The minor offenders (17 per cent of the total) tended to be greater nuisances than the petty offenders; although this group did contain some housebreakers, they were mostly persistent offenders whose records showed no evidence of planning, competence or substantial gain (Home Office, 1978e, p.15). Clearly, as many as one third of the prison population can be regarded as pathetically incompetent and rather trivial, though often persistent, offenders.

Second, medical records were examined in order to obtain information about the mental state of prisoners and, although this posed problems of variability, it was found that of all prisoners (including lifers) as many as 176 (21 per cent) were assessed as mentally disordered, with only 265 (33 per cent) assessed as showing no symptoms of mental ill-health. In between there was a large number of 370 men (46 per cent) classified as a mixed group who showed some signs of requiring psychiatric or medical treatment for such things as drinking problems and mild psychiatric symptoms, but did not meet the rigorous criterion for inclusion in the mentally disordered group of having their conditions described as 'gross' or 'severe' (Home Office, 1978e, pp. 16–17). Clearly, even with strict criteria as many as one in five of the prisoners were grossly mentally disordered, and by a more liberal assessment, as many as 546 (67 per cent) required some form of specialist intervention.

Finally, records were examined to see what proportion of prisoners had community ties as evidenced by a home to go to upon release, this being regarded as an index of social stability. Overall, a total of 232 men (30 per cent) were assessed as completely homeless, the proportion being even greater for petty offenders – 42 per cent – and those with over 20 previous convictions – 77 per cent (Home Office, 1978e, pp.17–19). Additionally, when the categories of homelessness and mental disorder were combined (see Table 5) it was found that 92 (12 per cent) of the prisoner population were both mentally disordered and homeless. The same number were mentally disordered only, 140 (18 per cent) homeless only, and a mere 447 (58 per cent) neither homeless nor mentally disordered. When these factors were related to post-prison experi-

Table 5

Mental state and homelessness in relation to reconviction: south-east prison population 1972. (Reconviction data derived from a sample of 575 discharged prisoners followed up for two years)

Category	*Number*	*Percentage*	*Percentage of each category reconvicted*
Mentally disordered and homeless	92	12	72
Mentally disordered only	92	12	61
Homeless only	140	18	69
Neither	447	58	30
Total	701	100	54

(Home Office, 1978e, Table 6, p.22 and text, p.23)

ence it was found that, of 575 prisoners followed up for two years after release, 310 (54 per cent) were reconvicted overall, though there were marked differences between the groups. Of the 176 who were neither mentally disordered nor homeless, only 30 per cent were reconvicted, but for other groups – the homeless and/or mentally disordered – the reconviction rates were in excess of 60 per cent.

What these data seem to indicate, looking at the sheer numbers of inmates who fall into one or more of the categories discussed, is that there is a sizeable proportion of the prison population (apparently about one in three) who could best be characterized as chronic social inadequates, more social casualties than sophisticated villains, whose pattern of offending shows persistence but no serious offences, no considerable gain and no competence in planning – and all this combined with homelessness and gross mental disorder. This is the group described by Mr Merlyn Rees as 'petty offenders within the prison system who are socially inadequate and whose criminality is more of a nuisance than a serious threat' (Home Office, 1977d, Foreword).

Faced with this portrait of a typical prisoner in England, the researchers went on to question what proportion of these offenders really required a custodial sentence. Using the twin criteria that their offending or criminal history was not sufficiently serious as clearly to warrant a protective, deterrent or retributive prison sentence, and that they were suitable for non-custodial sentences (so that even with reoffending they would not overstrain public tolerance), it was concluded that as many as 266 prisoners, or 36 per cent, were potentially divertible from prison. Most of these were classified as minor or petty offenders, a large proportion falling into the mentally disordered and homeless categories (Home Office, 1978e, pp.21–3). Putting it bluntly, on these data it looks as though a very large proportion of the English prison population comprises socially inadequate and mentally disordered petty and persistent offenders who, even by conservative penal criteria, really ought not to be there.

Evidence from other sources bears out this rather pathetic portrait of the average prison inmate. Work by Corden *et al.* on 107 petty short-term prisoners in the north of England reveals a strikingly similar pattern of gross social disadvantage, substantial personal problems and trivial patterns of offending. On a scale of offence seriousness, 55 prisoners (51 per cent) were rated as 'not serious', with only 16 inmates (15 per cent) rated as 'serious' offenders. Indeed, nearly half of all the committals to prison were for non-payment of fines, and as many as one in three of these were for offences related to drunkenness (Corden *et al.*, 1978, Appendix II, Table, 2, p.82, and Table 6, p.85). In addition, the sample was noticeably lacking in social ties: 29 (27 per cent) were assessed as social isolates, having little or no contact with friends or relatives whilst in prison and expecting little upon release; over a quarter were assessed as being homeless; and as many as 77 per cent were unemployed at the time of arrest (Corden *et al.*, 1978, Appendix II, Table 5, pp.83–4; Appendix III, pp.87–9; Appendix IV, pp.90–92).

A similar picture emerges from a recent study by Wilkins (1979, Chapter 6) of short-term offenders who showed a pattern of non-serious offending almost universally set against 'a background of overdrinking, social isolation, and employment and accommodation difficulties' (Wilkins, 1979, pp.67–8). The importance of this study, especially in view of the argument to be presented below, is that it dramatically confirms the earlier and very much larger-scale investigation conducted in the same prison by Sparks (1971, Chapter III), which portrayed the typical inmate of a local prison as a man serving a very short sentence for a petty offence, often a fine defaulter, who had already been in prison on a number of previous occasions without its having discernible impact on his criminal behaviour. Men like this made up a resident population aptly described as 'the lumpen-proletariat of the whole English penal system' (Sparks, 1971, p.90).

What, then, of the future for this type of offender? My prediction is that there will be little change in penal policy and that we will continue with a high level of unnecessary and ineffective incarceration. The argument for penal inertia in this area is that, whereas for the trivial occasional offender we could, without causing undue public alarm, make reasonable fiscal savings by endorsing decarceration, and for the more serious offender we could anticipate a degree of political advantage in advocating tougher measures, neither of these possible benefits would accompany the alteration of our present strategy of incarcerating this intermediate class of offenders.

As far as possible political advantage is concerned, there is none whatsoever to be gained by treating this type of offender – the offender with gross personal, social and psychiatric disadvantage – even more severely. The general consensus, certainly implied and often explicit (Home Office, 1977b; Home Office, 1978e, pp.12–24; House of Commons, 1978, vol. 1), is that this class of offender is more social nuisance than public threat, more to be pitied than to be punished, and in need of social welfare or psychiatric treatment rather than a punitive penal response. In the light of these general feelings, it would be an exceedingly rash politician who advocated an even sterner penal response. In addition it is very doubtful, given that local prisons are at present 42 per cent overcrowded (King and Morgan, 1979, Table 1, p.10), whether they are capable of absorbing the increased numbers of prisoners such a response would inevitably generate. Hence a more zealous approach is out of the question.

Equally, however, any substantial move in the opposite direction, towards decarceration of these offenders, seems fraught with political disadvantage. There is, I believe, little public goodwill to be exploited by acting generously. On the one hand these offenders, although clearly disadvantaged in the ways already mentioned, are equally clearly still criminal – a rough-and-ready assessment of adult male prisoners in local prisons suggests that, with a mean age of under 30 years, they will have amassed an average of twelve previous convictions and earned themselves more than three previous custodial sentences (Sparks, 1971, Chapter 3; Home Office, 1978c, Chapter 4; Wilkins, 1979, Chapter 6). Notwithstanding the rather pathetic and minor quality of their offending, its repetitive nature could well generate political, media and public resistance to any manoeuvre designed to see them decarcerated. To the extent that the penal system is in part founded on retributive principles, it will be very difficult indeed to argue that the most frequent offenders ought to receive the most lenient dispositions. And this restraint on decarceration is likely to increase as the retributive model or 'just deserts' approach to corrections takes precedence over reformation and rehabilitation (Von Hirsch, 1976). On the other hand, apart from any retributive reluctance to see offenders go unpunished, there is the more important point that the general public (or penal policy-makers on their behalf) would probably tend to resist measures specifically intended to release *this* sort of offender – the mentally disordered, the vagrant, the alcoholic, the socially incompetent – onto the streets of *their* towns and cities. As Hawkins (1976, p.164) correctly observes in relation to a Harris poll about correctional policy in the United States, although public support is very high for rehabilitative measures provided in prisons, this tends to crumble away when the measures involve contact with offenders in the community, and even more so when respondents are asked about hostels for offenders 'in your neighbourhood'. This aversion to offenders in the community would tend to counsel against decarceration. Thus there is clear political disadvantage both in being more severe and in being more lenient. Hence the tendency will be towards inertia.

With reference to any possible fiscal advantage, it is clear that this could only result from massive decarceration. Is it perhaps the case, then, that these cost benefits would more than compensate for any political disadvantage? At face value this seems quite possible, because there is certainly a large group of offenders who by common consent ought not to be in prison, who are not being helped by their experience of incarceration, and for whom decarceration seems desirable. Yet all these imagined fiscal savings through decarceration may prove illusory. On the one hand, as noted earlier, unless decarceration takes place on a large enough scale, sufficient to empty and close down some prisons, the upshot will be increased expenditure and no net savings, as government pays for both custodial and non-custodial measures. And, on the other hand, the various inadequacies of these offenders (personal, psychiatric, social) tend to suggest that, were they to be decarcerated, they would scarcely be capable of surviving on their own, often in a harsh and unforgiving urban environment. Measured by almost any yardstick, they are clearly a dependent group who, outside of prison, would have to rely on various forms of social aid and welfare to survive easily. The kind of social support which would enable them to stay out and make out would be the provision of hostel-type accommodation with continuous close support and supervision, meaningful trade training followed by realistically paid employment which would frequently have to be of a sheltered nature, and specialist programmes to control or eliminate specific problems such as illiteracy, alcohol or drug abuse and lack of social skill. To provide all this could turn out to be very much more expensive than the non-specialist and intermittent costs of imprisonment. In short, it is considerably cheaper occasionally to arrest and then briefly incarcerate these offenders than it would be to provide continuous and comprehensive community support and care. (In 1977 as many as 5,563, or 19 per cent, adult male receptions into custody under sentence were for sentences of up to three months (Home Office, 1978c, Table 4.5, p.38)). Thus, with respect to economic factors, there is gross disadvantage in decarcerating this particular type of offender. Hence, again, the tendency will be towards inertia.

Conclusion

It appears, then, that the development of penal policy is best characterized by inertia, with no prospect of an easy resolution to the present crisis in imprisonment, whether by a large-scale prison-building programme, which looks financially impossible, or by massive decarceration, which appears politically unacceptable. However, within this overall tendency towards inertia, certain developments are taking place. First, for relatively minor and occasional offenders there is moderate expansion of non-custodial measures, though this is viewed largely as the consequence of the very high costs of incarceration, rather than as a valued penal objective in itself, and is also subject to definite limits, beyond which a non-custodial sentence is seen as wholly inappropriate. Second, sentencing innovations have been proposed for so-called dangerous offenders, which, together with the increasing length of prison sentences, suggests that it has now become politically expedient or advantageous to urge a more rigorous approach to the minority of more serious offenders. And, third, there is a residual group of mentally disordered and socially inadequate petty persistent offenders who will in all probability continue to be imprisoned on an intermittent basis because community care turns out to be both politically unacceptable and prohibitively expensive.

References

American Friends Service Committee, 1971: *Struggle for Justice*, Hill & Wang, New York

Bottoms, A. E., 1977: 'Reflections on the Renaissance of Dangerousness', *Howard Journal of Penology and Crime Prevention*, vol. XVI, no. 2, pp.70–96

Brody, S. R., 1978: 'Research into the Aims and Effectiveness of Sentencing', *Howard Journal of Penology and Crime Prevention*, vol. XVII, no. 3, pp.133–48

Butler Committee, 1975: *Report of the Committee on Mentally Abnormal Offenders*, HMSO

Corden, J., Kuipers, J., and Wilson, K., 1978: *After Prison: A Study of Post-Release Experiences of Discharged Prisoners*, Papers in Community Studies No. 21, University of York

Greenberg, D. F., 1975: 'The Incapacitative Effect of Imprisonment: Some estimates', *Law and Society Review*, vol. 9, pp.541–80

Greenberg, D. F., 1977: 'The Correctional Effects of Corrections: A Survey of Evaluations', in D. F. Greenberg (ed.), *Corrections and Punishment*, Sage, Chapter 5, pp.111–48

Hart, H. L. A., 1968: 'Prologomenon to the Principles of Punishment', in *Punishment and Responsibility: Essays in the Philosophy of Law*, Clarendon Press, pp.1–27

Hawkins, G., 1976: *Prison: Policy and Practice*, University of Chicago Press
Home Office, 1969: *People in Prison*, HMSO
Home Office, 1970: *Non-Custodial and Semi-Custodial Penalties*, Report of the Advisory Council on the Penal System, HMSO
Home Office, 1974: *Young Adult Offenders*, Report of the Advisory Council on the Penal System, HMSO
Home Office, 1976a: *Report on the Work of the Prison Department, 1975*, HMSO
Home Office, 1976b: *Police Cautioning in England and Wales*, Home Office Research Study no. 37, HMSO
Home Office 1976c: *Report of the Parole Board, 1975*, HMSO
Home Office 1976d: *The Effectiveness of Sentencing*, Home Office Research Study no. 35, HMSO
Home Office, 1977a: *Report on the Work of the Prison Department, 1976*, HMSO
Home Office, 1977b: *The Length of Prison Sentences*, Interim Report of the Advisory Council on the Penal System, HMSO
Home Office, 1977c: *Prisons and the Prisoner*, HMSO
Home Office, 1977d: *A Review of Criminal Justice Policy, 1976*, HMSO
Home Office, 1978a: *Sentences of Imprisonment: A Review of Maximum Penalties*, Report of the Advisory Council on the Penal System, HMSO
Home Office, 1978b: *Report on the Work of the Prison Department, 1977*, HMSO
Home Office, 1978c: *Prison Statistics, England and Wales, 1977*, HMSO
Home Office, 1978d: *Criminal Statistics England and Wales, 1977*, HMSO
Home Office, 1978e: *Home Office Research Bulletin No. 5*, Home Office Research Unit
Home Office, 1979a: *Youth Custody and Supervision: A New Sentence*, HMSO
Home Office, 1979b: *Report on the Parole Board, 1978*, HMSO
House of Commons, 1978: *Fifteenth Report from the Expenditure Committee: The Reduction of Pressure on the Prison System*, vol. 1 (Report), HMSO
King, R. D., and Morgan, R., 1979: *Crisis in the Prisons: The Way Out: A Paper Based on Evidence submitted to the Inquiry into the United Kingdom Prison Service under Mr Justice May*, University of Bath and University of Southampton
Kozol, H. L., Boucher, R. J., and Garofalo, R. F., 1972: 'The Diagnosis and Treatment of Dangerousness', *Crime and Delinquency*, vol. 18, pp.371–92
Lerman, P., 1975: *Community Treatment and Social Control: A Critical Analysis of Juvenile Correctional Policy*, University of Chicago Press
Mitford, J., 1974: *The American Prison Business*, George Allen & Unwin; Penguin, 1977
Morris, N., 1974: *The Future of Imprisonment*, University of Chicago Press
Pease, K., 1978: 'Community Service and the Tariff', *Criminal Law Review*, pp.269–75
Scottish Council on Crime, 1975: *Crime and the Prevention of Crime*, HMSO, Edinburgh
Scull, A., 1977: *Decarceration: Community Treatment and the Deviant –A Radical View*, Prentice Hall, Englewood Cliffs, New Jersey

Sparks, R. F., 1971: *Local Prisons: The Crisis in the English Penal System*, Heinemann Educational

Steadman, H. J., and Cocozza, J. J., 1974: *Careers of the Criminally Insane*, D. C. Heath, Lexington, Massachusetts

Von Hirsch, A., 1976: *Doing Justice: The Choice of Punishments*, Report of the Committee for the Study of Incarceration, Hill & Wang, New York

Wenk, E., Robson, J., and Smith G. W., 1972: 'Can Violence be Predicted?' *Crime and Delinquency*, vol. 18, pp.393–402

Wilkins, G., 1979: *Making Them Pay: A Study of Some Fine Defaulters, Civil Prisoners and other Petty Offenders in a Local Prison*, National Association for the Care and Resettlement of Offenders

Wright, M., 1978: 'Law and Order – the Facts', *New Society*, 12 October, p.80

More about Penguins
and Pelicans

For further information about books available from Penguins please write to Dept EP, Penguin Books Ltd, Harmondsworth, Middlesex UB7 0DA.

In the U.S.A.: For a complete list of books available from Penguins in the United States write to Dept CS, Penguin Books, 625 Madison Avenue, New York, New York 10022.

In Canada: For a complete list of books available from Penguins in Canada write to Penguin Books Canada Ltd, 2801 John Street, Markham, Ontario L3R 1B4.

In Australia: For a complete list of books available from Penguins in Australia write to the Marketing Department, Penguin Books, Australia Ltd, P.O. Box 257, Ringwood, Victoria 3134.

CHILDMINDER

Brian and Sonia Jackson

Over one million children in Britain under the age of five have a mother who goes out to work. **Childminder** is the first national survey to estimate not only the number of childminders but also the quality of the care that a child may receive during the day. Brian and Sonia Jackson go beyond revealing the best and the most horrendous, further even than a wealth of practical and positive suggestions, to argue for a change in the whole status of childminding in the community. Beyond the news stories, the reviews and the television programmes that the hardback publication generated, **Childminder** did indeed change official attitudes to children. Brian Jackson explains in his preface to this edition that there is now a National Childminders Association, that there have been BBC TV programmes specially for minders, and that registration is becoming a sign of self-respect and pride.

FREAKS:
Myths and Images of the Secret Self

Lesley Fiedler

The renowned and controversial literary critic, Leslie Fiedler, writes about the Freak, from classical times to the present era of film and pop-culture 'freaking out': the Freak as a holy figure, an intermediary between men and the gods; as a living good luck charm; as a showpiece or source of entertainment; as an object of pity or antipathy; and as a symbol of the human condition of the alienation of all men. In a book which seeks to describe the psychological, cultural and religious place they have occupied in our consciousness, Fiedler writes: 'Only the true Freak challenges the conventional boundaries between male and female, sexed and sexless, animal and human, large and small, self and other, and consequently between reality and illusion, experience and fantasy, fact and myth'.

THE HISTORY OF SEXUALITY
Volume One: An Introduction

Michel Foucault

This, the first of six volumes looks at the repression of sex in Western countries from the seventeenth century onwards, and shows how our very eagerness now to analyse, investigate and discuss sex, constitutes a form of guilt in a society which has made a science of sex.

WHO'S WATCHING YOU?
Britain's Security Services and the Official Secrets Act
Crispin Aubrey

Stemming originally from the author's personal experience of the security system and the Official Secrets Act as co-defendant in the Aubrey Berry Campbell trial this book extends its scope to look at the secret agencies of surveillance which exist in Britain today – their methods, their targets and their uniquely privileged position outside the system of democratic accountability through parliament. There are countless examples of phone-tapping, surveillance and other such practices which emphasize the ever-increasing presence of these massive, anonymous security organizations intruding into our lives.

THE CONSUMER SOCIETY AND THE LAW
Gordon Borrie and Aubrey L. Diamond

This authoritative survey, now in its fourth edition, revised and updated, explains how the law relating to consumer protection evolved, and acts as a guide through the maze of ensuing legislation.

GUIDE TO SUPPLEMENTARY BENEFITS
Tony Lynes

Completely revised to take into account new regulations, this is a simple, comprehensive and up-to-date guide to the grounds on which claims can be based, to the likely response of local officials and to the machinery for appealing against first decisions. It does much to simplify the picture, both for claimants and for those who act professionally or voluntarily for them.

POVERTY:
The Forgotten Englishmen
Ken Coates and Richard Silburn

In this revised edition the authors look again at what is meant by the word 'poverty', at the impact of shifts in public policy, at the failure of the welfare services to alleviate poverty, and at the frequent failure of slum-clearance schemes. The impact of developments in the last ten years is analysed in relation to their detailed survey of St Ann's in Nottingham.

PSYCHOLOGICAL SURVIVAL:
The Experience of Long-Term Imprisonment
Stanley Cohen and Laurie Taylor

The authors taught and talked to the inmates of Durham's maximum security block, where they gained an insight into the problems peculiar to long-term imprisonment. In this book, which grew out of their experience there, they show how such prisoners fear psychological deterioration, how they react to disrupted emotional relationships, and how they manage to adapt to prison conditions without losing their sense of personal identity. In the substantial new introduction to this second edition, the authors discuss how their original forecasts on the treatment of long-term prisoners have been borne out by recent developments in British penal policy.

UNDERSTANDING AND HELPING THE SCHIZOPHRENIC:
A Guide for Family and Friends
Silvano Arieti

In clear and simple language, Dr Arieti, a world-renowned authority on schizophrenia, explains what is known about the illness. He offers invaluable advice on how to recognize the first signs, how to live with and talk to the patient day by day, what arrangements to make, what treatments are available, what hospitalization has to offer, and, in general, how to help as a family member, friend, or paraprofessional.